THE FORMS OF POWER

From Domination to Transformation

THE FORMS OF POWER

From Domination to Transformation

Thomas E. Wartenberg

Temple University Press
Philadelphia

For my parents
Hannah and Rolf Wartenberg
and
in memory of my grandmother
Rosa Schiller

Temple University Press, Philadelphia 19122
Copyright © 1990 by Temple University. All rights reserved
Published 1990
Printed in the United States of America

The paper used in this publication meets the minimum requirements of American
National Standard for Information Sciences—Permanence of Paper for Printed
Library Materials, ANSI Z39.48-1984

Library of Congress Cataloging-in-Publication Data
Wartenberg, Thomas E.
The forms of power : from domination to transformation / Thomas E. Wartenberg.
    p. cm.
Includes bibliographical references.
ISBN 0-87722-648-2 (alk. paper)
1. Power (Social sciences) I. Title.
HM136.W345 1990
303.3—dc20   89-37385
                                                                CIP

Contents

Acknowledgments

THIS STUDY has taken shape over a long period of time. Many people have contributed to it in various ways, and I would like to thank all of them for their help in shaping it, even if they do not find their names listed here.

A number of individuals read portions of the final draft of my manuscript and gave me many valuable suggestions for improving it. Lee Bowie, Steven Ellenburg, Ann Ferguson, and Iris Young gave me much needed advice about how to shape my ideas into a coherent manuscript. I thank them all.

Other readers gave me suggestions on specific sections of the manuscript at various stages of its development. I have benefited from the valued assistance of Wolfgang Balzer, Sam Bowles, Jay Garfield, Linda Nicholson, Paul Ricoeur, Ed Royce, and Robert Schilkret. I would like to thank Sandra Matthews for her help with the photos on the jacket.

I owe a very special debt of thanks to Richard Schmitt. Not only did he follow the development of this manuscript through a variety of different drafts but his comments and encouragement provided me with the necessary critical and emotional support to keep developing my analysis. I want to thank him very deeply for his help. Without it, this book would be far less adequate than it is.

I also benefited from comments received after reading portions of this manuscript to audiences at the following universities: the University of Massachusetts–Amherst, the University of Stockholm, the University of Uppsala, Munich University, Ljubljana University, Graz University, the University of Konstanz, Helsinki University, and the University of North Carolina–Chapel Hill. I have also read papers at a number of conferences and professional meetings. On all of these occasions, the reactions of my audiences—both supportive and critical—have helped me develop my thought. This book could not have been written without the generous support of Mount Holyoke College and the Fulbright Commission. Because of their support, I was able to spend the academic year of 1986–87 in Munich. The bulk of my research for this manuscript was completed during that year.

Finally, I owe an immense debt of gratitude to my wife, Wendy Berg. Not only did she agree to take time off from her own career so that I could be in Munich, but her emotional support enabled me to use that year in a productive way. Without her help, encouragement, and forthright criticism, I would not have managed to write this study, and I want to thank her very much for it.

Various portions of this manuscript have appeared in preliminary form elsewhere. Portions of Chapter 3 appeared as "The Concept of Social Power" in *Philosophy, Law, Politics and Society: Proceedings of the Twelfth International Wittgenstein-Symposium*, edited by Peter Koller, Alfred Schramm, and Ota Weinberger (Vienna: Hölder-Pichler-Tempsky, 1988), pp. 224–30. Portions of Chapters 4 and 5 appeared as "The Forms of Power" in *Analyse und Kritik* 10 (1988), pp. 3–31. An earlier version of Chapter 7 appeared as "The Situated Conception of Social Power" in *Social Theory and Practice* 14 (1988), pp. 317–43, and a version of Chapter 9 appeared as "The Concept of Power in Feminist Theory" in *Praxis International* 8 (1988), pp. 301–16. I am grateful to the editors and publishers concerned for permission to reprint this material.

THE FORMS OF POWER

From Domination to Transformation

Introduction

THIS BOOK arises out of my dissatisfaction with previous theories of power. It develops a theory of power that steers clear of two tendencies evident in such theories: treating power as an objective feature of an agent's situation and universalizing a particular form of power. The theory of power that I develop acknowledges the diverse forms that power can take in the social world, while also treating power as the result of the ongoing interactions of human social agents. It is for this reason that I call it a *field theory of social power*.

The term "social" indicates the specific focus of this study: to understand the forms in which power affects the interactions that human beings have with one another. This study only concerns the use of the term "power" in the human social world. There are other uses of the term "power"—for example, such natural occurrences as storms or earthquakes are called "powerful"—but I am only concerned with power as a specifically *social* phenomenon.

By using the term "social", I also refer to power in all its different forms as a social reality. All the more particular forms of social being such as the political, the economic, and the familial are encompassed by the idea of the social. A theory of social power conceptualizes the forms that power takes in intersubjective human life, abstracting from the specific character of more particular forms of power such as political and economic power.

Previous theorists of power, particularly political theorists, have failed to recognize that power can be exercised within all the different domains that constitute human social life. They have tended to limit their theories of power to the sphere of politics. While a decision made by a political leader might certainly qualify as a paradigm case of the exercise of power, so too might the decision of a corporate executive. By focusing upon social power in general, this study corrects the one-sidedness of such views of power.

3

The basic question for a theory of social power is, "How does power manifest itself socially?" No sooner is this question asked, however, than its coherence may be called into question. After all, questions about power seem to be empirical questions. It makes sense to ask such questions as: "Who has power?" and "How do those with power use it?" Once the meaningfulness of these questions has been granted, one might very well ask why there needs to be a theoretical study of social power, one whose task is different from the clearer, more empirical task of delineating the actual structure of power in society.

This challenge to the coherence of a theoretical study of social power raises many deep and important questions, questions whose ultimate answers can only be articulated in the course of actually developing my account of social power. Nonetheless, it is important to supply a provisional understanding of the aim and purpose of a theory of social power.

One reason it is important to develop a theory of social power is that the concept of social power plays a fundamental role in describing and evaluating social inequities. Just as the concept of justice plays a significant role in legitimating social institutions, the concept of power plays a fundamental role in their critique. By claiming that many of the relationships in society are power relationships, the social theorist intends to justify the claim that such relationships are not themselves legitimate. The concept of power, in its basic social use, indicates the presence of a hierarchical relation in society, one whose legitimacy is called into question.

A theory of social power cannot simply accept the idea that power is always illegitimate; it needs to specify the scope of illegitimate power relations, contrasting them with power relations that do have legitimacy. But even though a theoretical account of the concept of power challenges the idea that power relationships are always illegitimate, the most basic use of "power" within social theory is nonetheless as a means of criticizing a social relationship.

The goal of this study, then, is to provide a theoretical conception of social power that will enable social theory to make use of this concept as a fundamental one in articulating a critique of social relationships, practices, and institutions. Although social theorists have not always been reflective enough about the foundations for a critical theory of society, it has become increasingly clear that social theory needs to develop a more adequate basis for the theoretical claims that it wishes to make. This study is intended to provide one element for such a theoretical framework.

The idea that the concept of social power has a legitimate—indeed, a central—role in social theory is one that has emerged in the course of the twentieth century. Dissatisfied with the conceptual frameworks that previous social theorists had adopted in their attempts to provide a means of criticizing the structure and practices of society, recent social theorists have employed the concept of power as one that, in virtue of its comprehensiveness, could serve the purposes of social criticism more adequately.

There are, however, a number of problems confronting the theorist interested in exploring the nature of social power. The first is the diversity of grammatical phrases in which the term "power" functions. The social theorist must demonstrate that these different uses can be unified into a coherent theoretical concept of power.

The task that I undertake in the first chapter of this study is to show that there are two fundamental meanings of the word "power" that have significant uses within social theory. I distinguish two different concepts of power based upon two phrases in which the term appears: the concept of *power-to* and the concept of *power-over*. I show that each of these concepts has a legitimate use within social theory, but that, despite the connection between them, they need to be kept distinct by an adequate theory of social power. I argue that a theory of social power has, as a first priority, the articulation of the meaning of the concept of power-over because social theory employs this concept as a primary means of conceptualizing the nature of fundamental inequities in society.

The claim that power-over is a central term that social theory ought to employ is one that various social theorists would contest. According to such theorists as Hannah Arendt, power is a positive aspect of social functioning, one that enables groups to succeed in regulating their common lives, so that it is a mistake to focus upon the concept of power-over. In the second chapter, I expose the flaws inherent in this view. In particular, I show that this conception does not have the sort of priority that Arendt and others claim for it. Although their account does capture a certain aspect of social life, it does not analyze the primary meaning of "power" within social theory. Indeed, this account shifts the social theorist's gaze away from the set of phenomena that a theory of social power must comprehend, namely the illegitimate inequalities that exist in modern societies.

Having defended the goal of a theory of social power from an important set of challenges, I turn my attention to a particular debate within Anglo-American social theory that is concerned with the question of how to define the concept of power-over. I argue, in the third chapter, that this entire debate takes place within a conceptual framework that is fundamentally flawed. Its shortcomings are the conception of human social agency that it presupposes and the understanding of scientific theorizing that it seeks to satisfy. As a result of the inadequacy of these assumptions, none of the theories put forward in this debate can provide an acceptable theory of social power.

The balance of my study develops my own *field theory of social power*. It rejects the idea that power can be viewed either as the *property* of social agents who possess it or as a *quasi-subject* with aims and purposes of its own. My theory is based upon the idea that power relationships are the result of the ongoing interactions of human beings. Because of this perspective, it provides social theory with an understanding of power that explains why the presence of power constrains the actions of social agents in a way that those agents can challenge and even, under certain circumstances, alter.

I begin the development of the field theory of power in the fourth chapter by presenting my own definition of one agent's power over another agent. I show that the phrase "has power over" functions as a specific type of excuse for certain actions, making a social agent less liable to criticism, punishment, and so on. I then present an ontology of human social agency that is more sophisticated than that upon which previous conceptions of power had been based. I develop the basic concepts of such an ontology by means of the idea of an agent's *action-environment,* a term that I use to characterize the situation of a social agent. I then argue that the concept of one agent's power over another is to be understood as an agent's *constraint* of the action-environment of another agent.

This definition is only the first step in the development of the field theory of social power. Since a theory of social power seeks to develop an understanding of how power functions in society, my first task is to show how my definition of power can be used to develop a view of the basic types of power. I distinguish three basic types of power: force, coercive power, and influence. These three terms refer to different ways in which the action-environment of a social agent can be constrained by another agent, and, as such, they constitute three distinct types of power. Rather than seeing these three types of power as distinct types of social relationships, I argue that they form a tripartite strategy that a dominant agent needs to employ in order to maintain her power over another agent. Since a dominant social agent will necessarily extend her power basis from force to coercive power and to influence, I refer to this feature of social power as its *articulation.*

In Chapter 6, I undertake a systematic discussion of domination, showing that there are two strategies that a social agent can use to establish domination. I show that Hegel's discussion of the "lordship-bondage" dialectic in his *Phenomenology of Spirit* develops one such strategy. In it, social domination is based upon the use of force and coercive power. I also show that Marx accepts this model of domination and supplements it in an important manner. The second strategy for achieving social domination is developed by Nietzsche and extended by Foucault. It sees ideas themselves as the primary means by which such relationships are constituted. I argue that social theorists should

acknowledge the importance of each of these two accounts of social domination in their attempts to understand that phenomenon.

In the first six chapters of this study, my discussion is conducted within
the framework of a dyadic view of power. That is, it proceeds as if it were
clear that a power relationship is a relationship between two social agents that
is independent of the broader social context. In the seventh chapter, I argue
that it is important to acknowledge the role that the social context plays in the
constitution of social power. I use the term *situated power* to emphasize the
fact that a power relationship is constituted by a broad social context. I argue
that understanding the situated nature of power relationships entails a fundamental supplementation of the model of power and social domination that I
have so far developed.

Since an agent's power over another agent depends upon the continued
presence of other social agents, it follows that power relationships can always
be contested by changing the manner in which those social agents act. Power
relationships have a different ontological status than do natural facts, since the
objectivity of the attribution of power to an agent always presupposes a background of continuing action and behavior by other agents. In the eighth chapter, I argue that this entails that a theory of social power must be *dynamic*—
that is, must take into account the temporal aspects of power relationships.
Few social theorists have seen the need to incorporate temporality into their
account of power, resting content with a structural, atemporal view. I argue
that this distorts such views of power and show how the dynamic nature of
power can be incorporated into my account of situated power relationships.

In the ninth chapter, I call into question the assumption that power is a
negative feature of social relationships, one that ought to be done away with.
Contemporary feminist theorists have argued that it is a mistake to see all the
uses of power within society as serving social domination, and that power
plays a positive role when it is used in a transformative manner. A transformative use of power is one in which an agent uses her power over another
agent in order to help that other attain certain skills or abilities.

My discussion of the transformative use of power shows that it is an important use of power that has not been adequately acknowledged by most social theorists. Because feminist theorists have not presented this idea in general enough terms, in the final chapter I develop such a general account of
transformative power. Beginning with a close look at Socrates' mode of interaction with his interlocutors, I articulate a model of transformative power that
shows both its importance as a means of constituting social agents as independent beings and the highly problematic nature of its practice.

The view of power that emerges from my study, then, is one that sees power as a more variable and problematic social presence than most other theories of social power. By combining structural, situated, dynamic, and transformative aspects, my field theory of power recognizes and incorporates the complexities of power relationships. It shows that power can be both a detrimental and a beneficial aspect of social relationships.

Because the field theory of power recognizes such diverse forms of power, it has an important role to play in social theory. Only by means of a careful analysis of the forms and uses of power in the social world, an analysis that does not attempt to fit power into a preconceived understanding of its social role, can power be seen as it truly is: a set of distinct social phenomena that play essentially different but nonetheless related roles in the constitution both of individual social agents and of society as a whole. Without an awareness of the variety of forms of power, social theory is doomed to an eternal battle among theories of power that privilege a particular form of power as the essence of power. The virtue of the field theory is that it conceives of power in terms that avoid doing this. As a result, it provides social theory with a comprehensive view of social power, one that accounts for the negative as well as the positive role that power plays in the constitution of human social life.

1

The Problematics of Power

POWER IS one of the central phenomena of human social life. Yet no sooner does one begin to reflect upon what power itself means than one is confronted by a fundamental problem: It becomes unclear whether power is a positive or a negative feature of human social relations. The use of the term "power" within ordinary discourse seems to reflect a basic ambivalence about the nature of power. Sometimes power is spoken of as something that people think of as belonging to them, part of their proper inheritance. They have been "ripped off" when someone else has *their* power. A locution like "Power to the people!" implies that power is a positive characteristic of social life that has its proper location in the hands of the people. On the other hand, the term also functions to denote negative features of human social relations. When we speak of a dictator's power over the minds of his followers, the concept connotes a sinister aspect of human life, the ability of a charismatic figure to cloud the judgment of normal people and dominate them.

Although ordinary discourse is thus ambivalent about power, one might hope that social theoretic accounts of it would provide a more univocal account of this crucial social phenomenon. After all, social theorists generally attempt to introduce clarity and precision into our ordinary discursive practices. Since, as a result of the importance that phenomena associated with power play in the lives of human beings, social theorists have expended a great deal of effort in articulating a theoretically sound concept of power, one might expect to find more of a consensus among them about its nature.

If this is one's expectation, one will be sorely disappointed, for social theoretic discourse concerning power is, if anything, even more sharply divided than ordinary discourse. Indeed, the very precision for which social theorists strive makes their accounts of power more sharply opposed than is the case in ordinary discourse.

Thus, some social theorists have argued that power is necessary to the existence of society, a crucial means whereby human beings regulate their mutual lives. Hannah Arendt, for example, claims that power is an important part of the social world whose contribution to the functioning of human social life is all too often overlooked. In elaborating this view, she claims that "all political institutions are manifestations and materializations of power; they petrify and decay as soon as the living power of the people ceases to uphold them."[1] For other social theorists, however, power is a much more sinister phenomenon, a means whereby one group of human beings is able to use its relations with other human beings for its own benefit. These latter theorists view power as something that can and should be eliminated from human social relations. For example, David West says: "Distinctive of radical or critical approaches to the concept of power is the conviction that a theory of ideology must be central to them. Power is not always either coercive or blatant. It operates more subtly and more perniciously when it operates invisibly in the form of ideology."[2] In attempting to show the subtle means whereby power operates, West employs a concept of power that treats it as a negative feature of social relationships.

Thus, both in our ordinary discourse about power and in the more highly refined theoretical discourse of social theorists one finds a deeply problematic dichotomy. On the one hand, power seems a necessary and positive feature of both an individual's life and a society; on the other, it seems to be the root of many of the deepest problems of a society.

Nor is this the only problem confronting a theorist of power. A closer investigation of the various theories that have been put forward by social theorists in attempting to explain precisely what power is shows that these theories have no common point of agreement. Not only do they disagree about whether power is a positive feature of social relationships, but almost every assertion that is made about power seems grounds for further controversy, from the question of who or what is able to possess power to whether the idea of possessing power is even a coherent notion.

One likely result of contemplating the range of conflict among theories of power may be skepticism about the possibility of articulating a general theory of social power. Niklas Luhmann, for example, makes the following observation:

There are numerous contradictory attempts to bring the concept of power to a theoretically and empirically successful concept. In view of this situation, a theory of power cannot be satisfied with a descriptive explanation, with an analysis of the essence [of power] which more or less presupposes that which it presents as its result.[3]

Although Luhmann uses this observation as a means of justifying his own theoretical approach to analyzing the concept of power, it reflects a sense of frustration that many social theorists have felt when confronted by the range of disagreement that characterizes theories of power.

Some social theorists have argued that a general theory of power ought not to be an aim of social theory at all. In the work of Michel Foucault, for example, there are repeated suggestions to the effect that a general theory of power is not possible, that one ought to address the subject by considering particular domains within which power is present and showing how power has structured them.[4]

The question of whether the project of a theory of social power makes sense is one that becomes urgent in light of this theoretical situation. The range of conflicts among various discourses of power makes it hard to accept the idea that there could be a single theoretical explanation of what power is. Since I shall put forward a theory of social power despite my recognition of the problematic nature of the concept of power, it is necessary for me to explain why such a project makes sense.

In part, this requires that I explain why there is such variety among the views of theorists who have sought to refine our ordinary discourse about power. I shall argue that a wide range of problematic assumptions condition their disagreements. When these various assumptions have been investigated, the fact of disagreement will no longer seem like a barrier to developing an adequate understanding of power.

Although the specifics of my argument will only become clear in the course of my discussion, let me give an indication of the strategy that I shall use in investigating the nature of power. So far, I have shown that there is a great deal of disagreement among theorists of power in regard to such a fundamental question as whether power is beneficial or harmful as a social presence. If one felt compelled to determine which side of this thorny issue was correct, one might well despair about providing a general account of power. However, I see this disagreement as reflecting an important feature of social power, namely that it can be *either* a negative social presence *or* an importantly beneficial one depending on the nature of its use. This means that only by paying attention to the particular use of power that is at issue is it possible to specify whether power is harmful or beneficial.

Most social theorists have failed to reflect upon the discourses of power at

a general enough level. As a result, such social theorists have presented their
analyses at the wrong level of generality. The analysis of power as a social
phenomenon in general cannot treat the presence of power as in itself beneficial or harmful to society. As I shall argue in this study, the question of
whether power is beneficial or harmful can only be answered in regard to the
specific form that a power relation has in a particular situation.

But this means that the conflict over whether power is beneficial or harmful
is one that cannot be solved, because power is really both. In certain circumstances, it is a positive and necessary feature of society; in others, it is negative and eliminable. By looking at the disputes among power theories as themselves a means of understanding the nature of power, I develop a theory of
power that is able to resolve many of the issues over which theorists of power
have fought.

Essentially Contested Concepts

The fundamental nature of the conflicting assumptions made about power
has caused social theorists a great deal of concern. They have worried that, if
the empirical diversity of such theories cannot somehow be understood theoretically, doubt will be cast upon the possibility of developing a theory of
power that will do more than simply add another theory to a seemingly endless
multiplicity.

One way in which social theorists have tried to cope with this situation is
to claim that power is an *essentially contested concept.* An essentially contested concept is one of a set of special concepts used within social theory
whose legitimate use cannot be settled by appeal to theoretical criteria alone.
Disputes waged with essentially contested concepts are claimed to be un-
resolvable by discursive means alone; there are no purely theoretical criteria
for deciding which use of such concepts is the correct one. Thus, for example,
Steven Lukes begins the presentation of his "conceptual analysis of power"
with the claim that his view is "ineradicably evaluative and 'essentially contested'".[5] Similarly, William E. Connolly states that "attention to the grammar of 'power' makes it readily understandable why it is an essentially contested concept."[6]

By claiming that the concept of power is "essentially contested", these
two theorists emphasize a number of features of the theoretical dispute surrounding that concept. For one thing, the claim that power is essentially contested entails that there is no reason to expect a consensus about how to
employ the concept. Lukes and Connolly therefore commit themselves to articulating an internally consistent view of power, even though this will not

satisfy others who operate with a different meaning for "power". Although both of them claim that it is possible to give a rational defense of the positions that they put forward, their use of the thesis of essential contestability results in a limited conception of what can truly be accomplished by such a defense.

At the same time, the thesis of essential contestability provides a way of understanding the wealth of competing conceptions of power. Since power is essentially contested, debates concerning the correct concept of power will continue; but instead of seeing this as an impediment to their inquiries, Lukes and Connolly see it as a reason to advocate the particular conception of power that they think is most illuminating. Since the essentially contested status of power will always result in dispute about which theory of it is correct, a theorist is necessarily engaged in an attempt to influence others to accept that view of power which she thinks is the most perspicuous. As a result, there are bound to be numerous attempts to advocate the use of one or another theory of power.

I believe, however, that the thesis of the essential contestability of power is mistaken. I shall demonstrate my claim by showing that the thesis of the essentially contested nature of concepts does not explain the nature of the divergences among theories of power, but unjustifiably reduces all conceptual and theoretical disputes to a single mold, a mold that does not adequately explain the multiplicity of existing theories of power. So, despite its initial attractiveness as a means of explaining the seemingly bewildering variety of theories of power, the thesis of the essential contestability of "power" needs to be rejected.

To begin with, it is important to understand exactly what the thesis of essentially contested concepts asserts. The concept was introduced into philosophic discourse by W. B. Gallie in order to challenge the idea that there is always "an assumption of agreement, as to the *kind* of use that is appropriate to the concept in question, between its user and anyone who contests his particular use of it." [7] Gallie is concerned with situations in which theorists disagree. Although such a debate employs certain concepts, he claims that there is no consensus about the meaning of those very concepts. It is such concepts that he asserts are "essentially contested".

Gallie provides criteria by which to judge when a concept is essentially contested.

(I) It must be *appraisive* in the sense that it signifies or accredits some kind of valued achievement. (II) This achievement must be of an internally complex character, for all that its worth is attributed to it as a whole. (III) . . . The accredited achievement is *initially* variously describable. (IV) The accredited achievement must be of a kind that admits of considerable modification in the light of changing circumstances. . . . I shall call the concept of any such achievement "open" in character. (V) . . . Each party recognizes the fact that its own use of it [the concept] is contested by those of other parties.[8]

Examples that Gallie gives of essentially contested concepts include a "work of art" and "democracy".

I shall discuss the concept of democracy in order to illustrate Gallie's thesis. Democracy is generally regarded as an achievement of Western culture, and the term refers to a broad set of social institutions that such an achievement makes use of. As a result, to say of a society that it is democratic is to make a positive appraisal of it. However, in using that term, one can highlight various features of democratic societies. For example, in granting foreign aid, our government seems to view societies as democratic because they have public and secret elections of their leading officials. Many social critics, however, argue that such a characteristic is not sufficient to warrant calling a society democratic, and that a society that lacks "equality of all citizens, irrespective of race, creed, sex, etc., to attain positions of political leadership and responsibility"[9] is not democratic, whatever the nature of its electoral process. Gallie's thesis is that this sort of disagreement about whether a given society is democratic revolves around different understandings of the meaning of the term "democracy". Because there is no way to adjudicate between these two competing uses of the term by saying that one of them is *the* correct definition—that is, because there is no single, essentially defining feature of a society in virtue of which it can be called a democracy—this dispute reflects the essentially contested nature of the concept and cannot be settled by purely discursive means.

Because essentially contested concepts refer to things that have a complex structure, disagreements arise when these concepts are applied non-paradigmatically. In a non-paradigmatic application, not all the features of the complex reality are present, so that one feature is taken to be *the* essential one, the one that legitimates the application of the concept to particulars. Gallie's thesis is that the logic of the situation entails that there will always be disagreement about which features are the essential ones for the concept's application. Given the logic of such concepts, there will always be disagreement about which particulars fall under their extended use. But while such contested uses of these concepts are inevitable, this does not rule out the possibility of rational discussion. One disputant can still persuade another that her use of an essentially contested concept is superior even though she cannot prove that her disputant's use is illegitimate.

One can think of Gallie's thesis as a claim about how the meanings of concepts evolve. Gallie is arguing that the present use of a concept cannot settle the question of whether to extend its use to new cases in which not all of a given set of defining characteristics are present. The decision about whether we should extend the use of a concept to include a new particular that possesses a certain feature of the concept but that lacks certain other previously crucial features is precisely that: a decision that cannot be legitimated in a purely theoretical manner.

Gallie's thesis about the nature of such concepts is a development of the Wittgensteinian idea of family resemblance. Wittgenstein argues that certain concepts do not have a single defining characteristic in virtue of which particulars are classified as instances of that concept. This had been the traditional view of the nature of all concepts that were held to be susceptible to formal definition.[10] On this view, to say of some particular that it is an F is to have in mind certain characteristics f_1 through f_n in virtue of which that thing is classified as being an F. In the case of the concept "game", Wittgenstein argued that the logic of the concept did not work that way, that the most that could be asserted of all things that were classified as games was that they shared a certain family resemblance.[11]

Gallie emphasizes the fact that there are often important practical consequences involved in the question of how we classify. Although it may not seem to make a lot of difference whether we accept the classification of "new games" as games although they lack a competitive character that might be taken to be essential to a game, a lot does hinge on whether we characterize a certain regime as democratic. These practical consequences form the background for Gallie's discussion of the question of conceptual classification.

Given this understanding of the idea, does it make sense to think of "power" as an example of an essentially contested concept? The attractiveness of doing so is that it would explain why there has been such a proliferation of theories of power: Different social theorists are arguing with one another about how to extend the concept of power to cases that are non-paradigmatic. Since a good deal also hinges on whether power is seen to be present in a given situation, there is reason for various theorists to differ on their assessments of the case.

Nonetheless, not all social theorists have accepted the claim that "power" is an essentially contested concept. Anthony Giddens, for example, argues that this view is based on the mistaken idea that there is a special subset of concepts with a peculiar nature. As a result, the thesis of essential contestedness is "either mistaken or unenlightening. . . . It is mistaken if the implication is that some notions in the social science are *essentially* contested while others are not. . . . I would want to claim not just that a few especially contentious concepts . . . but the whole conceptual apparatus of social theory is in some sense 'ineradicably evaluative'." [12] Either the thesis of there being essentially contested concepts has to be enlarged to include all concepts in the social sciences, Giddens argues, in which case it is not enlightening since it does not explain the nature of the conflicts that arise concerning the use of certain peculiar concepts; or it may be interpreted as a thesis concerning the especially problematic status of a particular subset of the concepts employed within social science, in which case it is quite simply false.

While I agree with Giddens' rejection of the thesis that the concept of power is essentially contested, I think his reasons for rejecting it are not adequate. In fact, Giddens seems not to have properly appreciated the distinctive nature of Gallie's argument. In this respect, his view is like that of Lukes. Lukes uses the idea of essentially contested concepts in a much broader manner than Gallie in order to point to the fact that there are political disagreements within social theory that are reflected in the manner in which social theorists define the concepts that they use. But Gallie's thesis is not simply that the concepts used in social science are ones over which there is a lot of debate, or even ones over which debate is, in some sense, necessary. His thesis has to do with the open texture and hence indefinability of these concepts.

It is this aspect of his claim with which I disagree. While there can be fundamental and important dispute over the meaning of central terms in social theory, at least in the case of "power" I want to argue that such dispute does not follow the course it would if Gallie's thesis were true. "Power" is not a concept that has the sort of logic that Gallie attributes to concepts like "work of art" and "democracy". [13]

The central problem is that the thesis of the essential contestability of "power" is too general to explain the nature of the disputes that have arisen among social theorists about that concept. The thesis claims that a basic type of dispute concerning "power" is the result of the peculiar logic of essentially contested concepts. These disputes are due to social theorists' applying different criteria to non-paradigmatic cases of power. However, as I mentioned at the beginning of this chapter, theorists of power are divided on such fundamental questions as what the concept of power refers to. They do not agree about whether power is a positive feature of society or a negative one, whether it can be possessed by groups or only by individuals, whether it is measurable or not, and so on.

The depth and variety of these disagreements cannot be understood by means of the thesis of the essential contestability of "power". There is no level at which power theorists agree about the nature of "power".

The model that Gallie proposes for understanding theoretical disagreement will therefore not do as a model of the disagreement among social theorists concerning the concept of power. The differences among power theorists are not simply about how to classify borderline cases; they are about the basic core of a theory of power. The disputes among social theorists about how to conceptualize power are more basic and more diverse than can be accounted for by means of the idea of essentially contested concepts.[14]

The Meanings of "Power"

I have just argued that one attempt to explain the widespread and fundamental disagreement about how to understand the concept of power is inadequate. But this seems to leave us where we began: with a multiplicity of theories of power that call into question the very project of developing a theory of power that will not simply contribute another voice to an existing cacophony. As I have said, however, the project of this book is to demonstrate that it is possible to develop a conception of power that is superior to previous ones. In order to do so, I will argue that previous theorists of power have made a number of illegitimate assumptions. By exploring the manner in which these assumptions have given rise to inadequate theories of power, I will be able to show exactly in which respects my own account surpasses the views of previous theorists.

As a first step in my argument, I shall focus on the concept of power itself. Although ordinary discursive practice makes a distinction between two fundamental uses of the concept of power, since social theorists want to introduce a greater degree of precision into ordinary discourse, they have tended to stipulate a particular use of the concept of power as the single correct one. In doing this, they have, for the most part, ignored the fundamental duality of "power". As a result, it is not surprising to encounter theories of power that have fundamental differences, for such theories may be talking about different aspects of social reality.

My claim is that the concept of power is unusual because it has two basic but fundamentally different uses in ordinary language, uses that result in an essential ambiguity in the concept. We can see this if we consider two of the meanings of that term that are presented by *The Oxford English Dictionary*. The first meaning that *O.E.D.* gives for "power" is "ability to do or effect something or anything, or to act upon a person or thing."[15] As an example of this use of the concept, the *O.E.D.* gives Malory's "It shalle not lye in your power . . . to perysshe me as moche as a threde" (*Arthur*, XV, ii, 657). If we look at the grammar of this use, we can see that the concept power occurs as part of the phrase "has power to". In fact, this phrase is characteristic of the occurrences of "power" conveying this meaning of the word: "Power" here is a shorthand for the *ability* to do something; it is a characteristic of a particular. In this usage, it is not only human beings to whom power can be attributed: All entities possess powers of some sort or other. As a reflection of this contextual significance of the term "power", it has become commonplace within much of social theory simply to refer to this sense of the concept of power as power-to, as a means of distinguishing it from the other sense of power, that of power-over.[16]

Another meaning for the term "power" is given by the *O.E.D.* as follows: "Possession of control or command over others; dominion, rule; government, domination, sway, command; control, influence, authority."[17] One example given of such usage is John Stuart Mill's claim that "a man's power is the readiness of other men to obey him."[18] The basic idea of this usage is that power involves a specific type of relationship between human beings, one that is hierarchical in virtue of one person's ability to affect the other without the other's being able to reciprocate.

As with the case with the first meaning of "power", there is a particular grammatical phrase within which the concept occurs, namely "has power over". In such a phrase, the concept of power functions in a relational manner: It is limited to social agents, the sorts of entities that can be plausibly said to control or to command others. As I have mentioned, many social theorists, relying on this grammatical link, refer to this meaning of the term as specifying the concept of power-over.

It is my claim that, despite the appearances of unity of meaning conveyed by the term "power", these two different uses of the term have fundamentally different meanings, a feature of the term that has not been adequately recognized by social theorists. Hannah Pitkin is one of the few social theorists who have explicitly acknowledged the importance of this fact. Indeed, she makes a very clear argument that these two different locutions do indeed constitute two different meanings for the term "power":

> It is important to distinguish between the expressions "power to" and "power over." If "power" were a label for certain phenomena, such a distinction could not be of great importance, since the two expressions would necessarily involve the same idea of power simply set in different verbal contexts. But if the concept of power is built up out of, abstracted from, its various characteristic expressions and occasions of use, then the idea of power in "power to" may be *significantly different* from the idea of power in "power over." That is, indeed, the case. One man may have power over another or others, and that sort of power is relational, though

it is not a relationship. But he may have power to do or accomplish something by himself, and that power is not relational at all; it may involve other people if what he has power to do is a social or political action, but it need not.[19]

Pitkin's concern in this passage is to show that traditional political theory has been misled by a false view of the nature of language. Her claim about the nature of "power", however, can be separated from that more general point. She claims that there is a relational and a non-relational meaning of "power" and that these need to be distinguished from one another. The terms power-over and power-to capture this distinction, whose importance has been ignored by theorists because of an inadequate view of language.

In claiming that there are two meanings of the concept of power, one need not be claiming that there is no relationship between them. Indeed, since any attribution of an ability to an agent will involve attributing a power to her, the attribution of power-over an agent to another agent will involve some attribution of power-to. Nonetheless, the concept of power-over picks out a different aspect of reality than does the concept of power-to.

Many social theorists have conceived of their task as sharpening the manner in which "power" is used within ordinary discourse. For example, Talcott Parsons lists the "diffuseness" of most social theoretic conceptions of power as a defect that his own account will remedy.[20] However, in attempting to present a more specific and less diffuse concept of power as a tool for social scientific research, Parsons fails to notice that the diffuseness of the concept of power in ordinary discourse is not simply a result of the imprecision of ordinary discourse as a conceptual tool. Rather, as I have just argued, ordinary discourse uses the term "power" in two distinct contexts to make two distinct types of claims. It is this duality of use that may result in an apparent imprecision in the concept itself.

But simply stipulating a single, refined concept of power as *the* concept of power that it is appropriate to use within social theory will not do, for it ignores the other context within which the concept of power is employed. Many social theorists have argued that their own particular starting point and conceptualization is the only one adequate to an understanding of every use of the concept in general. It is this failure to acknowledge the dualistic nature of the concept of power that has resulted in the appearance that there are no common grounds from which to adjudicate the disputes in social theory about the nature of power.

In order to demonstrate this, I shall look at the ways in which philosophers have traditionally conceived of power, showing the presence of two different conceptions of power that also have been adopted by social theorists. I shall begin by considering philosophers who have primarily conceived of power by means of the locution "has power to". Interestingly enough, there are two similar, but distinct trends in the analysis of this particular concept. In the first, dating back to Plato's *Sophist,* power is analyzed as the ability to affect something, to bring about a change, or to be affected or changed: "I suggest that anything has real being that is so constituted as to possess any sort of power [*dunamis*] either to affect anything else or to be affected. . . . I am proposing as a mark to distinguish real things that they are nothing but power." [21] Plato uses the term "power" here as the basis of an entire metaphysics, one that characterizes the "being of beings" in terms of power. This understanding of power is one that treats it as a property that all existent things have in common with one another. Indeed, it is precisely in the context of attempting to develop a theory of what being is that Plato puts forward this account of power.

For my purposes, however, the important thing to notice is that he uses the concept of power to refer to an ability to affect another thing or to be affected by it. That is, the specific feature of a thing that Plato takes as a mark of it as an existent thing is its ability to interact with other things. It is this feature that he uses the term "power" to conceptualize.

This usage of the term remains active in the philosophic tradition. It is employed, for example, by Locke. In his famous discussion of power in *An Essay Concerning Human Understanding,* Locke defines it as a simple idea:

> Power. . . . is another of those simple Ideas which we receive from Sensation and Reflection. For observing in our selves, that we do and can think, and that we can, at pleasure, move several parts of our Bodies which were at rest; the effects also, that natural Bodies are able to produce in one another, occurring every moment to our Senses, we both these ways get the Idea of Power. [22]

Although Locke's intention in discussing power is to demonstrate that the idea can be abstracted from experience, he accepts the Platonic conception of power as an ability to affect or be affected by something else. It is this meaning of "power" for which Locke attempts to provide a genetic account.

Locke acknowledges his use of such a conception of power more explicitly when attempting to make a distinction between active and passive power: "Power," he says, "is twofold, viz. as able to make, or able to receive any change: The one may be called *Active,* and the other *Passive Power*." [23] Thus, while attributing an active power to the sun in virtue of its ability to melt ice,

Locke also attributes a passive power to ice, in order to indicate that ice itself is the sort of thing that could be melted by the sun's power. The core notion of power for Locke is that of the ability of a thing to affect another thing, to cause it to change, or to be affected by a thing.

This usage of the term "power" is clearly dispositional. That is, it posits an ability on the part of one thing to affect a change in something else. As such, there is a distinction between having an ability and actualizing it. Power is thus not always realized, but stands for an ability that a thing has, independently of whether that ability is realized.

One respect in which Locke's use of the term "power" differs from Plato's is that Locke explicitly views things as having different types of powers. Relying on a substance-attribute metaphysics, Locke refers to the various properties of substances as their powers—that is, as the abilities that they have to affect things and to be affected by them. Plato's use of the term "power" is necessarily bound by his historical context; for him, this articulated structure of existent entities is not available. As a result, Plato does not speak of an entity as having a number of distinct powers, but only of power as the mark of the being of an entity. This is an important difference, for it opens up the question of whether it makes sense to speak of a thing's power generally or only of its various powers.

Despite this difference, Plato and Locke alike use the term "power" to refer to both an active ability to cause change and a passive one to suffer it. This way of speaking has generally been regarded as problematic within social theory and, indeed, philosophy in general. To speak of both causes and their effects as powers blurs the distinction between such active and passive capabilities. Most theorists have agreed that it is less confusing if one limits one's use of the term "power" to refer to active capabilities. One thus finds most modern social theorists who operate with this particular sense of power simply limiting it to the capacity of a thing (or person) to produce a change in another.[24]

Having discussed the manner in which the locution "has power to" grounds one line of theorizing about power, let me now turn to a second approach, which begins by limiting the concept "power-to" to human beings, or social agents at most, and then employs a definition of it that involves an agent's ability to bring about a result that is beneficial to him. This view of power is introduced into modern philosophic and political discourse by Hobbes in the following terms: "THE POWER *of a man*, to take it universally, is his present means, to obtain some future good."[25] I have already noted that Hobbes is here limiting his discussion of the concept of power to power possessed by human beings; it is also worth noting that he limits the use of "power" to its active sense. In both ways, he is departing from the more general usage that characterized the claims of Plato and Locke.

But there is an even more fundamental change in Hobbes's conceptualization of power, for he understands power not simply as the ability to bring about a change in something else but as a person's ability to bring about a state of affairs *beneficial* to that person. This view of power narrows the sorts of ends that an effect can have in order for it to be an instance of power. Instead of the generalized view present in Plato and Locke, Hobbes counts only effects that bear a very specific relation to an agent as instances of that agent's power. It marks a more restricted understanding of power in that it treats an agent's power as relative to ends that are beneficial to him.

The use of the term "power" derived from Hobbes, like that in the Plato-Locke tradition, does not treat power as fundamentally a social phenomenon. Although the Hobbesian use of the term is only concerned with the power of human beings, it does not limit that concern to power possessed and exercised within the social realm—that is, in relation to other human beings.[26] A person's power is understood as her ability to bring about effects, whether or not these effects have some essential reference to other human beings.

It is this narrower, Hobbesian view of power as an individual's ability to bring about a state of affairs beneficial to her that forms the core of one notion of power-to that has been important in contemporary social theory. In seeking to develop a concept of power that would refine the imprecise nature of its ordinary use, social theorists have tended to see the idea of power-as-ability as the fundamental sense of the concept and thus have used it as the basis of their refined conceptualizations. For example, Bertrand Russell, one of the first twentieth-century philosophers in the Anglo-American tradition to discuss power systematically, also defines power in a manner that depends upon the Hobbesian tradition, namely as "the production of intended effects".[27] Russell's definition treats power as the actual exercise of an ability. In this context I simply want to note that Russell is here employing something like the Hobbesian conception of power as a person's ability to realize a state of affairs, although Russell's stress on the actual production of the effects rather than the ability to produce them makes his definition of power less adequate than Hobbes's account.[28]

The prioritizing of power-to is very common among social theorists, independently of their more specific ideological or political leanings.[29] Nicos Poulantzas is an example of a Marxist theorist who opts for a view of power as the ability of an agent. For Poulantzas, power is primarily attributable to social classes. He states, "By power, we shall designate *the capacity of a social class to realize its specific objective interests.*"[30] This clearly is a definition of power that treats it as an ability, here of a collective social agent.

So far, I have looked at two related strands of philosophic thought in which power is conceived of as the ability to effect a change in something. By focusing upon one specific locution within which the term "power" functions, this tradition has developed a single concept of power, but at the cost of obscuring the use of this term to describe other social phenomena.

The second tradition of philosophic reflection focuses upon the other basic locution involving power, the phrase "has power over". According to this second tradition, the primary meaning of the term "power" is the ability of one human being to control another, which is referred to within contemporary discussions by the term "power-over". The idea that power involves the control of one human being over another has figured prominently in social theoretic discourse.

Spinoza is an example of a writer who uses "power" in this latter sense. Spinoza begins his discussion with a metaphysical account of power that does not differ in fundamental ways from the Platonic one: A thing's "persistence in being, then, cannot follow from its essence any more than its coming into being can; it needs the same power [*potentia*] to continue in being as it needs to come into being."[31] However, he goes on to develop a different concept of power, that of "being in the power of another," an understanding of the term that departs significantly from the Platonic view:

> It also follows that one individual is subject to the right of another, or dependent upon him, for as long as he is subject to the other's power [*potestate*]; and possessed of his own right, or free, in so far as he can repel all force, take what vengeance he pleases for harm done him, and, to speak generally, live as his own nature and judgment dictate.[32]

In this passage, Spinoza introduces a conception of power that is new to the philosophic tradition: the ability of one person to control the actions and beliefs of another. It is this "relational" sense of "power", one in which the term refers to a particular type of relationship among human beings, that forms the contrast to the sense of "power" I have previously considered. Interestingly enough, Spinoza makes his claims about "power" by means of two different Latin words. He uses *potestas,* rather than *potentia,* to refer to this relational sense of power and, as a result, is able to distinguish power-to and power-over in a clear and systematic way, a feature of his theory that has been obscured in its English translations.

Spinoza's use of distinct Latin words to conceptualize power-to and power-over gives further support to my contention that "power" has two distinct meanings. While both *potestas* and *potentia* have their root in the Latin term *posse,* which means "to be able", it is a mistake to see this common etymological origin as providing a fundamental unity.

A cursory examination of other languages supports this claim. In Greek, Plato used the word *dunamis* in proposing his theory of power. However, the word *kratos* is also used to refer to power in the sense of political power. (Hence the origin of terms like "demo-cracy" and "aristo-cracy" to refer to different forms of political power.) In German, there are a large number of terms referring to power whose meanings do not correspond exactly with English terms. However, German does have two different words to refer to power-over and power-to: *Macht* and *Kraft,* respectively. While *Kraft* also means strength, it is the term that is used to refer to the "powers" of substances. In German, a conceptual distinction is made between these two senses of "power" without there being a single root, as is the case in Latin.

In the usage of "power" that Spinoza introduces via the term *potestas,* "power" is used in a relational manner in that it posits a relation between two individuals such that one is able to limit the ability of the other to act or think as she would in the absence of the first. The use of the term is the one that I have signified by means of the locution power-over and that I shall argue is the primary one for a theory of social power.

James Mill also adopts this usage. Particularly interesting for our purposes, however, is the fact that, in arguing for this concept of power, Mill acknowledges that there are other senses to the concept, but claims that this is the most appropriate.

> The desire . . . of that power which is necessary to render the persons and properties of human beings subservient to our pleasures, is a grand governing law of human nature. . . . The grand instrument for attaining what a man likes is the actions of other men. Power, *in its most appropriate signification,* therefore, means security for the conformity between the will of one man and the acts of other men.[33]

Mill's failure to notice his own stipulative actions is quite apparent in this quotation. He is attempting to specify a single meaning of the term "power" as that most appropriate to use in social theory. In making his point, however, he implicitly acknowledges that there are other uses of the term within ordinary discourse, so that his own theoretical use has to be seen as stipulative. Mill's practice in this regard is only more obvious than that of many social theorists.

This is the sense of power that many contemporary social theorists have attempted to develop. For example, Harold Laswell and Abraham Kaplan reject the Russellian definition of power in favor of a relational conception: "Power in the political sense cannot be conceived as the ability to produce intended effects in general, but only such effects as directly involve other persons: political power is distinguished from power over nature as power over other men."[34] Although Laswell and Kaplan wish to distinguish their own use of the term "power" from Russell's, they do not notice that he defines power-to rather than power-over. They mistakenly take his use of the term "power" to be a more general use of the idea of power-over than that which they favor. So although they see themselves as working with a more limited concept of power than Russell, they fail to notice that the real distinction between their views is their focus upon alternative concepts of power. Thus, despite their efforts, Laswell and Kaplan do not really see the basic ambiguity of the concept of power.

In contrast to Laswell and Kaplan, Robert Dahl does not even see that there is an issue about the concept of power at this level of discourse. Dahl simply assumes that the appropriate phrase to define is "*A* has power over *B*", thus accepting the Spinozan sense of the term. Most of the theorists who have contested Dahl's definition of power have likewise followed his assumption.[35] This concept of power also lies at the basis of the use of the term "domination" by social theorists. Although "domination" has a more specific meaning than power-over has—that is, the use of power to dominate others—the traditions of social theory that concern themselves with domination make an implicit use of the notion of power-over.

Despite appearances to the contrary, Max Weber is another theorist who has focused upon the Spinozan sense of power. Weber defines power as "the possibility [*Chance*] within a social relationship of realizing one's own will even against resistance, no matter what such possibility depends upon."[36] Weber's definition is a mixture of the two locutions. By limiting power to social relationships, he seems to be defining the idea of one agent's power over another. His incorporation of the possibility of resistance into the definition further confirms this impression. However, when he defines power by means of the notion of "realizing one's own will", he is relying upon the Hobbesian account of power in terms of one's own future well being. Although Weber's use of the concept of the will results in a more internalist conception of power than Hobbes's reference to beneficial results, it seems to fit clearly into this tradition of regarding power as an ability.

This appearance notwithstanding, Weber does not fit into the Hobbesian tradition. As I have already mentioned, any attempt to define power-over will posit an ability—that it, a power—on the part of the agent who has power over another agent. Weber's definition, however, concerns the question of which of two agents in a social relationship has power over the other, and he asserts that the criterion of such power is the agent's ability—that is, power—to realize his will even though the other agent is trying to keep this from occurring. Because Weber does not see that there are two different senses of "power" that have to be distinguished, his own definition has the appearance of being about the one that it is not about.

This brief look at the development of these two different conceptions of power within the philosophic tradition and their impact upon social theory help to explain why "power" is an especially problematic concept within social theory—because it does not have a single use within ordinary discourse. When social theorists have attempted to introduce a more precise discursive practice, they have tended to stipulate a single use on the only appropriate one. But given the two basic uses of the concept within ordinary discourse, this stipulative practice has resulted in the emergence of two distinct trends within social theoretic conceptions of power: one developed by those who have stipulated a theoretical concept that is derived from the ordinary use of the phrase "has power to" and another developed by those who have stipulated one derived from the phrase "has power over".

It is difficult to accept the idea that "power" is not a more unified concept. According to a pervasive model of what it is for words or concepts to have meaning, each word in a language has associated with it a single meaning. As Pitkin asserts, accepting this model can lead us astray in analyzing the concept of social power. The meaning of a sentence is not achieved by linking each word to an idea in the mind in a sequential manner, as Wittgenstein, among others, has argued. The phrases "has power to" and "has power over" are not, despite their lexical similarity, about the same concept—"power". The fundamental ambiguity of "power" is a fact that social theorists need both to accept and to allow to affect their understanding of what they are doing when they produce a "theory of power".

Recognition of the ambiguity of the term "power" thus provides an understanding of one dimension of the variety of competing social theoretic conceptions of power. Not always fully aware of the duality of "power", social theorists have tended to develop theories of power that have fundamentally different objects, although these differences have been concealed from them.

This is not to say that social theorists do not have serious conflicts and disagreements with one another about "power". But these disputes are no more serious than the disputes in other fields. Once one acknowledges the duality of "power", then the remaining disputes among power theorists should not be a reason to doubt whether there are rational grounds for the settling of such disputes. Indeed, in the balance of this study I shall consider various views of power that I believe to be mistaken, and show the problematic nature of such theories.

Analyzing Power-Over

One central set of disagreements about the concept of power consists in choosing the appropriate sense of "power" with which to begin one's analysis. As I have argued, the expressions power-to and power-over are a shorthand way of making a distinction between two fundamentally different ordinary-language locutions within which the term "power" occurs. Depending upon which locution one takes as the basis of one's theory of power, one will arrive at a very different model of the role of power in the social world.

Instead of proposing a general theory of power, I intend to focus upon only one aspect of power, that of power-over. Although this will involve me in discussing issues of power-to from time to time, the basic aim of this study is to understand the nature of social power in the sense of power-over. The view of power developed in this study is partial: It seeks to illuminate only a portion of our ordinary understanding of power, namely that part of power that impacts on the lives of human beings by means of hierarchical social relationships. I wish to understand how power is an external factor that impacts on the lives of human beings.

Human beings also have power in themselves, and by concentrating on the locution "power-over", I do not mean to deny that many aspects of power-to have an important role to play within social theory. For example, the idea of coactive power, the ability of people working together to achieve things that they could not achieve alone, is an important theme for social theorists to study.[37] So is the role of processes of empowerment, for example, as the result of social movements.[38]

Nevertheless, I shall focus upon power-over because the concept of power has been used within social theory as a means of talking about hierarchical social relations and attempting to discuss their problematic status as well as their legitimate function. If we accept the idea that hierarchical social relations are a fundamental problem for social theory and that the concept of power has an important role to play in theorizing about them, then it follows that the concept of power-over has a fundamental role to play within social theory.

In so far as social theory has as one of its objectives the understanding of the nature of human beings' control over one another in society as a means of justifying or criticizing the role of such control, social theory will have to adopt the concept of power-over as one of its fundamental concepts. There is simply no other concept that is able to subsume the variety of forms of social control and influence under one rubric. Theories of social power have as their object explaining, justifying, and criticizing the unequal amount of control that social agents have over one another. As such they form an essential part of a general theory of society.

In the balance of this study, then, my aim will be to understand the structure and dynamics of social relationships involving power-over. I shall show that previous theories that have attempted to understand such relationships have foundered because of the assumptions upon which they have been erected. Such assumptions include a lack of attention to the variety inherent in the concept of power itself, use of a flawed model for understanding the nature of social theory, and an objectified understanding of power. My own conception of power will be developed in such a way that it avoids these illicit assumptions and thus provides a firm foundation for an understanding of what power is.

Let me add a cautionary note concerning my use of the term "power": When there is no danger of ambiguity, I will sometimes use the term "power" rather than "power-over". In any context where there might be confusion, I will explicitly use "power-over" in order to remind the reader that I am giving a theory of this concept and not that of "power-to".

My explicit statement that my theory is an attempt to conceptualize power-over differentiates my attempt from that of many social theorists who claim to be developing a theory of power. Since many of these theories have already chosen a specific sense of power as their focus, they are not really giving as general a theory of social power as they intend or claim. Some of the conflict surrounding theories of power arises as a result of social theorists' assuming that a particular analysis of power is the only one that ought to be used within social theory.[39]

The idea of focusing upon "power-over" is one that has come under fire from a number of social theorists. Although there are certain issues that a theory of power-over will not address, I wish to contend that it is an important part of a theory of social power and should not be replaced by a focus simply upon power-to. Consequently, before proceeding, I would like to look at the objections of two of these theorists, C. B. Macpherson and Nancy Hartsock.

C. B. Macpherson argues that it is important for social theorists not to limit their concern to power-over. He states that it is important to "separate the two components of which a man's power may consist: his ability to use his own capacities, and his ability to use other men's capacities. The latter ability is power over others, the ability to extract benefit from others."[40] Macpherson goes on to argue that contemporary political theory has been hampered by its failure to consider power as a generic phenomenon. He claims that contemporary political theorists, unlike their classical progenitors, focus upon political power as the only form in which power exists. As a result, they are unable to ask certain questions that he thinks are crucial to the enterprise of political thought: "Focus on the *source* of political power puts out of the field of vision any perception of the necessary *purpose* of political power in any unequal society, which is to maintain the extractive power of the class or classes which have extractive power." [41] Macpherson here points out that the narrow focus of contemporary political theory makes it difficult to raise important questions concerning power. Treating political power itself as a given has left political theorists unable, according to Macpherson, to ask more general questions about the differentiation of social power into separate political and economic spheres.

After making this important observation, Macpherson goes on to argue that the way to remedy this problem is to address issues of power-to as well as power-over: "These shortcomings of current empirical approaches to politics might be remedied if more attention were given to the other concept of power: power as ability to use and develop essentially human capacities." [42] Yet Macpherson has not demonstrated that his suggestion is the correct one for dealing with the problem that he has isolated. He wishes to make it possible to discuss certain issues concerning the role of political power in maintaining a general social inequality of power. An alternative strategy for doing this would be to attack head-on the problematic assumption made by political theorists that political power is itself the central form of power-over in society. A theory of social power of the type that I develop in this book will allow the discussion of the very sorts of questions that Macpherson calls for.

Indeed, the terms in which Macpherson frames his discussion show its problematic nature. Macpherson distinguishes two types of power that a person can possess: power to realize certain abilities, and power over other persons. In so doing, he assumes, as do his adversaries, an individualistic conception of social power. It is individualistic because it treats individual human beings as possessors of power. While Macpherson is critical of his adversaries' acknowledgment of only a limited range of such powers, he accepts the idea that power can be thought of as the possession of discrete individuals—that is, as their powers.

But this individualist assumption is a problematic one. Although the presence of power may always be observed by means of its effects on individuals, power itself need not be the possession of individuals. There are forms of power in which power affects the lives of individual social agents but cannot be analyzed as the possession of individual social agents. As I shall argue, one needs to approach the question of what constitutes the power that is exercised over social agents without assuming that the answer can be formulated using a conception of power as the possession of individual social agents. Ironically, Macpherson's conceptual framework buys into the very individualism he has so tellingly criticized in his earlier work.[43]

Another theorist who argues for the need to consider questions of power-to as well as power-over is Nancy Hartsock. Hartsock criticizes traditional theories of power-over for being the result of a male perspective on the social world. She characterizes her own argument in the following way: "I argue that by adopting . . . a feminist standpoint, one can set out a feminist . . . theorization of power that . . . can point beyond understanding of power as power over."[44] Hartsock identifies male theories of power as ones that focus on the idea of power-over. This is because male theorists equate power with domination. Such a view of power is limited, according to Hartsock. By way of contrast, "theories of power put forward by women rather than men differ systematically from the understanding of power as domination. . . . I was unable to discover any woman writing about power who did not stress those aspects of power relating to energy, capacity, and potential."[45] In the terms that I have been using, Hartsock is here claiming that female social theorists have stressed the idea of power-to, while male theorists have concentrated upon the idea of power-over. Hartsock's argument is that the views of power put forward by women incorporate a dimension of power that male theories have left out.[46]

Hartsock's identification of the idea of power-over with that of domination causes her to see theories of power-over as more limited than they are. As I shall argue, this is a serious mistake, one that fails to recognize the diverse roles that relations of power play in society. Seeing male theories of power as having the conceptual mechanism for dealing only with issues of domination causes Hartsock to overlook the fact that power-over can also refer to many of the sorts of relations that she sees female theorists discussing.[47] Power-over is a much more general concept than that of domination, and conceptualizing the specific nature of relationships in which power is exercised over other human beings will help us understand both how human beings are dominated by other human beings and how they are aided by them.

Conclusion

In this chapter, I have taken the first step in developing a theory of social power by articulating exactly what the object of such a theory will be. In contrast to many theorists of power, I have argued that "power" is a fundamentally ambiguous concept and that it is this ambiguity that is responsible for some of the disagreement about what it is that a theory of social power should address. By acknowledging the fact that theories of power-to and power-over conceptualize different, though related, aspects of society, we see that these theories do not necessarily compete, as they would if power were an essentially contested concept. Despite the self-understandings of many theorists of power, not all theories of power are attempts to conceptualize the same phenomena, so that no one theory of power can be general enough to replace all others. The assumption that "power" is univocal is one source of confusion concerning the possibility of developing an adequate theory of social power.

2

The Consensual Model of Power

HANNAH ARENDT'S conception of power is an example of a theory of power that has been subject to a great deal of debate among social theorists. In her book *On Violence,* Arendt argues that power is a positive characteristic of social systems. While Arendt's theory has been dismissed by many social theorists for its failure to provide an adequate view of the phenomena normally thought of as associated with the concept of power, it has also found important adherents, such as Jürgen Habermas, who has integrated important aspects of Arendt's view of power into his own synoptic social theory.

Arendt's theory is controversial because she argues that it is a fundamental mistake to develop a theory of social power that relies primarily on notions of inequality and domination. She claims that "power", in its fundamental meaning, is a consensual notion, one that relies upon the agreement of a group of social agents about how to regulate their mutual lives. Failure to appreciate this, she argues, has led social theorists to present a one-sided and distorted conception of power in society, a conception that fails to recognize power as a positive social force.

Although Arendt presents her theory as a general view of power and asserts that her conception of power is the only legitimate one, I shall argue that her theory is best viewed as an attempt to develop a theory of specifically political power. As such, her theory is a perfect example of the phenomenon that I discussed in the last chapter: a contentious view of power that seems much less contentious when the actual object of its analysis is recognized. Once Arendt's theory is properly designated as a theory of political power, both its initial plausibility and its ultimate weaknesses emerge clearly.

33

Thus, in looking at Arendt's view I shall not only be assessing its own validity but shall also be using it as an example of the problems that result in social theory when the terms of discourse are not subjected to careful enough scrutiny. The argument of this chapter will therefore supplement my claim in the first chapter that the conflicts among theories of power do not need to be explained by any special hypothesis such as that of the essentially contested nature of "power". As I shall argue, Arendt's failure to specify accurately the object of her investigation gave rise to pseudo-conflicts based on specific problematic assumptions that she and other theorists of power have made about the nature and scope of their own theories.

The Ascendancy of Power

Arendt's central aim is to develop a concept of power that departs from the standard assumption of many social theorists that "power" refers to structures of domination and subordination. In place of such a concept, she proposes a concept of power that designates the ability of a group to realize its own ends through cooperation. This use of the term "power" departs radically from its usual use to conceptualize hierarchical social relationships. It will be useful to begin by asking why Arendt proceeds in this peculiar manner.

Arendt begins her argument by claiming that the usual understanding of power is inadequate because it links power to violence. She argues that most of the contemporary theorists concerned with the topic have made this linkage by claiming that violence is the ultimate foundation and rationale for the existence of power relations: "If we turn to discussion of the phenomenon of power, we soon find that there exists a consensus among political theorists from Left to Right to the effect that violence is nothing more than the most flagrant manifestation of power."[1] It is precisely this linkage of power and violence that Arendt views as problematic. In attempting to account for its prevalence, she traces it back to what she calls a "command-obedience model of power". According to such a model, an agent has power if she is able to issue commands that other agents will then obey. Arendt believes that social and political theorists have generally adopted this model of power. For example, she claims that Voltaire's definition of power as "making others act as I choose" relies on it, and that it is present in the writings of such diverse theorists as C. Wright Mills and Bertrand de Jouvenal.

Arendt sees the traditional command-obedience model of power as supporting the claim that violence is the ultimate form that power will assume in order to enforce its own decisions: "If the essence of power is the effectiveness of command, then there is no greater power than that which grows out of the barrel of a gun." [3]

The particular linkages that Arendt makes between power, violence, and the command-obedience model seem somewhat arbitrary. In order to see exactly what Arendt is worried about, we need to realize that she sees the question of power as tied to that of the nature of political rule. She is critical of the command-obedience model of power because she sees that view as entailing an inadequate understanding of the nature of political life itself. Her reasons for making these assumptions will emerge from a consideration of the view that Arendt is trying to counter.

The understanding of power and political life that Arendt wishes to criticize is one that received its paradigmatic formulation in Plato's *Republic*. In book 1, after Socrates has proposed that a just state is one whose rulers rule for the benefit of the ruled, Thrasymachus challenges this view by claiming that the rules of justice are nothing but rules laid down by the rulers in their own interest. Rather than seeing the rulers as caretakers of the ruled in analogy to doctors, pilots, and horse-trainers, as Socrates suggests, Thrasymachus sees them as powerful individuals who seek to benefit themselves by means of ruling other, weaker individuals, proposing that we see rulers as like shepherds who take care of their charges in order to benefit themselves. [4]

It is this view that Arendt sees as linking power and violence. Because power is conceived of as nothing but effectiveness of command, the use of violence to maintain command is seen as the logical strategy for power to employ if that is the only means available to ensure obedience. The effectiveness of a ruler is gauged by his ability to get the ruled to do what he wishes them to. Violence is simply the most extreme form that such rule can take.

Although Arendt phrases her criticism in terms of the inadequacies of the command-obedience model of power, her real worry is that this view of the nature of political rule is inadequate. That is, she sees the command-obedience model of power as grounding a particular view of the nature of political rule. Since she believes that this view of political rule is both widely accepted and deeply flawed, she seeks to undermine it by showing that it misconceives of the nature of power, and hence political life itself.

In order to defend her view, Arendt calls upon an alternative tradition in political thought, one in which she claims power and violence are seen as antithetical. In this tradition, she says, there is a recognition that, where violence is used, power has become inoperative. She traces this tradition back to the roots of democratic theory in Athens and Rome as well as to eighteenth-century political theory. The model of power that is presented by this tradition, she argues, is one that recognizes the fact that power is dependent upon the will of the people: "It is the people's support that lends power to the institutions of a country, and this support is but the continuation of a consent that brought the laws into existence to begin with." [5] If power is thought about in terms of a consensual model rather than a command-obedience model, Arendt argues, then the linkage of power and violence that has dominated much of political thought, both traditional and contemporary, will be seen to be mistaken. Indeed, once power is seen to require the prior consent of those over whom it is exercised, then it will also be recognized that power can never be exercised by means of the use of violence.

To prove her point, Arendt considers the case of a revolution, a situation that seems to offer the best example of a context in which violence is used to ground relations of power. One might be tempted to claim that, in a revolutionary situation, it is precisely violent acts that allow a group to achieve dominance, so that such a situation presents the clearest view of the violence that always forms the basis for power. But Arendt argues that a closer inspection of the facts reveals this not to be the case at all.

> In a contest of violence against violence the superiority of the government has always been absolute; but this superiority lasts only as long as the power structure of the government is intact—that is, as long as commands are obeyed and the army or police force are prepared to use their weapons. When this is no longer the case, the situation changes abruptly. . . . When commands are no longer obeyed, the means of violence are of no use. . . . Everything depends on the power behind the violence. [6]

Given Arendt's critique of the command-obedience model of power, it is surprising to find her employing it in this passage as a means of characterizing the nature of a government's power. Leaving this aside, however, we can see that Arendt is arguing that, even in the case of revolutions, the primacy of power can be demonstrated. Only if those who possess the means of violence are *willing* to use their weapons to enforce the orders of those in power will those in power be able to use violence to enforce their will. The ascension to political power by the victorious party is not due to its employment of violence itself, but rather to its ability to command the *allegiance* of those who possess the means of violence. The undoing of the dominant political regime can only come about, she claims, when the agents who enforce its decisions—that is, the police or the army—are no longer willing to do so. Contrary to the assumptions of most political theorists, Arendt argues, it is power that is a necessary condition for the effective use of violence and not the reverse. Without the consent of those capable of committing acts of violence, the commands of those "in power" are futile.

Arendt takes this discussion to prove "the fundamental ascendancy of power over violence." [7] That is, she holds that, even in the case of revolutions, the relation between power and violence is the reverse of what contemporary theorists have assumed: Power—in her newly defined sense as based upon the consent of those over whom it is exercised—is actually the reality behind the use of violence. She holds that political theory needs to adopt such a new sense of power in order to achieve an adequate understanding of the nature of political rule. The usual Thrasymachian assumption that power is based upon violence causes social theorists to give a reductive analysis of the nature of human social life and to misunderstand the importance of power as a consensual phenomenon.

Situating Arendt's View

Arendt seems to be offering a fundamentally different conception of power from that which has been developed by other social theorists. However, a great deal of the provocativeness of Arendt's view is merely apparent. It is achieved because she ignores the conceptual setting for her own view of power. Contrary to Arendt's own claims, her account of power needs to be understood as an attempt to explicate the nature of political power and not of social power in general. Only in this light is the point of her seemingly peculiar claims about power apparent; but once it is viewed in this light, Arendt's theory is not as radical as she would have her readers believe. For her view does not amount to an alternative conception of power, but merely an argument for acknowledging a form of power that is not adequately stressed by many contemporary theorists. The problems that result from Arendt's failure to observe the distinction between the concept of power in general and the more particular forms of power are paradigmatic of what happens when social theorists do not reflect upon the aims and objects of their own theories in an adequate manner.

Because of its surprising content, many social theorists have rejected Arendt's conceptualization of power as deeply flawed. Steven Lukes, for example, argues that Arendt's view of power lacks persuasiveness because it was developed in order to support her general theoretical program. One of the basic claims of Arendt's political philosophy is that there has been a decline in the importance of a "public space", a space in which individuals can come together and argue with one another without fear of sanctions. It is this space

that she feels comprises the essence of a healthy society that will remain free
of the disease of totalitarianism. This is an important and influential idea that
has played a significant role in much of Arendt's writing and has been picked
up by Habermas and transformed into the center of his critical theory in the
guise of the ideal speech situation.

Lukes argues that Arendt's conception of power serves more to support
this general view of society than to give an adequate analysis of power itself.
He claims that Arendt is offering a stipulative definition of "power"—that is,
seeking to get social theorists to revise their usual manner of thinking about
it—in order to render her own theory of society more plausible. He states that

> [Arendt's] conceptualisation of power plays a persuasive role, in defence
> of her conception of "the *res publica,* the public thing" to which people
> consent and "behave nonviolently and argue rationally", and in opposi-
> tion to the reduction of "public affairs to the business of domination" and
> to the conceptual linkage of power with force and violence.[8]

Lukes goes on to argue that such a stipulative definition of the concept of
power has serious problems. Arendt's recommendation that we revise the role
that "power" plays in our usual conceptual framework legislates an entire
sphere of concern out of existence, resulting in a conceptual framework that
lacks an important capability: If Arendt's recommendation was accepted,
issues that had previously been designated by means of the concept of power
could no longer be referred to by that means. Since Arendt does not offer
any compelling reason for adopting such a new form of discourse, her idiosyncratic usage of the concept of power is simply a mistake, one that is caused
by her attempt to bend this concept to her own systematic concerns. Pointing
out similarities between Arendt's view and that of Talcott Parsons, Lukes
states: "All that Parsons and Arendt wish to say about consensual behavior
remains sayable" in a theory that sticks to the usual conception of power, "but
so also does all that they wish to remove from the language of power."[9] Since
our ordinary conceptual framework has all the resources available to Arendt—
plus the ability to refer to other phenomena by the use of the traditional concept of power—Lukes argues that there is no persuasive reason to adopt a new
stipulative definition.

Although Lukes makes many important points in his criticism of Arendt's
program, one serious problem in his view results in his making too sweeping a
dismissal of her ideas. Lukes fails to see that Arendt's recommendation about
how to revise the conceptual practices regarding "power" has two aspects.
The first is the development of a certain understanding of the nature of politi-

cal power. The second is the claim that this is the only sense of power that social theory ought to recognize. While Lukes argues that the second claim is inadequate, he fails to address Arendt's argument for the first one.

By accepting Arendt's own view of the scope of her theory, Lukes is able to criticize it tellingly. Ironically, however, once one recognizes that Arendt is actually mistaken about this aspect of her theory, her own theory of power takes on more plausibility. That is, in order to see that Arendt's view of power is not as arbitrary and self-serving as Lukes claims it to be, it needs to be understood as a view of the nature of political power that Arendt misleadingly presents as a general theory of power.

To see this, it is important to realize that Arendt's use of the term "power" to refer to political power is not simply idiosyncratic. Many social theorists, and political theorists in particular, use the term to stand for political power. For example, Talcott Parsons, with whom Lukes and others associate Arendt's view,[10] in an article entitled "On the Concept of Political Power" offers a definition of the concept of power in general that suffers from shortcomings similar to Arendt's. Parsons defines "power" as follows:

Power then is generalized capacity to secure the performance of binding obligations by units in a system of collective organization when the obligations are legitimized with reference to their bearing on collective goals and when in case of recalcitrance there is a presumption of enforcement by negative situational sanctions—whatever the actual agency of that enforcement.[11]

Parsons, like Arendt, trades on an ambiguity about what the object of his definition is. As the title of his paper suggests, it is political power only, and not social power in general, that forms the concern of his analysis. He presents a definition of such power that he believes to be superior to other attempts. However, like Arendt, Parsons then argues as if the concept of power that he has developed were the only legitimate use of the concept within social theory. As a result, he mistakenly concludes that his analysis of political power amounts to an argument that all other conceptions of power have no place within social theory.[12]

Jürgen Habermas also operates with a discourse that elides the distinction between social power in general and specifically political power. Although he is critical of certain aspects of Parsons' view of power, Habermas accepts Parsons' use of money as a model for understanding the nature of power. Habermas agrees with Parsons that, "considered as a steering medium, power represents the symbolic embodiment of amounts of value without itself possessing any intrinsic value. . . . Nominal claims to compliance with binding decisions can be redeemed in real values and are backed by reserves of a particular kind." [13] Habermas claims that power is a symbolic medium that regulates the interaction of social agents without requiring that they interact in a communicative manner. Just as money provides a medium for the systematic interaction of agents in the economic realm, power regulates their interaction in the political realm.

There are many features of Habermas' view that call for discussion. For my present purposes, however, I simply want to call attention to the fact that Habermas views the concept of power as one that has meaningful application only within the political domain. Perhaps as a result of the influence of Arendt and Parsons, Habermas simply accepts the conventions of their use of the term "power" without noticing how problematic those conventions are. His own discourse shows the same problematic elision of political and social power that I have demonstrated in regard to Arendt and Parsons.

This particular use of the term "power" is not just arbitrary; it has a basis in a specific discursive practice involving the term that I have not yet discussed. This practice involves a locution that refers to certain political offices as being the location of power itself, as when we say that two political parties are vying for *power* in an election. In such a locution, "power" is used to refer to certain positions in the government itself. Since the occupants of these positions can make certain important decisions, it is these positions that are the object of political struggle. For a party to be "in power" is for it to have its members in these central positions. In the United States, such power is often associated with the presidency. A party is said to be in *power* if its candidate has won the presidential election.

The discursive practice of Arendt, Parsons, and Habermas can be seen as an attempt to treat this particular use of the term "power" as the basic one for social theory. Such a view is tempting in view of the fact that the term occurs without a preposition in this usage. This fact can easily give rise to the impression that this use of the term is basic, the one upon which social theorists should concentrate.

In fact, the situation is rather the reverse. This use of the term "power" is really a localization of power to a specifically political realm. Although it is an important use of the term "power", one that any general theory of power needs to acknowledge, it is not the most general use of the term. As I argued in the previous chapter, there are other uses of the term that are more general in that they do not limit power to the specifically political realm. It is such uses of the concept of power that are most basic in a theory of social power in general.

There are two conclusions that I shall draw from my discussion of the discursive practice of Arendt, Parsons, and Habermas. The first is that one aspect of the conflict between these theorists and a critic such as Lukes has its source in their privileging of different uses of the term "power" within ordinary discourse. Once the divergence in the use of the term "power" has been noted, it is possible to resolve the conflict between these theorists by showing that they are not advocating discourses that actually compete with one another. Rather, each discourse can be shown to have an important place within a general theory of social power. "Power" is less contested than it first appears.

But, secondly, Arendt's theory cannot be critically assessed so long as it is considered to be a theory of social power in general. To do so is to fall prey to the very conflation that she makes as part of her attempt to reform the discursive practices of social theorists. Since we have seen that she is trying to provide an understanding of political power, it is necessary to ask whether her proposal make sense when viewed in this light.

Once Arendt's view of power is considered this way, it can be seen that it has more plausibility than Lukes and other critics allow.[14] Only the conflation of the object of investigation, caused by the multiple locutions in which the word "power" is used, makes Lukes's dismissal of Arendt's view plausible. Although it is true that Arendt's view of power does not make sense as a general analysis of the concept of power, it does not really compete with such analyses. The universalistic aspect of Arendt's presentation of her claims needs to be rejected, but once this is done, her other claim—that political power is best understood as a form of power grounded in the consensus of the governed—emerges as a distinct claim that cannot simply be dismissed as a result of the problems in her first assertion. This claim requires an independent assessment.

The Plausibility of the Consensual Model

I have been arguing that Arendt should be taken to claim that political power results from a mutual decision made by a group of people to create a social hierarchy in order to run their common life efficiently. The dominant position in the hierarchy is one that is referred to as "having power". I shall now present an argument for Arendt's view, an argument that shows that the power that an agent has in such a hierarchy is not a form of domination at all, but rather *an artifact of social life* in that it is a means for enabling agents who desire to cooperate with one another to have an effective means of making group decisions. The establishment of a specific type of social hierarchy is simply a solution to what might be called a "technical" problem of group life, namely how to make decisions in an efficient and well-defined manner. As such, political power—in the sense of the concentration of decision-making in the hands of a specific sub-group—emerges as the result of a group's decision about how to order its own affairs.

To illustrate this, I will use a simple example drawn from sports. Say that a group of people are playing touch football and that they have decided on the particular positions that each one will play. As they come into the huddle to decide on what play to execute at a particular time, there may be a lot of confusion, with everyone trying to argue that his favorite play is the best one to try next. In such a situation, it might be possible to decide on plays democratically, listing all the proposed plays and then voting on their favorite ones, eventually choosing one play by majority vote. It is clear that such a decision procedure will not work; the exigencies of the game make it impossible to execute democratic decision-making procedures in a speedy and efficient manner. Even in informal game situations, a particular participant is usually chosen as captain, at least temporarily, with the result that she is given the responsibility of making the final decision about what plays to make and how to handle the input from others. She has the "power" on the team in that she is the one who makes the decisions about how the team will act.

This example provides a clear legitimation for the claim that a power hierarchy, by concentrating decision-making for a group in the hands of a single agent, solves a problem of coordination in group life. Only if the various agents that compose a group have a means for coordinating their actions can they really act as a group at all—that is, have a means of arriving at a single plan of action. In order to make group action possible, at least in certain situations, a single agent needs to be given the right to decide what is to be done. At this level, the need for a decision-maker is a purely formal need. Tossing a coin would do as well. Nonetheless, what this shows is that the establishment of a social hierarchy can serve the function of enabling group actions to take place.[15]

This example supplies an argument for Arendt's claim that power can have a consensual basis. It shows that the Thrasymachian view of political power as necessarily exercised by the rulers in their own self-interest is false. Political power can have a grounding other than the desire of a powerful group to assert its own interest at the expense of those whom it rules. Political power can be the result of a group's decision to handle its own affairs in an efficient manner.

Arendt's view of political power, then, makes an important criticism of the Thrasymachian assumption that political power is necessarily an instrument of social domination. She has pointed to an alternative account of the origin of political power, one that I have given more precision. It is an account of political power that shows the consensual basis that such power can have.

But even in making these claims, I have misstated the conclusion of Arendt's argument slightly. While I have spoken of the possibility of political power's having its origin in a consensus, Arendt speaks of the necessity of such grounding, of power's necessarily excluding relations of violence. I turn now to a criticism of Arendt's illicit extension of the idea of consensus from a possible to a necessary ground of political power.

Power and Violence

A good way to approach the problems with Arendt's account of political power is to focus upon the terms she uses. Her argument progresses using only the terms "power" and "violence", employing these terms in rigid opposition to one another. This practice is highly suspicious and justifiably has attracted a good deal of critical attention.

For example, Dennis Wrong criticizes Arendt's terminology in the following manner: "In effect, she equates power with legitimate authority and places it in stark contrast to violence without distinguishing violence and the threat of violence". [16] Wrong attempts to locate the problem with Arendt's discourse in three separate but connected issues. The first is the rigid opposition between "power" and "violence." In Chapter 5, I shall argue that there are various other forms of power that an adequate theory of power must include. By operating with a conceptual framework with only two terms, each conceived as excluding the presence of the other, Arendt brings to the study of power a rigid dichotomy that does not do justice to the rich texture of power relationships in society.

But Wrong also claims that each of the terms in this opposition is inadequately conceived by Arendt. While I believe that there are problems with Arendt's use of the terms "power" and "violence", I do not think that Wrong has adequately demonstrated what they are.

First of all, Arendt does not make a simple equation of power with legitimate power, as the following quotation demonstrates: "Even the totalitarian ruler, whose chief instrument of rule is torture, needs a power basis—the secret police and its net of informers." [17] While we shall have to investigate the nature of the point that Arendt is making in this quotation, she clearly does not equate power with legitimate political power (what Wrong calls "legitimate authority"), since she claims that the totalitarian ruler, the paradigm of illegitimacy, requires a power basis. Second, while Arendt does fail to distinguish the exercise of violence from the threat of its use, there is another problem that Wrong does not notice: Arendt's very use of the concept of violence to describe all non-consensual political phenomena lumps together various things that need to be kept separate. The real issue for Arendt is to deny that power is grounded in relations of force. But not all uses of force are violent. Arendt's use of the word "violence" carries with it the unjustified assertion that the use of force is necessarily suspect. But this is precisely what Arendt needs to argue in order to establish her thesis. Arendt's use of the word "violence" attempts to use semantic connotations in the place of argumentation. Had she used the terms "force" and "coercion" to make her claims, she would not have been able to make the argument for the mutual exclusiveness of consensual and non-consensual aspects of political power.

The point of focusing on Arendt's use of this single, stark conceptual dichotomy between "power" and "violence" is to show that it obscures many of the issues that Arendt ought to face. With a more sophisticated and nuanced framework with which to conceptualize issues surrounding political rule, one would not be tempted to make the oppositional claims that Arendt does. Once again, we can see the importance of subjecting one's theoretical vocabulary to careful scrutiny.

But showing the problems with Arendt's theoretical vocabulary is only the prelude to an investigation of her more substantive claims. The central shortcoming of Arendt's view of power is that, by adopting a rigid dichotomy, Arendt precludes herself from giving an account of the role of coercive relationships in the maintenance of political power. As a result, she presents an account of political power that is as one-sided as the Thrasymachian view she wishes to counter.

To see this, I want to return to the football example. The point of that example was to show that a certain type of power relationship could be seen as solving a problem of group rule by delegating decision-making to a single social agent. Arendt wants, however, to assert more than that. She wants to show that political power is necessarily consensual. This is an unjustifiable extension of the argument I have given. That this is so can be seen by reflecting on the fact that the political power that the dominant agent in a social hierarchy has is simultaneously a form of power-over. By restricting her use of the term "power" to the power inhering in a role, Arendt obscures the element of power-over in the constitution of social hierarchies. While it is true that there is a consensual basis to the power that the captain of the team has in this example, the relationship that is constituted is one in which she does have *power over* her team members. That is, it is the captain's decision about which play to run in a particular situation that determines what a particular player must do. As a result of the team's decision to let her decide which play to call, the captain's decisions are binding on the team members. She has power over the team members in that she determines which play they will execute. The fact that a team member who fails to follow her instructions can be criticized as having made a mistake shows that the captain does have power over her teammates.

Arendt's use of the term "power" focuses upon only one of the two aspects that are essential to this situation. For her, "power" refers to the concentration of decision-making in the hands of the captain. Her analysis fails to provide a means of referring to the other aspect of this situation—namely, that the captain's decision-making power gives her power over her teammates in that her decisions are binding upon them.

One reason that Arendt would deny that the dominant agent in a consensual power relationship has power-over is that she identifies power-over with domination. As I have already stated and will demonstrate more fully in the course of this study, this is simply a mistake. There are relationships in which power-over is used in order to enhance the life of the subordinate agent rather than to dominate her. Arendt's blindness to this possibility causes her to resist the idea that political power includes an aspect of power-over.

That political power entails the presence of power-over can be seen by returning to the example of the football team. Let us ask what would happen if one player decides that he does not like the agreement that he made and wants to opt out of the consensual power relationship to which he earlier consented.

If the decision that the group made to appoint a captain is held to, it is clear that the team cannot tolerate this player's decision. There must be some means available to the team to enforce the players' decision upon each player. A team that had to reforge its consensus at every instant would be unstable. Since there is a real need to make social decisions in an efficient manner in sports, whatever form of decision-making is adopted must be one that will not continually have to be renegotiated. The only way to ensure this is to have some means of enforcing the decision-maker's decisions. An agent cannot be allowed to opt out of the solution he has accepted, for this will vitiate the effectiveness of the solution.

Coercion is the simplest means for enforcing a player's obligation to his teammates. If a player who had previously agreed to have one player be captain decides that that decision was a bad one, but none of the other players do, one effective means for retaining the power relationship is for all the other players to make a threat—for example, by offering the dissident player an ultimatum: Either accept the captain we all have designated or get off the team. Such an ultimatum would keep the team functioning even in the face of the dissent of a single player (assuming, of course, the presence of a sufficient supply of players). The dissenting player would have to decide which alternative to accept, whether to continue playing with a captain he did not approve of or to stop playing. By including in its structure a coercive aspect, such a form of power acquires a means for handling the problem of dissension.

Even a consensually generated hierarchical form of political power, then, has a need for some means of coercion. The ability to threaten to use force (recall that this means the presence of violence, given Arendt's terminology) is necessary to keep a consensually based form of power operating despite dissension. A power relationship cannot maintain itself if the subordinate agent can simply opt out of it whenever he chooses to. Once agents have accepted the idea of a common form of life, they cannot opt out of that life whenever they choose.

If political power is viewed in an exclusively consensual manner, then there can be no way to handle the problem of dissent. Although political power can originate in a consensus of those who become governed by such power, it is always exercised with their de facto consent. There will be times when recalcitrant agents have to be coerced to keep to the terms of their original consent.

Viewed from a purely political point of view, the American Civil War can be seen to be an example of the coercive use of political power. In this case, the federal government was unwilling to tolerate "opting out" as an alternative that it would allow the Southern states to adopt. On its view, the decision to enter into the Union was not one that could be opted out of when a state chose to. From a theoretical perspective at least, that war was fought in order to establish a particular conception of the power of the federal government as the ruling one.

The examples of sports and of the Civil War show that even consensually constituted instances of political power can have coercive aspects. Indeed, without such a coercive mechanism, a power structure would be helpless in the face of dissension. The purely consensual model that Arendt advocates abstracts from this crucial feature of political power and, as such, is unsatisfactory. Instead of seeing political power simply as a form of consensus, both the consensual and the coercive aspects need to be seen as integral to the maintenance of political rule.

A second problem with Arendt's model is that her single-minded focus on the consensus that she correctly argues is essential to the constitution of political power obscures another fundamental issue—namely, whether that consensus is a universal or only a partial one. Indeed, as I shall argue, one who accepts the Thrasymachian view of society need not deny that there is a consensus at the basis of the political power in a society; she can simply argue that that consensus is a consensus among the rulers only and hence does not entail the legitimacy of the political system itself. Arendt's discussion of power does not undermine this claim, because she fails to distinguish this issue from the question of whether power needs to have a consensual basis.

We can see this problem in Arendt's own discourse, for she claims not simply that political power can involve consent but that it necessarily does and, hence, can never be grounded in forms of violence. She assumes that her view of political power is sufficient to account for all the structures of political power in contemporary society. This is a mistake with serious consequences. Just because power sometimes can arise as an artifact of social life, as a solution to a problem of social decision-making, not all forms of political power need share such an origin.

This problem will emerge if we reconsider the example Arendt gives of a revolutionary situation. Recall that the point Arendt wishes to make is that even in a revolutionary situation power grounds violence and not vice versa. The ability of a government to command the means of violence is possible, she claims, only because those possessing arms are willing to follow commands that other agents give them. Arendt wants to prove by means of this example that even violence is founded on a form of power. She wants to be able to maintain that such a form of power cannot be analyzed as a form of domination. The government is able to remain in power only so long as its own agents, those possessing the means of violence, faithfully execute its commands.

Arendt is correct to point out that the government only has power so long as those who actually will exercise its commands are willing to do so. In a revolutionary situation, there may come a time when the agents of the government are no longer willing to do so, and when they align themselves with the revolutionaries instead. It is this possibility to which Arendt is calling attention, and it is indeed an important point, one that illustrates the importance of adopting a more dynamic understanding of power relationships than many theorists of power have.[18]

The problem with Arendt's argument, however, is that she conflates the claim that power depends on the consent of those who exercise it with another one, namely that the existence of a power relation in a social group is based upon the universal consent of those who make up that group. She takes her example of the revolutionary situation to show that the existence of a particular form of political power depends upon the consent of a certain group of agents to continue to play their customary role. According to Arendt, while they consent to the rule of the pre-revolutionary government, they empower it; once they change their allegiance, they disempower it.

In making this claim, Arendt simply replaces a view of power in which political rule is identified with domination with a view of power that identifies political rule with consensus. Although she is correct to deny the adequacy of the identification of political power with domination, she simply supplants that conception with one that is equally flawed.

There are really two problems here. The first is that Arendt conceives of the situation of those who carry out the orders of the political rulers as one in which they consent to those orders. The second is that she takes such consent to show that violence is never the basis of political rule.

An adequate analysis of the situation of those agents who carry out the orders of the rulers requires a more adequate social ontology than Arendt employs, one that shows that agreement is not the only factor in constituting social power. It is such an ontology that I will develop by means of the idea of a situated power relationship in Chapter 7 of this study. But even at this point, it is possible to see the weaknesses of Arendt's account.

Arendt conceptualizes the situation of those agents who enact the dictates of the rulers in too simple a manner. Just because an agent chooses to follow the order of another agent does not mean that she consents to the legitimacy of that order. Arendt wants to deny that an agent in a political community is in a power relationship with her leaders. But as I have argued, the presence of political power does not rule out the presence of a relationship of power-over. In fact, both aspects of power are present. A subordinate agent may be in a situation where not following an order made by a dominant agent can be so detrimental to her own welfare that she will choose to follow the order even while wishing that there were other options open to her.[19] Arendt simply conflates the failure of an agent in a political power relationship to resist an order with her consenting to its legitimacy. Only by means of such a conflation does her view have any plausibility.[20]

In the example of a revolutionary situation, Arendt conceptualizes the situation of the agents in the army or police as one in which they are free to give their allegiance to the government or not, depending upon their view of its legitimacy; according to Arendt, they are simply faced with two groups competing for power, the government and the revolution. In reality, however, these agents find themselves within a more complex power dynamic. In normal circumstances they would be faced with serious harm should they choose not to follow the orders of their rulers. The special nature of the revolutionary situation is that the entire social structure that constitutes the power of a political regime is called into question, with the result that it becomes highly unlikely that the current rulers will be able to actualize their power over their subordinates in the form of sanctions. At that point, because the coercive structure of the regime has been weakened, subordinate agents are able to pursue with impunity courses of action that would result in serious harm in normal circumstances. To conceptualize this as simply the question of whose rule one consents to is to misunderstand the dynamic nature of social power relationships.

Arendt's failure to heed these distinctions leads her to treat what she calls "power" and "violence" as two different phenomena. In fact, however, they are really aspects of the same social phenomenon. While Arendt would claim that a citizen who decides to obey the law shows the presence of power and one who is shot while breaking it shows the presence of violence, really both actions show the nature of political power. As my analysis of the articulation of power in Chapter 5 will show, the threat that constitutes a dominant agent's power only needs to be *exercised* in those cases where that threat is *not effective* in altering the actions of the agents to whom it was made. Arendt's abstract distinction between power and violence sunders this complex relationship. While Arendt does see that the exercise of power is only necessary in situations in which it has not been effective in altering the choices that agents make, she misconceptualizes this fact as entailing a radical dichotomy between violence and power.

As a result of this failure, Arendt does not see that power is often constituted by the threat of the use of violence (or force). Only a failure to distinguish the *exceptional* violent exercise of power from the *routine* possession of power based on the threat of such an exercise accounts for Arendt's failure to see violence and power as intimately linked.

But even if we pass over this problem in Arendt's account, there is still the problem of what her account actually proves. Even if Arendt could demonstrate that the agents who carry out the orders of the rulers do actually consent to those orders, what would it show? At best, she would show that political power requires a partial consensus of the rulers and their agents. But this would not show that such power did not have a basis in violence or, more appropriately, coercion. For Arendt fails to show that the consensus upon which power is based must necessarily be a universal one.[21]

Acknowledging the possibility that the consensus that brings a particular form of political power into existence could be partial calls into question the attempt by Arendt and, following her, Habermas to see actually existing political power as a distorted form of a consensual relationship. The fact that such power could be the result of a partial consensus means that such relationships can have an origin other than the distortion of a universal consensual relationship. The presence of a partial consensus does not, in itself, assure us that such a partial consensus is but a distorted form of a universal one. With equal plausibility, such a partial consensus can be viewed as essential to the nature of the power relationship.

Arendt is thus unable to dismiss the Thrasymachian view of power by pointing to the consensual element of power relationships. The Thrasymachian can acknowledge the consensual element in political power but deny that, even in principle, this consensus could become universal. This view of political power, which sees such power as depending upon the exclusion of certain groups from the consensus that generates it, cannot be dismissed by means of an analysis of the nature of power relationships. Nor is pointing to such a consensual basis enough to assure such excluded agents that resorting to violence is an incorrect approach to the problems they face.[22]

Conclusion

In this chapter I have explored Hannah Arendt's view of power with two goals in mind: to demonstrate that power theorists often disagree with one another in part because they are using the single term "power" to talk about different phenomena, and to show that the consensual view that Arendt advocates does not pay sufficient attention to coercive aspects of political power. I have suggested that any adequate conception of political power will need to treat it as having both consensual and coercive aspects.

3

The Power Debate

THE CONCEPT of power-over is a central one for social theory to understand and analyze. This is because locutions involving this phrase allow social theorists to refer to hierarchical social relationships in a clear and specific manner. Since a central use of the concept of power is precisely that of characterizing such relationships, it is important for social theorists to provide a clear language for so doing.

It is therefore not surprising to find that there has been a significant amount of discussion among social theorists about how to analyze this concept. In fact, there has been an on-going debate within recent Anglo-American social theory concerning the proper manner of defining the notion of one social agent's having power over another social agent. I shall subsequently refer to this debate as the power debate. My goal in this chapter is to show that the positions defended by the participants in the power debate concerning the appropriate manner of defining an agent's power over another are inadequate precisely because of faulty assumptions they make about the nature of social theory in general.

Ontology and Power Theory

In presenting the views of the theorists in the power debate, I shall show that the conceptions of power that they put forward are articulated within a space that is determined by their conceptions of the ontology of human social agency. In order to clarify this idea, let me take a moment to explain the conception of ontology that I am using.

By "an ontology of human social agency" I mean to indicate the basic understanding of the nature of human agency that a given theorist has. When-

51

ever a social theorist talks about human beings and the nature of their roles in society, she necessarily conceives of the human being in a certain way, and assumes that a particular manner of conceptualizing the human being is the appropriate one to use. In a certain sense, even our so-called ordinary ways of speaking and thinking about ourselves as social agents are based upon such an ontology of human social agency. In our ordinary discourse, we use a whole set of intentional concepts in describing and theorizing about our behavior. Such concepts include those of deliberation, intention, and responsibility. By calling the set of such concepts "an ontology of human agency", I highlight the fact that even our ordinary mode of discourse contains certain assumptions about the nature of the human being that can legitimately be called "ontological", since they posit the human being as a certain sort of being in virtue of their use of certain concepts to describe and delimit that being's possibilities.

It is my claim that the theories of power developed within the power debate also have such an ontological understanding of human social agency at their base. In this case, however, the ontological understanding of human social agency is one that departs from our ordinary one. This is because the power theorists see it as their task to provide a conception of power that can function within a *scientific* social theory. In order to do so, they believe it to be essential to use terms and theories that have more clarity than does our ordinary conceptual framework.

Although the power theorists therefore depart from the ontology of human social agency inherent in ordinary discourse, they do not themselves discuss this feature of their theory. Their own ontology of human social agency is itself not an explicit object of inquiry, but simply something that they presuppose in giving their particular analyses of power. Nonetheless, since these theorists are attempting to define the power that one agent has over another agent, they necessarily presuppose some conception of the nature of human agency in presenting their views. Only on the basis of a certain understanding of human agency is it possible to put forward a particular definition of an agent's power over another agent. By closely examining the way in which these theories conceive of human beings, I shall be able to demonstrate the presence of such an ontological view in their claims.

My use of the term "ontology" in this context has affinities with Heidegger's use of the term. In *Being and Time,* Heidegger argues, among other things, that metaphysical theories often have an unacknowledged understanding of "Being" behind them, an understanding that Heidegger himself seeks to make explicit.[1] I am likewise trying to demonstrate the unacknowledged presence behind a theory of an understanding that conditions the terms within which the theory is developed. Such an understanding is not explicitly articulated by the theorist, and yet it determines the conceptual space within which her theory operates. Indeed, once the implicit understandings are made explicit, the theories with which one is concerned appear in a fundamentally different light, for one is able to see how the implicit understanding of the nature of the human being controls and limits the accounts under investigation.

The Power Debate

The power debate is a particular discussion of social power that stems from certain criticisms of C. Wright Mills's seminal work, *The Power Elite*.[2] In that work, Mills attempts to demonstrate the existence of a group of "men" whom he dubs "the power elite" and whom he characterizes as occupying "the strategic command posts of the social structure, in which are now centered the effective means of the power and the wealth and the celebrity which they now enjoy."[3] Mills's claim that there is such an elite depends upon a conception of those in power as "those who decide whatever is decided of major consequence."[4]

In response to Mills's claims, a number of social theorists, dubbing themselves "pluralists" or "democrats", have argued that his account of the stratification of modern society is inadequate both theoretically and empirically.[5] Foremost among these critics is Robert A. Dahl. Although Dahl puts forward a variety of criticisms of Mills's work, the important feature of Dahl's critique from our point of view is that he stresses certain theoretical problems that he sees there.

Instead of arguing that Mills's claims about the distribution of power in the United States are simply false, Dahl argues that they suffer from a methodological flaw. Dahl asserts that Mills fails to develop his argument in a manner that would allow his claims to be established as a well-confirmed empirical theory. In order to do this, Dahl claims, Mills would have to show, by "the careful examination of a series of concrete decisions", that in cases where there is a conflict over the alternative to be chosen, "in all or very nearly all of these cases the alternative preferred by the ruling elite is actually adopted."[6] Since Mills has not done anything of the sort, Dahl argues that Mills has not established the thesis that there exists a power elite in the United States.

In his article "The Concept of Power", Dahl moves beyond his criticism of Mills and attempts to provide a positive definition of power that would satisfy the criteria he himself uses in his criticism of Mills. That is, he is concerned to develop a concept of power that would allow claims employing that term to be subject to the sorts of empirical testing he claims are necessary to establish the existence of a power elite.

In making this argument, Dahl is conditioned by his adherence to the general research program known as *behavioralism*. Behavioralism is a theory about the proper method of conducting social scientific research. The methodological motivation for such a position is that of making social theory as fully scientific as the natural sciences. As Dahl says, "The behavioral approach is an attempt to improve our understanding of politics by seeking to explain the empirical aspects of political life by means of methods, theories, and criteria of proof that are acceptable according to the canons, conventions, and assumptions of modern empirical science."[7] Although framed in terms of the canons of scientific rationality *tout court,* behavioralism has adopted the view of scientific theories that was standard at the time of its development, the general empiricist conception of scientific theories known as "the deductive-nomological model."[8]

One important aspect of the behavioralist program is that of defining theoretical concepts by reference to human behavior. The rationale is that such a practice is a suitable application of the operationalist view of the role of theoretical entities in a scientific theory. According to operationalism, a theoretical concept, in order to be meaningfully employed within a scientific theory, must refer to a specific set of observable phenomena. What this means is that the terms of a scientific theory are divisible into two distinct classes: the theoretical terms and their observational basis. The observational basis is the real "meat" of the science, with the theoretical terms serving as ways of relating statements made in terms of the basis. Operationalism is thus usually allied with the ontological thesis that the referents of the theoretical terms of the theory do not refer to genuine existents but are merely instrumental or calculational devices.

Behavioralism can be seen as the application of this general view of the nature of theoretical terms in the sciences to the particular context of the social sciences. What the operationalist model requires is that all the theoretical terms of a science be given an observational basis. The behavioralist specifies this general view by arguing that all the theoretical concepts of social science be given an operational definition in terms of actual human behavior. Behavioralists claim that, without such a reference to human behavior, the theoretical terms of social science are not precise enough for empirical employment. As one political theorist puts it, "Political behavior . . . represents an orientation or point of view which aims at *stating all the phenomenon of government in terms of the observed and observable behavior of men.*"[9] Although phrased in terms of government and, hence, political phenomena, this statement represents the general behavioralist point of view for all social sciences.

The idea that the concepts that social science uses must refer to the behavior of human beings is reminiscent of the philosophic position known as "behaviorism", which claims that all human action can be understood simply as the behavior of the human organism. Nonetheless, at least some of the proponents of the behavioralist point of view in political science wish to distance themselves from philosophical behaviorism as they understand that term. For example, David Easton, in his article "The Current Meaning of Behavioralism", [10] argues that behavioralism in political science does not involve the eschewal of reference to the subjective states of political actors. Despite this disclaimer, he argues that the scientific statements of political science have to be generalizations about political behavior that can be verified by means of "reference to relevant behavior". As a result, his claim to reject the philosophic position of behaviorism notwithstanding, Easton winds up advocating a complex form of behaviorism, similar to that developed by Gilbert Ryle in *The Concept of Mind,* [11] rather than the more reductive forms in which it was first developed. As Easton himself notes, behavioralism rejects the "stimulus-response" model of the human being in favor of a "stimulus-organism-response" model. In accepting the latter model, behavioralism commits itself to an understanding of that organism in terms of selective responses—that is, behavior—and nothing else, a fact whose significance Easton seems to underestimate.

That behavioralism involves an ontological thesis becomes clear when one moves from the general position of behavioralism to its application to the problem of understanding power. This thesis is that the human being can be adequately understood as a social agent by means of a set of concepts that have a behavioral basis. Although this does not mean that no intentional concepts can be applied to the human being, it does mean that any concept that is introduced into the theoretician's vocabulary has to have a behavioral operationalization. I am pointing out that this epistemic stricture entails an ontological one, namely that the human being qua social agent is intelligible as a complex behavioral system.

This discussion of behavioralism as a general position in the social sciences allows us to see why Dahl argues as he does in regard to the concept of power. What becomes clear is that, because of his commitment to the behavioralist program that he uses as the basis for his criticism of Mills's conception of power, Dahl is forced to provide a concept of power that will meet the constraints of that program. According to Dahl's own strictures, if power is to be a meaningful concept in social science, it must itself fit into the general behavioral program; that is, it requires an operational definition.

Dahl's own attempt to provide a concept of power that meets the strictures of his own methodology is as follows: After remarking that he is not trying to give a general theory of power but only a particular theory of limited scope, Dahl introduces what he calls his "intuitive idea of power". According to this intuitive idea, "*A* has power over *B* to the extent that he can get *B* to do something that *B* would not otherwise do." [12] This intuitive idea of power is intended to present a conception of power that will fulfill the demands of the behavioralist by defining power in terms of human behavior.

A first problem with Dahl's intuitive idea of power is that, in it, he uses the word "do", which presupposes the concept of an action. From the point of view of the behavioralist, such a concept is not acceptable, for strictly speaking one cannot observe the fact that a human being is actually doing something. To do something one has to perform an action, and not all forms of behavior count as actions. All that is available for our observation on the operationalist model, however, is the "behavings" of human beings. Some of these behavings are interpreted as "do-ings" in the attempt to construct a general account of human behavior. Therefore, to be consistent, Dahl ought to restrict himself to human behavior, and not human actions, as the observational base upon which to confirm claims about power. Dahl is not consistent, however, switching more or less arbitrarily between the language of action and the language of behavior when talking about this observational basis.

There are two ways in which one could modify Dahl's view in order to handle this point. One could make it more consistent with behavioralism, arguing that he is really talking about changes in the behavior of human agents. This is indeed the line that was followed in the power debate itself and the one that I shall follow up in a moment. However, I also want to note that the use of the concept of human action in this context suggests that Dahl smuggles into his observational base forms of human agency that are not limited to mere behavings. Since I will suggest in the sequel that this is the correct way to develop a concept of power-over, I want to point out that there is a tendency in Dahl's writing, albeit a suppressed one, to treat the concept of power-over in the context of meaningful human action.

Dahl's work on power has been criticized from many directions. These criticisms have attacked both the empirical results that Dahl argues for and the theoretical claims upon which they are based. [13] For many purposes, however, it will be sufficient to consider only Dahl's theoretical account of power. I shall begin by considering the relation between Dahl's rather restrictive conception of power and the behavioralist ontology of human social agency upon which it is based.

Although Dahl uses the term "actor" to refer to human beings in society, his behavioralist commitment entails that all the concepts that are used to describe human beings as social agents have their ultimate rationale in human behavior itself. Such a conception of the ontology of human social agency is rather restrictive. In ordinary language, when we talk of human actions, we presuppose a range of categories including intentions and deliberations within which the concept of a human action has a specific place. For Dahl, however, all such concepts have meaning only in so far as they refer to a form of behavior. As a result, although Dahl talks of human *actors,* he has a limited conception of what their *agency* amounts to. When it comes to questions of power, the only thing that Dahl is able to countenance as evidence for the exercise of power is the fact that human behavior has changed. Any claim to the effect that an actor has exercised power over another actor can only be justified by referring to an actual change in the behavior of the actor over whom power was exercised. All other manners in which power might be claimed to be a factor in an agent's situation are ruled out by Dahl's ontological presuppositions.

Given these rigid strictures on what counts as an exercise of power, it is not surprising that Dahl's view has been seen to be seriously limited. One of the most interesting initial critiques of Dahl's claims was put forward by Peter Bachrach and Morton S. Baratz. They argue that Dahl ignores what they termed a "second face of power." [14] Bachrach and Baratz agree with Dahl that one agent is able to exercise power over another agent by bringing about a change in the second agent's behavior. However, they argue that this is not the only "face" that power has; power can also appear in situations in which, from a superficial point of view, nothing happens. An agent can also exercise power, according to Bachrach and Baratz, by keeping something from happening—for example, by keeping an issue that affects the welfare of the other agent from coming up for a political decision. Because Dahl uses decision-making as a particularly clear context in which one agent can actually affect the behavior of another, thus exercising power, Bachrach and Baratz argue that "non-decisions" are as much a domain for the exercise of power as the "decisions" that Dahl highlights. Dahl's commitment to behavioralism results, according to Bachrach and Baratz, in a one-sided perception of the two faces of power.

The idea that guides Bachrach and Baratz is that human beings' continuing to act as they previously had might itself be the result of power's being exercised over them. When a powerful agent is able to keep a particular issue from being one that will be decided politically, and where such a political decision, were it made, would result in a change in the less powerful agent's behavior, the powerful agent would be exercising power over the less powerful agent precisely by keeping his behavior from changing. For example, the Central Intelligence Agency exercises power over the Senate Intelligence Committee by keeping certain of the C.I.A.'s activities from being scrutinized by that Committee. Were the Committee to find out about these activities, it would move to halt them. However, because the C.I.A. is able to structure certain of its activities in such a way that the Committee is unable to have jurisdiction over them, the C.I.A. exercises power over the Committee in regard to these activites. It is just such political scenarios that Bachrach and Baratz see as a prime domain in which power is exercised, but that they believe Dahl's emphasis on changes in overt behavior and decisions fails to encompass.

The view that Bachrach and Baratz put forward concerning the nature of power certainly points out a weakness in Dahl's account. Although Dahl recognizes an agent's effect upon decision-making as a paradigmatic exercise of power, his methodological commitments keep him from recognizing the ability of an agent to keep an issue from being decided upon as likewise an exercise of power. Bachrach and Baratz argue that both these contexts are ones in which power can be exercised and that it is possible to give an empirically sound justification of the application of the concept of power to both types of situations. Dahl's restriction of power to overt changes of an agent's behavior is simply arbitrary, according to Bachrach and Baratz.

The conception of power put forward by Bachrach and Baratz thus sees power as inherently dualistic in structure. The concept of power has two faces, according to them, in that it has two distinct realms of applicability.

Let me just note in passing that Dahl's as well as Bachrach and Baratz's discussions reflect the same peculiarity we already saw in the case of Arendt: When political scientists discuss the issue of power, they tend to restrict it to political power. For them, issues of power have to do only with questions of governance and the democratic nature of government. This particular limitation of the concept of power to political contexts is not limited to Anglo-American theorists alone. Bertrand de Jouvenal, for example, in his study *On Power,* uses the term "power" as synonymous with "government".[15] Social power is, however, a much broader phenomenon than simply that reflected in the governmental sphere. As I have argued, this peculiarity of usage is reflected in deficiencies in political scientists' theories of social power when these are taken as general theories concerning the nature of power in society as a whole.

As Steven Lukes has pointed out, Bachrach and Baratz only partially succeed in developing a conception of power that is not subject to the arbitrary limitations of Dahl's attempt. On the one hand, their critique of Dahl's view points out that Dahl limits the applicability of the concept far too severely; on the other hand, their own critique remains partial and ad hoc. Rather than subjecting Dahl's behavioralist ontology to a critical scrutiny, Bachrach and Baratz seem content to point out another context in which the concept of power has a meaningful application. As such, their view remains incomplete. Although they show a limitation of Dahl's view, their own view cannot be a satisfactory alternative in that it simply places another type of context next to that which Dahl privileges as an appropriate context in which to observe the exercise of power. Bachrach and Baratz thus rest content with the metaphor of two faces of power in place of a more general theoretical explanation of the nature of power itself. While they conceive of themselves as criticizing Dahl's behavioralist orientation, the view that they present is itself not a fundamental challenge to that position. Their legitimation of the concept of a non-decision takes place within the ontological space of the behavioralist program.

Lukes self-consciously attempts to rectify what he sees as shortcomings in Bachrach and Baratz's view. He claims that he is going to introduce a new conception of power, one that is based upon a "*thoroughgoing critique* of the *behavioral focus* of the first two views"—that is, those of Dahl and Bachrach and Baratz.[16] It may seem surprising that Lukes then goes on to put forward a "third dimension of power" to supplement those put forward by Dahl and Bachrach and Baratz. However, a close look at Lukes's argument reveals that his view entails a significant departure from the ad hoc supplementation of Dahl effected by Bachrach and Baratz.

As a first step in his argument, Lukes proposes that a "third dimension of power" be recognized. In addition to the overt conflicts that Dahl recognizes and the exclusion of issues from the political agenda or "non-decisions" that Bachrach and Baratz add to the domains in which power can be exercised, Lukes argues that there is a third such domain, namely "*latent conflicts . . .* in [which] a contradiction between the interests of those exercising power and the *real interests* of those they exclude" exists.[17] Lukes's argument here is quite simple: Even when supplemented with the claims of Bachrach and Baratz, Dahl's view does not provide an extensive enough conception of the sorts of phenomena in which power is a factor. One agent can exercise power over another agent by making that agent believe that something that is really harmful to that agent is actually not so. As Lukes puts the point: "Indeed, is it not the supreme exercise of power to get another or others to have the desires you want them to have—that is, to secure their compliance by controlling their thoughts and desires?"[18] In cases of the sort Lukes is concerned with, power is exercised over an agent, but not through either an overtly political action of the sort recognized by Dahl or the exclusion of an issue from the political agenda of the sort recognized by Bachrach and Baratz. Central to Lukes's concern are exercises of power in which the subordinate agent does not even recognize the fact that power has been exercised over her. An advertiser who persuades a consumer to buy a product with the false promise that it will result in his acquiring the woman of his dreams is a prime example of an agent whom Lukes sees as having power of a kind that cannot be understood by means of either the one- or the two-dimensional view.[19] By including the idea of latent conflicts as another context in which it makes sense to use the concept of power, Lukes extends the applicability of the concept of power beyond the arbitrary borders set by Dahl as well as Bachrach and Baratz.

Had Lukes's analysis ended there, it would share the ad hoc character that I have attributed to the view of Bachrach and Baratz. Lukes, however, takes his argument one step farther: He argues that these three "dimensions" of power can be seen to have their source in a single "conception" of power. Lukes begins his presentation of this concept by claiming that the core idea involved in the notion of power-over is that one agent "in some way affects" another agent and that he "does so in a non-trivial or significant manner". He goes on to argue that this idea provides a single "underlying concept of power, according to which A exercises power over B when A affects B in a manner contrary to B's interests."[20] It is this particular conception of power that Lukes sees as providing unity to the three-dimensional view. The power that the three-dimensional view sees as being exercised in three distinct social domains is itself analyzed by this single conception of power. Despite the different domains in which it can exist, power itself is a unitary social phenomenon.

In assessing Lukes's conception of power, let us consider Lukes's claiming to be giving a fundamental critique of behavioralism. The central idea of Lukes's view of power is that the idea of an agent's objective interest can be used as the basis for giving a definition of power. Indeed, from Lukes's point of view, the concept of interest is one that lies at the heart of the three different conceptions of power: "In brief, my suggestion is that the one-dimensional view of power presupposes a liberal conception of interests, the two dimensional view a reformist conception, and the three-dimensional view a radical conception."[21] Lukes's own use of the concept of interest is a rejection of behavioralism because it extends the set of basic concepts used in social science beyond those which can be specified simply in terms of human behavior. To say of a social agent that she has a certain objective interest is to make a claim about her that cannot be legitimated by referring to her actual or possible behavior. The concept of an agent's interest transcends the limitations behavioralism seeks to put on the meaningful employment of concepts in the social sciences.

As a consequence of his enlargement of the basic concepts of social science, Lukes also rejects the basic understanding of human agency that Dahl as well as Bachrach and Baratz accept. Whereas they hold that the concepts that are necessary to understand human agency can be operationalized in terms of human behavior, Lukes rejects this idea, since he thinks that it is both legitimate and necessary to conceive of social agents as having objective interests that cannot be specified simply by reference to their behavior. Thus, by rejecting behavioralism, Lukes also rejects the ontology of human social agency that characterizes that view.

As a result of this rejection, Lukes is able to give a very different definition of power than his behavioralist predecessors do. Because he understands human beings to be agents with interests, Lukes is able to see those interests as the target of exercises of power. As a result of his enlargement of the ontology of human social agency to include the concept of the interests that social agents have, Lukes is able to articulate a conception of power in which the affecting of such interests plays a central role.

Despite this advance, the concept of power that Lukes develops on the basis of this enlarged ontology is inadequate because Lukes has not developed a complex enough ontology of human social agency. Lukes is forced by his own ontology to adopt a notion of power according to which power can be exercised by an agent only when he affects the interests of another agent. However, such a conception of power is not adequate.

One problem with Lukes's conception of power can be seen by considering the example of paternalism. Paternalism is a phenomenon in which one agent exercises power over another agent precisely when the latter agent is deemed incapable of knowing what his interests are. The dominant agent then seeks to get the subordinate agent to act in a manner that realizes his real interests even though the subordinate agent does not or cannot recognize them. The case of a father who keeps his daughter from going to town with her friends so that she can practice the piano instead is an example of a paternalistic use of power. Because the father believes he knows better than his daughter what her real interests are, he sees his exercise of power over her as legitimate. On Lukes's view, however, if the father is actually right about what the real interests of his daughter are, his paternalistic treatment of her is not even an exercise of power.

Clearly, any view of power that fails to conceptualize paternalism adequately has serious shortcomings. Paternalism is a morally and socially problematic practice precisely because the dominant agent acts out of a conviction that he understands better than the subordinate agent what is good for her. Even though a dominant agent may be correct in his assessment, paternalistic treatment cannot be legitimated by simply denying that it is an instance of the exercise of power over another agent. Paternalism needs to be included among the phenomena of power, not ruled out of existence by definitional fiat.

If the case of paternalism shows that Lukes's definition of power is "too narrow", it can also be shown to be "too wide". There are many examples of "significant affectings contrary to an agent's interest"—which are properly conceptualized as harms—that are simply not cases of the exercise of power. For example, consider the case in which two agents have a car accident and are seriously injured. This does not seem to be a case in which one would be willing to say that the agent who caused the accident exercised power over the injured agent. Because the two agents in the crash have been placed in a situation in which the harm that comes about happens as an incidental result of the actions of the two agents, the car accident does not qualify as an exercise of power. It is not the ability to harm *per se* that constitutes an agent's actions as an instance of power. For a case of harming another agent to constitute an exercise of power, it must fit into a different pattern of explanation than that which Lukes's definition provides. For example, a harm that befalls an agent might be an exercise of power if the harm was intended by another agent as a means of keeping the former agent from doing something. The "objective situation" of the agents involved is insufficient to warrant the judgment that a particular harm that befalls one of them because of the actions of the other is a result of the exercise of power over that agent. Like Bachrach and Baratz, Lukes is unable to articulate an adequate conception of power because he retains too much of Dahl's behavioralist orientation, seeking to provide an operationalization of the concept that does not refer to any intentional features of the agents' situations.

Thus, Lukes's failure to incorporate intentional concepts into his understanding of human social agency results in a conception of power that has serious flaws. Left only with the notion of interest as a means of characterizing the nature of the human being qua social agent, Lukes is more or less forced into using the idea of a significant effect upon those interests as the key to defining "power". But such an operationalization of the concept of power, while more adequate to the task of providing a conception of power that is not arbitrary and limited, still does not provide a conception that fulfills the demands of social theory.

This understanding of the problems inherent in Lukes's manner of proceeding also lets us see why Anthony Giddens' critique of Lukes, though substantially correct, does not really show us the reason that Lukes's definition is inadequate. Giddens argues that Lukes's attempt to use the concept of interest as the basis for defining "power" is a mistake.

I should want to say, as against Lukes, that the concept of interest, like that of conflict, has nothing logically to do with that of power; although substantively, in the actual enactment of social life, the phenomena to which they refer have a great deal to do with one another.[22]

Giddens is certainly right that there are cases involving the exercise of power that do not involve actions contrary to the interests of the agent over whom power is exercised. As my discussion of paternalism shows, there are situations in which one agent may exercise power over another where the latter is mistaken about what is in her real interests.[23]

What Giddens' criticism does not make clear, however, is the motivation behind Lukes's use of the notion of interest in his definition. Giddens simply makes the point that "power" and "interest" are two distinct concepts that have no necessary connection with one another, a point that I have made by means of specific counter-examples to Lukes's definition. What Giddens fails to bring out is the source of Lukes's idea that power might be definable in terms of interest.

As I have argued, Lukes's use of the concept of interest depends upon his acceptance of certain aspects of the behavioralist program even as he has attempted to reject it. In the next section of this chapter, I will continue to explore this issue by looking at the model of scientific theories that Lukes shares with his behavioralist adversaries.

The Basis of the Power Debate

In justifying my claim that Lukes's definition is too broad, I argued that he still adheres to one tenet of behaviorism, namely its focus on "objective" features of the social world. This suggests that, despite the differences among the power theorists I have considered, they all share a certain basic model of how to understand power, a model that is inadequate. This is, in fact, the case.

The model that the theorists of power accept has two characteristics. The first is that it tries to find an objective basis for ascriptions of power to an agent. As a result, such a model fails to see that the ascription of power to a social agent takes place within a framework of intentional concepts that cannot be reduced to any non-intentional basis. The second characteristic is that it conceives of power as something that is exercised in discrete interactions between social agents. As a result, it is unable to conceptualize ongoing social relationships and social roles as fundamental domains in which power is exercised. Because of these two features, the very terms within which the power debate has been conducted are insufficient for formulating an adequate conception of power; an adequate conception of power, therefore, needs to begin with a fundamental reassessment of this general framework.[24]

My first claim is that, despite their differences, all the theorists in the debate have accepted a similar, flawed model of how the theoretical terms of a social theory need to be legitimated. In the case of Dahl, I have already shown that his commitment to behavioralism causes him to develop an account of power that makes no reference to intentional states of a social agent that cannot be cashed out in terms of behavior. I have also argued, following Lukes, that Bachrach and Baratz do not confront Dahl on this aspect of his view, remaining with the basic behavioralist model while they critique Dahl's exclusive focus on overt conflicts.

As I have argued, despite his explicit attempt to critique Dahl's behavioralist orientation, Lukes remains within the horizon of the very conception of scientific methodology that grounds behavioralism. Lukes's use of the notion of an agent's objective interest, while an explicit break with behavioralism about what to count as constituting the basis for power ascriptions to an agent, is continuous with behavioralism in its attempt to isolate "objective" features of an agent's situation that form the basis for the theoretical ascription of power to that agent. Lukes's choice of the concept of interest as the central one to use in defining power is conditioned, as I have already indicated, by his understanding of that notion as referring to a feature of an agent's situation that is determinable without any reference to the agent's intentional states. The appeal of this concept is that it allows him to define power in terms of a non-intentional concept while breaking with the specific focus on behavior that is characteristic of the behavioralist views. In attempting to provide such a non-intentional basis for an understanding of the concept of power, Lukes's view is continuous with that of his behavioral opponents.

Lukes opts for a non-intentional conception of power because he, like his fellow theorists in the power debate, is under the influence of a faulty model of scientific theorizing. According to this model, science is characterized by the presence of a level of discourse that is free of interpretive activity. The power theorists all accept the idea that social theory ought to model itself on the natural sciences by attempting to formulate theories in accordance with such canons.

The idea that scientific theorizing proceeds by elaborating a theoretical language upon an observational language is one that the participants take for granted as a standard to be imported into the social sciences. The work of such philosophers as W. V. Quine, Wilfrid Sellars, Thomas Kuhn, and Paul Feyerabend[25] has shown that the empiricist model of science—and its operationalist form in particular—cannot give us an accurate model of how science actually works. Theory and observation are much more intimately linked than this model of science acknowledges.

Once one realizes that even the natural sciences do not conform to a certain picture of the norms of scientific rationality, the desire to make the social sciences conform to that model loses all its motivational force. The work of such outstanding social theorists as Jürgen Habermas and Charles Taylor,[26] in which they argue that the social sciences have an irreducibly intentional component, gains strength from these developments in the theory of the physical sciences.

These theoretical reflections help explain the impression that developments in the power debate are not getting us closer to an adequate definition of power. The attempt by theorists to ground ascriptions of power in some sort of observational basis involves an inadequate appreciation of the interplay between theory and observation in science. The obvious rejoinder to their attempt is the claim that power must be grounded in intentional discourse and not in a privileged "objective" realm. The lesson to be learned from a consideration of scientific methodology is that the concept of power has a place within an intentional language dealing with social agents. The attempt to deny this leads to an inadequate understanding of power as well as of human agency itself.

This conclusion, although negative, points the way to a more positive outcome. For it establishes the following as a desideratum for any account of the concept of power: It needs to place itself within the realm of intentional discourse from the very beginning. In order to achieve a more adequate understanding of what power is and how it functions in society, an interpretive stance in regard to the nature of society must be adopted and the concept of power must be located within a framework of interpretive concepts.

An examination of a second faulty assumption that guides the theorists in the power debate will provide another clue about how to proceed in developing a conception of power that is more adequate than those put forward within the power debate itself. The assumption concerns the question of what sorts of relations between social agents actually count as relations in which power can be a factor. A central problem with the views of power put forward by the theorists in the power debate is that they tend to think of power in terms of what I shall call "an interventional model." A theorist who accepts the interventional model of power thinks of power as something that is present as a factor in the relations between two social agents only as a discrete event in which the relation between the two agents changes. I call this an "interventional" model of power in order to focus attention upon its assumption that power is a factor in social relations only when an agent *intervenes* in a previously constituted situation and changes it. Power is therefore conceptualized as an agent's intervention in a previously given social relation. When two agents interact in a particular social event, there can be an exercise of power; in the absence of such an intervention, however, there is no power.[27] Thus, the primary locus of power, on the interventional model, is a specific social interaction between two social agents.

Recalling Dahl's insistence that an agent has power only if she is able to affect the behavior of another agent, one can see that Dahl is thinking of power in an interventional sense—as something that is present in the social world only by means of the discrete acts of a social agent. These are the sorts of things that he is looking for as a necessary condition for the ascription of power to a social agent. His criticism of Mills is precisely directed to Mills's failure to show the specific mechanisms whereby power is exercised by a social agent in precisely this interventional sense.

Although both Bachrach and Baratz and Lukes make a variety of criticisms of Dahl's framework for thinking about power, they do not challenge this particular aspect of his thought. For them as well, power is thought of on the interventional model, as an event in the social world. What they differ on is simply the sorts of events that can be thought about as involving power.[28]

As I have said, I call this manner of thinking about power "interventional" in order to highlight the fact that it views power as primarily a factor in non-routine interactions between social agents. According to this model, power is only a factor in human social relations when two social agents encounter one another and interact in a manner that is not predetermined by their social roles. It assumes that the understanding of the human being as a social agent without specific social ties is the appropriate one for the analysis of power.

As a result of their adherence to this model, these theorists of power have focused on power as a factor in the following sort of scenario: Two social agents, each of whom is constituted as a social agent independently of the other, meet in a certain context. Power is a factor between them only when the agents have opposing agendas or interests. The exercise of power between them is an event that changes something about their relation to one another, but that does nothing to change their status qua social agents. The fact that an agent has exercised power over another agent does nothing to our understanding of their agency.

Once the presuppositions of the power debate's model of power are made explicit, it becomes clear that the terms within which the debate is conducted are problematic, for they do not allow the theorist a clear means of conceptualizing some of the fundamental phenomena that are usually associated with the concept of power. In particular, the idea that the most fundamental use of power in society is its use in structuring the basic manner in which social agents interact with one another is ruled out by the interventional model.

In order to see the need to adopt an understanding of power that acknowledges its fundamental rule, consider the idea that men have power over women in our society. For the purposes of this discussion, I will simply assume that this idea is a valid one that any theory of power would accept as something for which it had to account. On the interventional model, such a claim would have to be interpreted in either of two ways. On the first interpretation, this is really a claim about the social classes "men" and "women". What it asserts is that one class actually acts so as to affect the possibilities of the other class. But this seems a problematic way of understanding the claim that men have power over women, for there does not seem to be a specific action that the class of men takes in order to exercise power over women. There are some cases in which a group does exercise power over another group by means of a general action—war is a good example. In a war, the individual agents who make up each of the warring social agents perform a series of coordinated actions that amount to the collective action of waging war. The exercise of power by men over women does not seem to be amenable to such an analysis. There is no obvious candidate for the group action that men undertake by means of their particular actions and that results in their exercising power over women.

On the interventional model of power, then, the only interpretation left for the claim that men have power over women is that it is an empirical generalization of more particular interactions between men and women in which individual men have power over women. But this reading of the claim is just as implausible as the collective one. The power that men have over women in this society is not simply constituted by the actions of particular men in which they exercise power over particular women. A particular man's ability to exercise power over a woman may depend, for example, on that woman's inability to get her fellow workers to stand up for her. Such general social facts are themselves part of what constitutes men's power over women. The actual interventional uses of power by men are dependent upon a more systematic structure of power that allows them to exercise power over women in the first place.

As a result of this analysis, we can see that the interventional model of power is not an adequate manner of conceptualizing a fundamental use of power in society, namely its use to structure the basic terms of interaction of social agents. As a result, the terms within which the power debate is conducted can be seen to be inadequate to understanding the most basic aspects of power in society.

In order to bolster this claim, I shall turn to Hegel's discussion of the "lordship-bondage relationship" in the *Phenomenology of Spirit*. Although this is one of the most well known of all Hegel's philosophic discussions, not all of its ramifications for an understanding of power have been recognized by social theorists. Here, I shall only use it to illustrate my claim that power cannot be limited to interventions.[29]

Hegel begins his discussion of lordship and bondage with a discussion of a different form of consciousness,[30] namely that of the life-and-death struggle. In the life-and-death struggle, two consciousnesses encounter one another and seek to validate their own "self-certainty" by means of a struggle to the death. While one might be tempted to see Hegel as giving an analysis of warrior societies, this is a mistake. Hegel's discussion is intended as a criticism of a certain way of thinking about human life and, in particular, power. He is arguing that a conception of power that posits power as existing as a result of the conscious decision of two consciousnesses to engage in a struggle for survival does not provide an adequate understanding of how power functions in society.

The fact that Hegel begins his discussion of human social life with a critique of this manner of thinking about human beings is not surprising, for Hegel sees Hobbes, the first modern theoretician of society, as having conceived of power in just such a manner. Hegel is arguing that Hobbes's picture of human beings in the state of nature is a picture of human social life, but one that does not understand its own social nature. As a result, it is an abstract and inadequate picture of how power works in social life.

Hegel does not make an external critique of this view of power showing that it cannot result in the formation of an objective social order as Hobbes wished, although Hegel believes that it cannot. Instead, he proceeds by showing that there is a logic of development immanent in this form of consciousness that drives it into another, more adequate form of consciousness, one in which power is conceived of according to a different model. The lordship-bondage relationship incorporates, according to Hegel, this more adequate means of thinking about the nature of power.

The lordship-bondage relationship is portrayed by Hegel as one that results from the encounter of two consciousnesses in a life-and-death struggle. When one of the two consciousnesses decides that life is more important than establishing its own certainty for itself, it chooses slavery over death and thus moves into a life of bondage. Hegel's point here is that the lordship-bondage relationship involves a fundamentally different model of power, one in which power is a factor that structures the *ongoing social relationship* between two consciousnesses. I shall call this model of power a "structural" one, one that conceives of power as a fundamental factor in structuring the two agents' relationship to one another.[31]

We can therefore understand Hegel to be giving a critique of an interventional model of power. His discussion of power involves an explicit critique of the sort of thinking about power that has characterized the power debate. Hegel argues that, when power is thought about as something that two discretely constituted agents attempt to wield over one another, an inadequate understanding of power is employed, one that must be supplemented by a more adequate one. The lordship-bondage relationship is this more adequate model of power, one in which power is conceived of not as an event in which one independent agent tries to affect another independent agent, but rather as something that structures an ongoing relationship between two social agents in which the identity of each of them is established.

Thus, Hegel's discussion of the lordship-bondage relationship supports my claim that the power debate has a specific focus that fails to provide an adequate conceptualization of the role of power in society. In the power debate, power is conceptualized as something that exists only within specific events that take place between two independently constituted agents. This results in a focus on specific events as the sole "locations" at which power is exercised in society. In so doing, relationships between agents are ruled out as proper domains in which power can be a constituting factor. Although all the theorists in the debate see power as relational—indeed, even as dyadic—they do not provide a conception of power that is adequate for understanding the nature of power relationships—that is, long-term patterns of mutual interaction that are shaped by the power of one agent over another. Since these sorts of relationships are one of the primary things that a theory of power must conceptualize, the power debate's focus on discrete events as the locus of power in society obscures many real issues that are at stake in a theory of power.

Conclusion

In this chapter, I have examined the power debate in order to show that the discussion of power by the theorists in that debate suffers from an inadequate understanding of the ontology of human agency that is itself conditioned by an inadequate view of scientific method. As a result, I have shown that the debate takes place within a set of assumptions that need to be rejected. The question that I would like to address in concluding is where this leaves one in the search for an adequate concept of social power.

Although I think that the theoretical commitments of the theorists in the power debate doom their attempts to articulate a concept of power-over that can be an adequate one for social theory, unlike other critics of this debate I do not think that the entire project of providing a more adequate conception of power is itself misguided. For example, Terence Ball argues that it is a mistake to focus upon the locution of power-over rather than power-to.[32] While I share Ball's reservations about the adequacy of explaining social power *tout court* by a theory of power-over, I do think that the latter has important things to tell us about how power works. What is needed, however, is a theory of power-over that rejects the blinders caused by adherence to an empiricist model of scientific theorizing. As I have said before, the failures of the power debate should not cause us to reject the attempt to explicate the meaning of the phrase "*A* has power over *B*", but rather should provide us with a clear sense of both the terms within which such an explication can be made and the phenomena that such an explication will have to elucidate. I reject the idea that the project motivating the power theorists' attempts should be given up because it has been discussed on the basis of misguided assumptions. Indeed, in the following chapter I will present my own explication of the concept of power-over, one that does not fall prey to the sorts of problems that I have identified in the attempts within the power debate.

4

Power-Over as Constraint

HAVING SHOWN the inadequacies in the ways in which power has been conceptualized by previous social theorists, I shall now proceed to articulate my own theory of power-over. The theory that I shall develop here is one that I call a *field theory of power*. I use this terminology in order to indicate that this theory treats power as having a fundamentally different structure than do the theories I have considered so far. It treats an agent's power over another agent as a field within whose effect the subordinate agent acts.

This theory, I shall argue, is an important advance over previous theories of power-over for various reasons. First, unlike them, it is self-conscious about the place of the concept of power-over within a general theory of power. It recognizes the existence of other forms of power, but nonetheless asserts the importance for social theory of the phenomena associated with the term "power-over". It is therefore articulated with a sense of the broader philosophical landscape that is missing in the particular theories of power that I have investigated in previous chapters.

But most centrally, the field theory of power is an important advance in the development of an adequate theory of power-over because it uses a different ontological model for understanding the nature of such power and therefore is able to solve many of the puzzles that have plagued previous attempts to analyze the concept of power-over.

The balance of this book develops the field theory of power-over. Because it departs from other conceptions of power in a number of crucial respects, I shall articulate the field theory gradually, justifying each of its features in turn. The present chapter contains the first elements of this theory. After an explanation of the basic ontology of a field, I shall develop an ontology of

71

human social agency. This ontology will allow me to give a definition of one agent's having power over another agent that is superior to previous attempts.

The Ontology of a Social Field

In order to convey the idea that an agent's having power over another agent ought to be conceived of by means of the idea of a field, I would like to explore various ontological models that have been used in the analysis of one agent's having power over another. My argument will be that the idea of a field emerges dialectically from a consideration of certain problems inherent in other ontological models that have been used to conceptualize power relations.

To begin, let me return to the power theorists whom I discussed in the last chapter. As I argued, those theorists analyze one agent's having power over another agent as an occurrent event. For them, power is something that exists primarily in its exercise—that is, as the result of a discrete intervention by a social agent in the life of another social agent.

This particular focus causes those theorists to give a one-sided analysis of what it is for an agent to have power over another agent. Having such power is not simply something that can be analyzed in terms of particular occurrent events. To attribute power to an agent is to claim more than that the agent exercises that power. Of course, an agent who has power over another agent typically affects the way in which the latter agent acts. But these effects cannot be reduced to actual exercises of power that the dominant agent undertakes.

To see this, consider a traditional marriage. It is generally agreed that husbands have social power over their wives in such marriages because they have control over the family's income. But it is a mistake to see this power as a factor in the husband-wife relationship only at times when, for example, a husband explicitly prohibits his wife from purchasing something. Such exercises of the husband's power over his wife are only the most overt expressions of the power differential between them in the relationship.[1]

As I argued in the last chapter, for the power theorists, general laws are seen as empirical generalizations based upon a set of observation statements. Claims about an agent's having power over another agent are then viewed as a type of generalization about the first agent's actual exercise of power.

The inadequacies of their analysis demonstrate the need to base an analysis of power-over on a more sophisticated ontology. A more complex ontological model that suggests itself is one that analyzes an agent's having power over another agent as a dispositional property that an agent has which can be actualized in an exercise of power.[2] A disposition is a property that a thing has but that it does not manifest at all times. A clear example of a dispositional property of a person is her knowledge of a language. A speaker who knows a language has that knowledge even when she is sleeping.

Conceiving of objects as having dispositional properties as well as occurrent ones involves attributing a more complex ontological structure to such objects. When such a model is employed, objects are posited as having both an overt and a covert structure. The covert structure of dispositions accounts for the nature of their overt characteristics. This structure is seen to be present even when the overt characteristics do not indicate it.[3]

To see how this ontological model broadens the scope of power beyond its actual exercise, let us return to the example of a husband's power over his wife. This model analyzes a husband's power over his wife as something that he could exercise at various times and in various ways. His power cannot be reduced to the actual moments in which it is exercised. Rather, such power is a property that can be manifested when he chooses.

Although this analysis of power-over is an improvement over the empiricist model of the power theorists, it still does not provide an adequate analysis of what is involved in having power over an agent. There are two problems with it. This first emerges when we consider once more the example of the husband-wife relationship. When we say that a husband has (economic) power over his wife, we are not simply making a counterfactual claim to the effect that he could exercise his power over her should he choose to do so. While this claim is entailed by the claim that the husband has such power, it is not identical with it: The husband's power is a factor in the life of his wife even when he is not actually exercising that power by making particular decisions that affect her. The fact of the husband's control of resources affects every aspect of the interaction between him and his wife.[4] The husband's power structures the space of possible interactions between them and cannot be understood by means of the ontological model of a dispositional property.

Another problem with the dispositional analysis of power-over is that it attributes to an agent power over another agent whenever the former has the ability to exercise power over the latter. But having power-over is an occurrent state of affairs, not simply an ability that an agent could actualize. One agent may fail to have power over another agent not because he could not exercise power over that agent should he choose to, but rather because there is no reason for him to do so. A Mafia boss has no power over me because he has no reason to exercise power over me. This is true even though, should he come to have such a reason, he certainly would be able to exercise power over me. The analysis of power-over in terms of a dispositional property of an agent uses too simple an ontological model for understanding the existence of this complex phenomenon.

The more sophisticated ontological model of a field provides a means for understanding the nature of an agent's power over another agent and solves the problems that I have raised for other accounts of the nature of such power. This is because a field has a different type of "being" than that which is normally attributed to objects and their properties. For this reason, to conceive of power-over on the model of a field is to conceive of it in a more complex fashion, one that allows us to see more clearly its mode of existence.

To understand exactly what is entailed by my use of the metaphor of a field, consider the nature of a magnet. We use the concept of a magnetic field to describe the manner in which a magnet is able to affect the motion of an object that is susceptible to magnetism. The concept of a magnetic field provides a means for conceiving of the array of specific effects that a magnet has upon susceptible objects. The fundamental aspect of the "objectivity" of the field is just this presence, one that cannot be explained simply as the manifestation of a disposition. The reality of a field can be reduced neither to an occurrent nor to a dispositional property of the magnet. Rather, the reality of the field lies in its alteration of the space surrounding the magnet in such a way that the motion of any susceptible object is affected.

This idea of an alteration of space by the presence of a field is the basic notion that I shall use in explaining the idea of power-over. According to this model, an agent's power alters the social space for acting that is occupied by the social agents over whom she has power. The mere presence of a powerful agent will be conceptualized as analogous to the presence of a magnet in that it changes the social space of the agents over whom she has power.

If power-over is analyzed by means of the model of a field, the two problems I raised for the dispositional analysis are easily solved. This is because the ontological structure of a field is fundamentally different from that of a dispositional property. A field is an occurrent reality that affects the behavior of objects within it. Thus, it is not like a disposition, which needs to be actualized in order to have an effect. Furthermore, a field is not simply reducible to its particular effects, so that by using the model of a field for understanding what it is for an agent to have power over another agent, I am not reducing such power to its actual manifestations.

At this point I have only indicated that the ontological model of a field provides a more adequate means for understanding the nature of power-over than do the more usual models employed by social theorists. It is not enough, however, simply to suggest that such a model would help to conceptualize this type of power. To complete my argument, I need to have a more developed account of what sorts of realities count as the social field that power is able to affect. In the remainder of this chapter, I will introduce an ontology of human social agency that will provide us with a conception of the structure of human social relationships in such a way as to provide a concrete means for understanding how to make sense of the metaphor of power as a field.

Terminological Remarks

In the last chapter, I showed how the theories of power developed by the power theorists were marred by their unselfconscious use of terminology. Before developing the field theory of power any further, I shall therefore take a moment to discuss my own choice of terminology within which to develop this view of power.

While most of the theorists in the power debate are concerned to develop an understanding of what it is for one agent to have power over another agent, they are not attentive to the variety of assumptions that are made as soon as one begins one's analysis by focusing upon a particular locution in which the term "power" occurs. For most of them, the explication of the phrase "*A* has power over *B*" determines the range of issues that an adequate theory of power has to face. The central problem, from their theoretical vantage point, is simply how to provide a definition of this phrase that will not violate certain strictures on the employment of concepts within a social scientific theory.

The power theorists fail to recognize that they have made a number of theoretical commitments in the very choice of this phrase as *the* one they will analyze. Although I have already discussed some of these in the previous chapter, one that I have not yet called attention to is the assumption that power is dyadic. That is, they assume that the concept of power-over can be analyzed in the relational form of the phrase "*A* has power over *B*". Although I will not pursue this issue further at this time, I will take it up in Chapter 7, arguing that important features of power are concealed by this dyadic assumption.

Another issue that is passed over too quickly by the power theorists is how one ought to understand the variables *A* and *B* in the phrase "*A* has power over *B*". Although it makes sense to attribute power to non-human agents, as when I say that the weather exerts a great deal of power over my moods, I shall be limiting these variables to a range of human beings and entities that are made up of them. In particular, I shall only consider social agents to be the sorts of things that can stand in the relationship of having power over one another. By making this limitation, I am explicitly acknowledging my attempt to define the social power of one social *agent* over another social *agent*.

I am calling attention to this usage not simply because it defines the range of phenomena that my analysis is attempting to clarify, though it does do that; I also wish to point out the ontological assumptions that are made in using this terminology. The term "agent" makes a specific characterization of the sort of entity that is capable of having power in society. To speak of an agent is to speak of a being that is able to act, not simply to behave. Part of what this means is that it is possible for a social agent to have done other than as it did.[5] The terminology of agency considers such beings as are able to act in an abstract manner, leaving aside any characterization of them other than this ability of theirs. An agent is simply a being capable of performing actions.

There are two types of beings that are typically thought of as being agents. The first is an individual human being. An individual human being is an example of a social agent because human beings are paradigmatic cases of agents. To be a human being is to be able to act. Indeed, one of the ontological characterizations of the human being, from Aristotle to Marx, has been the ability to act.[6] But individual human beings do not act only in isolation; there are certain groups of human beings that are capable of performing actions. Unions can go out on strike, and countries can wage war. By employing the terminology of a social agent, one allows oneself to refer to both individual human beings and social groups with a single term in so far as both of these types of entities are characterizable as able to perform actions.

The fact that the terminology of social agency allows one to refer, without further specification, to both individual human agents and to such collections of agents as are able to act in a unified manner is an important benefit of its use. It has therefore been widely used by power theorists.[7] For example, although Dahl uses the term "actors" rather than "agents" to refer to human beings in his theory, he goes on to say that such "actors may be individuals, groups, roles, offices, governments, nation-states, or other human aggregates."[8] Lukes also thinks that it is useful to adopt a terminology that allows him to refer to individual human beings as well as social groups. Although Lukes believes that "everyday usage [has the] unfortunate connotation . . . that the exercise of power is a matter of individuals consciously acting to affect others", he nevertheless decides "to abandon these assumptions and to speak of the exercise of power whether by individuals or by groups, institutions, etc."[9] Although I do not think that "everyday usage" is as univocal as Lukes maintains, I agree that it is useful to have a mode of discourse that allows one to refer to both groups and individuals. My use of the concept of agent is intended to allow me to do just that.

Such usage, it should be noted, is not unproblematic. Although the concept of a social agent makes sense when applied to individual human beings, its use to refer to groups raises many important issues about the logic of group actions. Although I shall not discuss these issues further, I do want to register my awareness of the problems to which such usage gives rise.[10]

There is one further terminological issue, namely how to refer to the two agents in a power relation. I shall refer to the agent who has power over another agent as the *dominant agent* and to the one over whom power is possessed as the *subordinate agent*.[11] I am somewhat hesitant about using the term "dominant" in this regard, for it might be taken to carry with it the assumption that all power relations are also relations of domination. Since I shall actually argue in Chapters 9 and 10 that there are power relationships that are not characterizable as relations of domination, I want my terminology to be neutral in this regard. I shall therefore use this terminology, but only after making the explicit statement that being in the dominant position in a relationship does not necessarily entail the substantive conclusion that the relationship is describable as one of domination.

The Attribution of Power-Over as a Discursive Practice

In developing an account of the concept of power, it is important to reflect on the way in which that term is used within ordinary discourse. As I have argued at length in the previous chapters, an adequate analysis of power needs to be self-conscious about how that concept functions within the specific discursive practices of ordinary language. In developing my own analysis of an agent's having power over another agent, I shall begin by considering the role that this locution plays within our usual discourse.

In order to do so, it will be useful to look at a passage from Aristotle's *Nichomachean Ethics* that I believe accurately registers one practice within which the concept "power-over" functions. At the beginning of book III, Aristotle distinguishes between voluntary and involuntary actions. He describes the latter in the following manner:

Those things, then, are thought involuntary, which take place under compulsion or owing to ignorance; and that is compulsory of which the moving principle is outside, being a principle in which nothing is contributed by the person who acts or is acted upon, e.g. if he were to be carried somewhere by a wind, or by men who had him in their power.[12]

In this passage, Aristotle treats those actions that result from a person's being in someone else's power as analogous to actions that occur because of physical compulsion. Although Aristotle does not say much more about this analogy, we need to inspect it very carefully.

When a sudden gust of wind blows a pedestrian into another person, the "action" of that pedestrian takes place through an external cause—that is, the wind. Such an "action" is not imputed to the person as something that he did, so that he is not blamed for causing harm to the person whom he bumped into. Thus, the presence of physical compulsion provides a reason to excuse a person from responsibility for the results of his behavior. Although a person may "do" something that normally would result in punishment or censure, when that "action" is the result of physical compulsion, the action is not deemed to be voluntary, and hence the agent is not normally blamed for his or her "actions". This is the point of making the distinction between voluntary and involuntary actions, as Aristotle points out.

Aristotle goes on to claim that actions that proceed from the power of other persons are, or should be, treated as similar to cases of physical compulsion. That is, Aristotle claims that such actions are also involuntary and should not be treated as making the agent subject to moral approbation or disapproval for performing them. His rationale for this claim is that, as in situations involving physical compulsion, actions that an agent performs as a result of the power of another agent are ones whose "moving principle" is not "within" the agent. In cases of physical compulsion this is clear: The person does not really even act, but his body behaves in a certain way because it is caused to do so by a physical force over which the person has no control. Aristotle claims that the same, or something similar, is true of actions resulting from the power of other persons. The question is why we should treat actions that result from an agent's being in the power of another as likewise caused by something external to the agent.[13]

Intuitively, Aristotle's claim makes a great deal of sense. When an action is caused by either physical compulsion or another person's power, an agent engages in a form of behavior as a result of a cause external to himself. To see this, consider a case in which a friend, call him Fred, takes part in a demonstration and performs a violent act that is judged to be uncharacteristic of him. One of the things that might be said in attempting to explain Fred's behavior is that the charismatic leader of the group had a great deal of *power over* Fred. As a result, when the leader urged Fred to undertake the violent action, Fred did so. By saying that the group leader had power over Fred, one is explaining the cause of Fred's unusual behavior. Because one judges Fred to be in someone else's power, one judges his actions not to be *fully* his own, but rather *to have been caused* by the agent who had power over him. By making such a claim one implicitly makes the judgment that, had Fred not been in the power of the group's leader, he would never have committed such an action.

Aristotle's claim does not occur in an attempt to analyze power, but rather in an attempt to use the idea of being in someone's power as a criterion for claiming that an action that someone performed was not a voluntary action. As a result, he passes over a significant problem by simply assimilating cases of power to those of physical compulsion. While it is true that there is an analogy between power-over and physical compulsion, they are not simply identical phenomena. That is to say, although the wind may literally cause me to bump into someone and thus to "do" something totally against my will, my acting as a result of someone else's power over me has a different structure. When the wind blows me into someone, it is really my body that is being acted upon. I have no conscious control over my "action". Such is usually not the case when someone else has power over me.[14] Although someone may cause my action, as Aristotle claims, she does not do so without my participating in that act to a greater degree than I do when the wind blows me. Thus, Fred's violent act is something that he did, while my bumping into someone is not something I did.

Thus, I think that Aristotle is right to claim that to say of a social agent that someone had power over her is to say that her actions were caused or controlled by that other agent in some manner and to a certain degree, and, conversely, to say that someone has power over another is to say that that agent has the ability to cause or control the actions of the other. The concept of power-over is used to register the judgment that an agent's action (or inaction) is caused by someone other than the agent herself. The point of ascribing power-over to a social agent is to judge that the normal circumstances of social agency have been altered. By recognizing the fact that the concept of power-over occurs within a specific discursive social practice with a specific point to it, one is able to see precisely how that term functions.

But Aristotle's analysis is only the starting point for a theory of power-over. While Aristotle accurately reflects the manner in which the concept of power-over is used in one discursive practice, he does not provide an explanation of why this practice is a legitimate one. In particular, his analogy between power and physical compulsion leaves open the question of the manner in which one agent's power can cause another agent to do something of which he is not, in an appropriate sense, the cause.

Aristotle's claim, then, sets up a goal for a successful analysis of power-over: namely to explain how an agent can, in a suitable sense, both undertake a certain course of action and yet be said to have been caused to do so. While Aristotle is right to say that we use the concept of power-over in precisely this way, he does not provide a satisfactory account of why such usage is legitimate.

The Ontology of Human Agency

The argument of the previous section sought to develop a provisional understanding of the sort of conceptual practice within which the attribution of power-over to a social agent has a place. As a first step in providing a more developed understanding of the legitimacy of this practice, I shall present a more sophisticated account of the agency of a social agent.

In thinking about the basic ontological structure of the situation of human beings considered as social agents, there are a number of general observations to be made. First of all, human beings always exist in a social and natural context that determines a set of possible courses of action that are available to them as agents. All sorts of different factors determine the courses of actions that are available to an agent in a given situation—for example, the physical limitations that a given social agent has. If she had a different set of physical capacities, there would be other courses of action that she could pursue. A first aspect of an agent's situation, then, consists in the possible courses of action that she has available to her.

However, the objective situation of a social agent is not all that determines how an agent will act. A second aspect of the structure of human social agency is the agent's assessment of her situation. The agent's interpretation of her situation is a significant element of human agency that must be acknowledged in a theoretical account of such agency. This assessment itself is composed of two elements. The first is the agent's understanding of the alternative courses of action that she might pursue in a given situation. Such a set of alternatives is not always active in the sense that an agent acts only after deliberately "running through" these alternatives. Nonetheless, the presence of such alternatives in situations where an agent does deliberate about which course of action to pursue gives us a clue to their role in human action. The second aspect of an agent's assessment of her situation is her evaluation of the alternative courses of action with which she is faced. For example, an agent may choose one action over another because of the consequences that accrue to her from pursuing it rather than the other action. On the other hand, an agent might follow one course of action because it is the sort of action that she believes she should pursue. In such cases, the agent's evaluation of the courses of action that she sees as available to her is the basis for her acting as she does.

I shall analyze these ontological features of human social agency by means of the concept of an *agent's action-environment*. In its most general sense, the concept of an action-environment specifies the structure within which an agent exists as a social actor. The actions that an agent engages in can be specified in terms of the options available to her in her action-environment.

The idea of the *action-alternatives* that are available to an agent in a given situation needs to be characterized more precisely. Intuitively, this idea is a perfectly clear one. In a given situation, an agent has a number of courses of action that she could engage in. For example, in my present situation as a writer of this book, I can continue writing or I can stop working and attend to other matters, such as paying some bills. Each of these courses of action represents a genuine possibility for how I might act in my current situation.

These reflections show that *an agent's action-environment in a certain situation* includes, first of all, of a set of *action-alternatives, a_i.* An action-alternative is simply a course of action that is available to the agent in that situation. I shall say that two courses of action a_i and a_j are alternatives in a specific situation if and only if an agent's pursuit of action-alternative a_i in that situation entails that pursuing alternative a_j is foreclosed to her at that time. Thus, my continuing to write this book at the present time entails that I cannot also go to the bank to pay my bills. Courses of action are genuine alternatives when an agent's engagement in one of them keeps her from being able to engage in other ones in a specific situation.[15]

This definition uses the idea of a course of action as the basic notion in defining an action-environment. In this sense, an agent's action-environment is defined by alternative courses of action and not simply by single actions that are available to her. Although I will not attempt to specify the scope of such courses of action, I will treat an agent's action-alternatives as constituted by courses of action, each of which is made up of many single actions. This definition also treats courses of action as alternative to one another only in a context. I am not using any general notion of incompatible action-types, but only of choices in a concrete context that rule out other choices. The incompatibility of action-alternatives is based solely on the fact that an agent cannot pursue all the possibilities that are available to her at a given moment of time.

It is important to recognize that my use of "availability" in this definition conceals an important problem. The action-alternatives that compose an agent's action-environment cannot be interpreted as the actions that an agent *could* engage in, if that is taken to mean actions that are physically possible for the agent in a given situation. Such a set of actions is much too wide to constitute an agent's action-environment in the sense that I intend. Although I could, for example, blow up my car by dropping a lighted match into the gas tank, such a course of action is not a genuine action-alternative for me in my present situation, since there is no reason for me to do so.

Such a consideration shows that not all the courses of action that an agent could follow in a given situation form genuine action-alternatives for that agent. In order to make sense of a more restrictive notion of an action-alternative, I shall rely on the notion of an agent's having a reason to pursue a course of action. I shall say that a course of action is an *action-alternative* for an agent in a given situation if and only if there is a *reason* for her to follow that course of action in the situation in which she finds herself. This specification of the notion of an action-alternative limits that notion to those courses of action that have some actual possibility of being pursued by an agent in a situation.[16]

There are many situations in which an agent may be unaware of all the alternatives for acting that she really has. For example, I might believe that I was not in a position to make an impact on a certain local social policy by writing a letter to my town government when I would have affected town policy had I chosen to write the letter. In such a case, although writing the letter is an action-alternative available to me, I may not regard it as such, seeing it simply as an exercise in futility. Agents do not always understand the full scope of possible courses of action that they could engage in.[17]

Considerations such as this make it clear that an agent's action-environment needs to include among its components the agent's interpretation of her situation. I shall call this aspect of her action-environment her *assessment* of her action-alternatives. By including this component in my conceptualization of the ontology of human agency, I acknowledge the fact that human beings act in light of an awareness of the alternatives that they have for acting, but that such an awareness does not always accurately reflect the actual nature of the set of action-alternatives available to them.

An agent's assessment of her action-environment itself involves two distinct features. First, there is the *understanding* that the agent has of the alternative courses of action that are open to her. Making this an explicit element in an agent's action-environment acknowledges the fact that an agent's sense of what it is possible for her to do may be more or less extensive than what she actually can do. In the letter-writing example I mentioned previously, I conceive of my action-environment as more limited than it actually is. Agents also see themselves as able to accomplish things that they in fact cannot. For example, a man might think that by using a certain after-shave lotion he will be able to attract the woman of his dreams when, in fact, this is simply not so. It is therefore important to distinguish between the action-alternatives that an agent actually has and that agent's understanding of what his action-alternatives are. As we shall see, the gap between actuality and an agent's understanding of it creates a crucial domain for the exercise of power.[18]

Equally as important to a full specification of the ontology of human social agency is the agent's *evaluation* of the alternatives that she has. By considering an agent's evaluation of her action-alternatives an element of her action-environment, I draw attention to the fact that, although agents act for various reasons, such action can be thought of as proceeding from an evaluation of the course of action that is followed. Such evaluation takes different forms in different contexts. An agent may perform an action because she thinks it will bring her great pleasure—indeed, because this action will bring her more

pleasure than any other alternative she sees. However, an agent may also perform an action that she thinks is the right thing to do and not worry about the
consequences of her action at all. Very different types of evaluations are possible as grounds for an agent's pursuing a course of action.

An agent's evaluation of her action-alternatives is an important aspect of
her action-environment. Reflection upon a situation in which an agent makes a
decision about what course of action to pursue by actually considering two
alternative courses of action will allow the importance of an agent's evaluation
to emerge. An agent who chooses to go to college, for example, rather than to
get married and raise a family, might do so on the basis of her evaluation of
these different action-alternatives. All sorts of different factors can enter into
such an evaluation: questions of the desirability of the courses of action themselves; questions of the consequences that will result from pursuing them;
even questions about the right mode of conduct for a contemporary woman to
engage in. All these different sorts of factors result in the agent's differentially
evaluating these two action-alternatives. By seeing the role of such considerations in the decision-making process, we can see that the evaluative component
of an agent's action-environment is as fundamental to it as the alternatives
themselves.

As I have said, many different factors can affect an agent's evaluation of
her action-alternatives. For example, an agent's sense of the sort of person
that she is functions to make certain alternatives that are available to her unacceptable and others desirable. A person who views herself as a woman of class
might find working as a cleaning woman demeaning, whereas another person
might find this to be a meaningful activity. An agent's sense of herself conditions her assessment of her action-alternatives.

How other agents will react to a person if she performs a certain action is
another sort of factor that can condition an agent's evaluation of her action-
alternatives. A man may not be willing to see a therapist even though he would
like to, because his close friends and family would see him as weak and ineffec-
tual if he did so. Here, an agent's view of the opinions of others affects his
evaluation of the options that he has for acting.

Real (as well as imagined) responsibilities, demands, and commitments to
others can also affect an agent's evaluation of her action-alternatives. If I have
promised to help my wife pick out a bathing suit, I may decide not to play
tennis with a friend even though I find such an action-alternative very desirable in itself.

Although I have used "negative" examples to illustrate a variety of factors
that can affect an agent's evaluation of her action-alternatives—that is, examples in which these factors cause an agent to refrain from performing cer-

tain actions that she might perform in their absence—such factors can also cause an agent to act in a positive manner. For example, I might decide to play tennis, even though I don't particularly like to do so, out of a desire to spend time with a friend. The point of giving these examples is to show that agents' evaluations of their options for acting depend on a wide range of factors having to do with their own sense of themselves and their relations with others.

While I have isolated one aspect of an agent's action-environment as evaluative, it is important to recognize that an agent's understanding of her action-environment is also evaluative in nature. As I have mentioned, agents make judgments about what courses of action are available to them. They may not believe themselves to be capable of performing certain actions that they could in fact perform. In so far as their understanding of their action-environment reflects these judgments, it too is evaluative.

At this point in my discussion of the proper set of concepts for conceptualizing the nature of human social agency I would like to introduce a very important *caveat*. Although I am conceptualizing an agent's engagement in a course of action as taking place in the context of an assessment of various alternative courses of action, I wish to avoid the intellectualist fallacy of assuming that every pursuit of a course of action can be represented as a conscious "running through" of a set of possible courses of action and the selection of one of them as the one to be engaged in. While I claim that human action takes place within a context of certain alternative possibilities, I am not claiming that all such action should be modeled on explicit decision-making. As both Heidegger and the pragmatists have argued, it is crucial to avoid such intellectualist misconceptualizations of human action.[19] By analytically distinguishing different elements of an agent's action-environment, I do not mean to claim thereby that all human action takes place by means of a process of explicit calculation of which alternative is the best one to pursue.

The Definition of Power-Over

The goal of this chapter is to present a definition of power-over that is superior to previous attempts. So far, I have presented a number of strands of thought as preparatory to this undertaking. At this point, I shall present my own conception of an agent's having power over another agent by weaving together these strands of analysis.

The central notion that I have developed in this chapter is that of an agent's action-environment. In so doing, I have showed that an agent's actions are the results of a complex structure that includes an awareness of various alternative possibilities for acting. I have also claimed that power is exercised over an agent when he is not able to act freely, that is, with a full set of possibilities available to him. In order to capture this idea more precisely, I will define an agent's power over another in the following manner: A social agent *A* has *power over* another social agent *B* if and only if *A* strategically constrains *B*'s action-environment. Since an agent's action-environment constitutes the "space" within which an agent acts, we can see why this definition of power-over can be called a field theory. We can think of the presence of a magnet as "constraining" the motion of a body. In the absence of the magnet, the body would move "freely", that is, without being affected by an alien presence. What this definition suggests is that an agent's power over another agent has an effect on the latter's action analogous to the effect of a magnet on the motion of a body.

By defining an agent's power over another agent in terms of the *constraint* that the first agent imposes upon the action-environment of the second, I depart from a number of central assumptions that were made by the theorists in the power debate. Most importantly, I do not privilege discrete interventions as the primary context within which power is exercised. Although a discrete intervention is one way in which an agent is able to constrain the action-environment of another agent—for example, by making it impossible for an agent to embark upon the action-alternative that she desires—an ongoing social relationship between two agents can also result in the constraining of one of their action-environments. Thus, when one agent systematically misleads another agent about what she is able to accomplish, he has power over her although such power need not be the result of a discrete intervention that he makes into her already constituted action-environment.

The presence of the word "strategically" in this definition is another respect in which it differs from more behavioristic accounts. It indicates that attributing power to an agent involves an understanding of the reason why an agent acts as she does. As I argued in the previous chapter, not all situations in which certain effects impact upon an agent are instances of power. In the present context, this means that, for an action through which an agent constrains another agent's action-environment to be one in which power is used, the agent's action must fit into a general pattern that I am calling a *strategy*. Thus, constraining an agent's action-environment by ruining his car in an accident is an exercise of power over that agent only if that accident fits into a more general strategy that the dominant agent is pursuing, such as keeping the agent from turning over secret documents to a third agent. A random traffic accident, although it does constrain the action-environment of an agent, is not an exercise of power.

There are a number of other features of this definition to which I would like to call attention. First of all, since an agent over whom power is exercised acts as a result of the exercise of power, the agent is not fully responsible for what she does. When we looked at Aristotle's exposition of the nature of involuntary actions, we saw that the claim that an agent acted because power was exercised over her functioned to diminish the agent's responsibility for acting as she did. My definition of power-over explains precisely why this is so: An agent who acts in a context in which someone else has power over her is not able to do as she wishes, but faces a situation in which the structure of her action-environment is in the control of someone else. She is therefore not in the normal circumstances of human action and, as a result, her responsibility for her actions is modified.

This explication of one agent's power over another also provides the necessary specification of the idea that an agent's action can be caused externally to her. By using the concept of an agent's action-environment, this definition provides a more concrete way of thinking about how an agent's action can be caused by another agent. An agent's constraint of either the action-alternatives that another agent faces or of that agent's assessment of those alternatives is what constitutes the power that the former has over the latter. By changing the circumstances within which an agent exists, another agent assumes responsibility for the actions that that agent performs.

Although this definition of power-over appears similar to the definitions I criticized in the last chapter, because it involves the notion of an agent's action-environment, it is situated in an ontology of human action that is more comprehensive than that posited by the behavioralistically influenced attempts to define power-over in terms of behavior, decisions, and interests. This reflects my claim that attributions of power over an agent make sense only as a contrast to situations in which an agent is taken to be acting without the presence of power. By locating the concept of power-over within the domain of concepts used for describing human social activity, I am able to make sense of the practice of judging that an agent's actions were what they were as a result of the presence of power.

At this point, I have presented the basic features of my conception of power-over. As I have argued, this conception of power has a number of important differences from the attempts by the theorists in the power debate to define the idea of power-over. My focus upon power as a field as well as my use of the framework of concepts pertaining to human social agency distinguishes my account from theirs at a fundamental level. It is my contention that the account that I have provided—because of its generality—is able to ground a more adequate theory of power-over than that which the theorists of power have articulated.

In a certain sense, I have not demonstrated the truth of this assertion in any but the most general terms. Although this definition does explain what is involved in attributing power to an agent, it does so in a very abstract manner and does not explain exactly how such power works in a particular situation. That is, this definition leaves open the question of exactly what aspect of an agent's action-environment is affected by the presence of power. Before the advantages of this definition can truly be perceived, it will be necessary to specify the various different forms that power can take, a task which I will begin in the next chapter. Only after seeing how this definition can actually be specified will the reader get a clear sense of the advantages of adopting it.

Power and Freedom

There is one possible objection to my account of an agent's power over another agent that I would like to consider. According to this objection, there is a fundamental incoherence in my account. I argue that to judge that power has been exercised over an agent is to judge that the action of that agent has been caused by another agent. However, my account of the concept of power allows that power can be exercised over an agent when the agent's assessment of her action-environment is constrained by another agent. This means that an agent can still freely choose how to act and thus that she is the cause of her own actions. My account of power, according to this objection, cannot have it both ways: Either power results in someone else's causing an agent's action or else it does not.

I shall begin my discussion of this objection about the relation of power and freedom by making an important distinction. Except in the sorts of cases that I shall use the term "force" to designate, human beings always act freely in the sense that they could have acted differently.[20] Only by literally objectifying the human being—that is, by treating her like a physical object and literally causing her state to be what it is—is it possible to take away her freedom in this sense. Aristotle's example of the wind is an example of such an objectification of the human being. Most of the time, however, despite the presence of power, human beings act freely in the sense of being able to have acted differently.

Human freedom does not, however, consist simply in the ability to have done otherwise; as Aristotle points out, the role of another person in causing one to act as one does may show that one is not completely free. When one chooses, for example, on pain of death, to reveal the location of one's comrade to an enemy, one could have done otherwise, but one is not free in that the alternatives between which one has had to choose are not themselves under one's own control.[21] In Aristotelian terminology, one's action is not voluntary. In such cases, although one could have done otherwise, and is thus free in one sense, one is not fully free in that one's action is not voluntary.[22]

In order for an action to be freely undertaken in a given situation, a human social agent needs to have at least two things. First, the agent must be in a position to do other than as she in fact does. This is a formal or metaphysical notion of freedom, one that attempts to characterize the human being as having a different type of existence than other entities in the world. Second, the agent's action must take place in view of a full set of options that she is capable of realizing. If an agent lacks the relevant set of options, then she will not be free, even though she may have the freedom to do other than she does in fact do.[23]

In the context of my discussion of power, this means that there is no contradiction between saying that someone chose to perform the action that she performed and saying that nonetheless the choice was itself caused by someone else. If the action-environment of a social agent is constrained by another agent in a manner that results in a different action's being undertaken by the first agent, then she will not freely engage in that action. To be a social agent in the full sense of the word does require that one be able to engage in activity that one has chosen to engage in; but it is equally important that one's choice not be made as the result of a structuring of one's options by another agent. Only if one conflates these two senses of freedom will one believe that the account of power that I have given is troubled by a conceptual incoherence.

Conclusion

In this chapter, I have developed a definition of what it is for one agent to have power over another agent. By means of an articulation of a set of concepts that are necessary for understanding the nature of human social agency, I put forward a definition of power that explains why the discursive practice of attributing power over an agent to another agent has a legitimate function.

The definition of power that I have presented is a very broad one. It states that an agent who exercises power over another agent does so by affecting the circumstances within which the other agent acts and makes choices. It does not, however, specify exactly how such effects are brought about. Indeed, it is a virtue of this definition that it is so general and that it allows of further specification.

The task to which I shall turn in the following chapter is that of showing that the types of power typically discussed by Anglo-American social theo-

rists can be distinguished from one another on the basis of this general definition. The differences among them concern the way in which the dominant
agent constrains the action-environment of the subordinate agent. The successful development of such an account will show a specific advantage of
adopting the definition of one agent's power over another agent that I have
presented in this chapter.

5

The Articulation of Power

IN THIS chapter, I shall argue that power-over is articulated. The articulated nature of power is an important aspect of the field theory of power because it posits power as having a more complex structure than the interventionist model recognizes. By characterizing power-over as articulated, I am claiming that an agent's power over another agent is constituted by the simultaneous presence of a number of different types of power.

The claim that power-over is articulated can be broken down into two more specific claims. The first is that power-over exists in a number of different types, specifically those of force, coercion, and influence. The second is that these different types of power are not simply specifications of the generic concept of power-over but are internally related to one another, that each type of power creates a "demand" that the subsequent type "fills". As such, these types of power are elements in an overall structure in which each functions to support the others.

In order to demonstrate the articulated nature of power, I shall present a typology of different forms of power. In presenting this typology, I shall continue to employ the categories used by power theorists in the Anglo-American tradition to understand the notion of power. I shall show that my definition of power-over can be used to distinguish such different types of power as force, coercive power, and influence by specifying the manner in which the subordinate agent's action-environment is constrained.

In so doing, I seem to be following the lead of these theorists for whom power-over is essentially a form of social domination. This is not the case, however. The types of power that I shall distinguish in this chapter are not necessarily forms of domination; they are types of power that can be used by social agents for a variety of purposes. Domination, as I shall argue in the next chapter, is a particular use of power, one in which the dominant agent affects the subordinate agent in a negative manner. The case of paternalism is an example of a use of these same types of power in order to benefit the subordinate agent. These types of power are neutral in that they can be employed by social agents in different ways and for different purposes.

I shall be doing two things at once in this chapter. On the one hand, I shall be showing that the general definition of power-over that I developed in the previous chapter can be realized in a variety of types of power depending on two variables: what aspect of an agent's action-environment is the specific target of the type of power at issue, and what means are used for such targeting. The different ways in which power can be a social presence can be specified by an attention to how a subordinate agent's action-environment is affected by the dominant agent.

At the same time, however, I shall be arguing that it is a mistake to think of these different types of power as mutually exclusive categories that determine the form that actual power relations can take. It is not the case that any power relation will necessarily be of one and only one of these types. As I have said, I shall argue that there is a "natural" tendency for a dominant agent to articulate her power—that is, to incorporate all the various types of power as a means of maintaining it. Actual power relations between social agents will not exhibit one of these types of power in separation from all others but will, at a minimum, consist of an array of these types, consolidated into the field that is a concrete power relation. This observation needs to be borne in mind as a means of interpreting the significance of the typology as it unfolds.

Let me also call attention to the fact that, in developing this typology, I shall use concepts that are derived from ordinary discourse and that function within it as ways of speaking about power. Such terms as "force", "coercion", and "influence" are used within ordinary discourse to conceptualize the existence of power. The definitions that I develop, however, should not be thought of as simply clarifications and regimentations of our ordinary conceptual scheme. I shall develop a set of theoretical concepts that distinguish among different types of power in a clearer and more systematic manner than normal usage allows. This typology is thus a step removed from ordinary discourse and is not intended simply as a clarified version of it. The clear-cut theoretical distinctions that I draw cannot be traced back without remainder to the use of these terms within ordinary discourse.

For example, the first type of power that I shall discuss is force. In so doing, I shall not attempt to conceptualize all that falls under the ordinary use of the term "force" in English. In particular, the usual use of the word "force" includes many things that I will conceptualize by means of the concept of coercive power. In discussing force, I aim to isolate a specific aspect of power that needs to be kept distinct from others. Although our ordinary conceptual practice does not neatly mark this distinction, there are important theoretical reasons for so doing.

Force

Force is the first type of power that I shall attempt to explicate. An exercise of power by an agent A over an agent B is an exercise of *force* if and only if A physically keeps B from pursuing the action-alternative that B wishes to pursue or causes a certain behavior to apply to B that B would avoid if possible.[1] Force achieves its ends by keeping an agent from doing what she wishes. An exercise of force relies on the physical ability of an agent to keep another agent from doing what she would prefer to do or to get something to happen to the agent that she would prefer did not. A simple example of force occurs when a parent forcibly opens a child's mouth and pours some medicine down the child's throat, despite his continuous attempts to resist taking the medicine.

The first thing to notice about force is that it exists only through its exercise. Although one may have a "means of force", such a means is a factor in B's action-environment—*at the level of force*—only if it is actually being employed. I say "at the level of force" because the possibility of being able to force someone to do, or refrain from doing, something is one of the primary grounds of more complex relations of power. The threat to use force, for example, is a more complex type of power than the simple use of force itself. Force, then, is the most basic way in which one agent is able to alter the action-environment of another agent and exists only as an occurrent event, an actual intervention.

Force is therefore not a real form of *relationship* between two agents. While it makes sense, from a logical point of view, to say that force is a *relation* between the two agents A and B, since force exists only in its exercise it cannot ground any long-term interaction between social agents. In itself, it is an occurrent item that serves to restrict an agent's ability to realize her own volitions and is thus the paradigm of an interventional form of power.

A second distinctive feature of force, one that follows directly from the first one, is that it has a primarily negative mode of appearance. It is much easier to use force to keep an agent from doing something than it is to use force to get something to happen to that agent. (Force can never make an agent *do* anything. It functions precisely by keeping an agent from doing something.) Although force is frequently used in the relationship between parents and their children, such a use of force is most often negative, keeping the child from performing actions that the parents do not want, and only in rare cases, as the one mentioned above, getting something to happen against the child's will. For instance, locking a child in his room is a use of force that restricts the child's ability to go where he wishes. Further examples of the negative structure of force abound. When an employer locks his employees out of a plant, he is using force to keep them from working. Similarly, when a saboteur ties someone up to keep him from revealing the existence of a bomb that he has just discovered, the saboteur is using force to keep the agent from acting on the basis of his discovery.

Although the saboteur's tying up of his victim is a clear example of an exercise of force, not all uses of force involve such direct physical domination of another's body. One can also use force to attack another's possessions, thus keeping her from using those possessions as means to realize her action-alternatives. For example, if a saboteur blows up his enemy's means of transportation, he is using force, but not directly on the body of his enemy. Similarly, an agent could burn down another's fields in order to keep him from paying the mortgage. Such exercises of force are *mediate* in that the actual target of the use of force is some possession that the agent would use for the realization of his preferred action-alternative. Force, then, can have as its target either the body of the agent or those possessions that the agent uses as a means to realize his intentions.

A crucial feature of the exercise of force is that it does not involve a mutual understanding between two agents. Unlike other forms of power, force is solely an *external* relation. Rather than trying to change the mind of another agent, in an exercise of force the dominant agent keeps the subordinate agent from being able to act as she would wish to. The subordinate agent is placed in a situation in which she is not capable of acting on her own; her situation is changed, but it is changed by her being placed in circumstances in which she is no longer able to use the same means of action as she previously could. In this sense, we can speak of force as requiring an *objectification* of a human being, for the subordinate agent is being treated as an object whose actions must be hindered, much as one might keep a rock from falling. To use force against another is to treat her in an objectified manner, not allowing her to act as she wants, without attempting to make her consent to such an occurrence in any manner.[2]

This analysis of the structure of force relations shows why force is not as pervasive a phenomenon as it is often assumed to be. While relations of force can be used to ground more complex relations of power, they are, because of their "uneconomic" character, inefficient means of affecting other people.[3]

Force is uneconomic for a number of reasons. In the first place, it requires that the dominant agent make some physical effort in order to keep the subordinate agent from doing what she would otherwise do. But this means, as we have seen, that force only exists when it is actually being exercised. As a result, maintaining the use of force requires a constant expenditure of energy by the dominant agent. This feature of force is one that, as I shall argue, distinguishes it from other types of power.[4]

Force is also uneconomic because it inherently occasions resistance. Since force proceeds without any attempt to alter an agent's own assessment of his action-environment, it is always perceived by those over whom it is used as a hostile presence, an alienating experience that restricts their ability to act. Because of this, it engenders a dynamic of resistance in those over whom it is exercised.

Although I have claimed that the actual exercise of force in social relations is not as extensive as is usually thought, I want to guard against one misinterpretation. I am not saying that force is not widespread, but that force *by itself* is less effective as a means of power than is often assumed.[5]

The validity of my claim will emerge from a consideration of the instrumental use of force. In its instrumental use, force is not used simply to keep an agent from acting as she intended; it is used as a sign of a more complex relationship of power. The important distinction here is that the instrumental use of force does not simply keep an agent from realizing a particular action-alternative. Rather, such a use of force is self-referential in that it alters the subordinate agent's action-environment in order to symbolize the fact that the dominant agent has the ability to do just that. For example, in the film *The Pope of Greenwich Village,* an irate gangster has the thumb of a young punk cut off as a warning to him, and to others, that those who attempt to steal from him will be made to pay, that his power extends even to their bodies. This expression of force, the ability to maim another's body, to cut off the thumb of the hand that has stolen, functions in this case as a sign of the more inclusive and complex power relations in which individuals stand with the gangster and is meant to serve as a symbol of those relations. The use of force in such cases is primarily instrumental; that is, it is used as the means of making a threat. In this case, the gangster is saying, "Steal from me and I will make you unable to steal!" Not only is the maimed youth punished by this use of force, but both he and others are warned of the extent of the gangster's power. The instrumental use of force is a potent form of power, one that is simultaneously an exercise of force and an attempt to constitute another type of power relation.

Many cases of bombing and terrorism have a similar structure. In them, force is used instrumentally to register the larger context of power that a group or nation has. These examples point toward the fact that force, although a reality in many social situations, achieves its full scope by undergirding other types of power. The instrumental use of force demonstrates my contention that force is normally a factor in a set of power relations that are more complex and varied than can be captured at the level of force itself.

Force, then, although a particular type of power, has an effect in social relations that transcends its own specific nature. One can have an understanding of the nature and efficacy of force in society only if one sees force as existing in actual conjunction with other, more complex types of power.

Coercive Power

Coercive power, the second type of power that I shall discuss, targets the set of action-alternatives that constitutes one aspect of an agent's action-environment. When an agent is in a position to threaten to use a resource or ability to affect the action-alternatives of another agent, then the agent can exercise coercive power. Coercive power can be exercised by an agent if (1) she is able to alter the set of action-alternatives available to another agent, and (2) she uses this fact to make a threat to that agent.[6]

Coercive power can only be exercised by an agent, however, when the threat that she makes is *effective*—that is, when it is recognized by the threatened agent and gets her to alter her anticipated course of action. Otherwise, although the threatening agent will be able to harm the threatened agent, the relationship between them will not be constituted at the level of coercive power. I will therefore say that a social agent A exercises *coercive power* over social agent B if and only if (1) A has the ability to affect B in a significant way; (2) A threatens to do so unless B acts in a certain way; and (3) B accedes to A's threat and alters his course of action. One example often used to illustrate the nature of coercive power is a thief with a gun. Although the possession of a gun gives a thief a means to use in coercing his victim, I think that this example obscures certain fundamental features of the exercise of coercive power in social relationships. I will therefore illustrate coercive power with an example that gives a clearer presentation of its nature.

Suppose that a local government refuses to issue a parade permit to a local environmental group that has asked for one and threatens the group by saying that anyone who demonstrates will be arrested and jailed. The local government is clearly attempting to coerce the environmental group.[7] What is the exact structure of such a use of coercive power?

We first need to consider the pre-threat action-environment of the group. Let us suppose that the group, G, has a limited set of financial and temporal resources, R. This set of resources constitutes the group's initial situation, S_0. The initial situation can therefore be represented as follows:

$$S_0 = R$$

Since the environmental group is dedicated to using its resources to fulfill its objectives, it wants to expend those resources in the most effective way possible. Let us assume that there are two options for the group: either holding a demonstration, D, or conducting a house-to-house survey, H. Let us also suppose that R is such that it will be fully expended by either undertaking, so that it is not possible for G to split R between them. In this case, we can represent the group's initial action-environment in terms of the following transformation:

$$S_0 = R \rightarrow S_1 \begin{array}{l} \text{-----}\blacktriangleright a_1 = D - R \\ \text{-----}\blacktriangleright a_2 = H - R \end{array}$$

Let us suppose that the group, after much deliberation, decides to pursue the option of demonstrating as more likely to realize its goals, and therefore applies for, but is denied, the permit for a demonstration.

At this point, we need to consider the impact that the government's threat has upon the action-environment of the group. I interpret that threat (T)—"Those who demonstrate will be jailed!"—as entailing the following conditional:

$$T = D \rightarrow J$$

where J stands for the arrest and imprisonment of the members of G.[8] But this means that one branch of the action-environment of G in S_1 is changed. It is no longer possible for the group to simply expend its resources on the demonstration; it must now reckon with its members' being arrested if the demonstration takes place.[9] I shall represent the effect of the threat in the following manner:

$$a_{1'} = D - R + J$$

It is this altered action-alternative that the members of G must deliberate about in S_0, so that their transformed action-environment can be represented as follows:

$$S_0 \rightarrow S_{1'} \begin{array}{c} \text{-----}\rightarrow a_{1'} = D - R + J \\ \text{-----}\rightarrow a_2 = H - R \end{array}$$

In other words, the set of action-alternatives the group now faces is transformed by the government's threat. Although the group is still able to conduct its house-to-house survey unhampered, it is faced with the prospect of being jailed if it chooses to demonstrate.[10]

It is this transformed set of action-alternatives about which the group must deliberate. In deciding how to react to the threat, there are two courses of action available to it. Either the members of G can decide that the threat of being arrested is sufficiently serious to keep them from demonstrating—in which case they can pursue the option of conducting the survey—or they can decide to go ahead with the demonstration and face the consequences. In the former case, the government's efforts at coercion will have been successful; in the latter, the failure of the attempt to coerce the group will put the government in a position where it can only use force over the group by arresting and imprisoning its members.

Although it may seem strange to say that someone who resists an attempt at coercion and suffers for such resistance has not been coerced by the threatening agent, I think such usage is appropriate. By making a threat, one attempts to coerce someone else into doing something. The coercion is successful only when the threatened agent accedes to the threat. Otherwise, although the threatening agent is able to harm the threatened agent—and such harm can itself involve other types of power being exercised over the agent—the threatening agent is unable to exercise coercive power over the resisting agent.[11]

This analysis of the effect that a threat has upon the action-environment of a social agent shows that there are a number of conditions necessary for the establishment of a coercive power relationship. The first is that the threatening agent A must have some means at her disposal through which she is able to affect the action-alternatives of the subordinate agent B in a manner that B is unable to counter. In the present case, it is the government's ability to jail the members of the group that constitutes its ability to affect B's action-alternatives. Second, A must be able to communicate to B her ability to affect B's action-environment. This condition is important, for it shows that coercion, unlike force, requires that the agents involved share an understanding of the significance of their interaction. The coercing agent must be able to communicate to the coerced agent her ability to control his situation depending upon how he reacts to her demands. This is a somewhat complexly structured interaction, one whose rules are not as self-evident as some social theorists have assumed.[12] Third, B must have reason to believe not just that A has the ability to affect his situation adversely, but that A has reason to do so should he fail to comply with the threat. Without this condition, there would be no reason for the threatened agent to take the threat seriously. If, for example, the environmental group knew that jailing the members of the group for demonstrating would result in a governmental crisis, then it would not take the threat as more than a bluff, something announced to keep the group from staging the demonstration but not indicating a seriously intended course of action. Similarly, an agent confronted by a masked person threatening, "Your money or your life!" who believed that the "thief" was really a friend playing a practical joke would have no reason for taking the threat seriously, even though he might play along. Finally, the negative consequences that A is able to inflict upon B must be sufficiently undesirable that they outweigh the benefits that would have accrued to B in the absence of A's threat. This means that not being jailed $(-J)$ must be desirable enough to make the benefits of demonstrating (D) no longer preferable to those of conducting the survey (H). The following example can clarify this condition. Contrary to the usual circumstances in a mugging, if the thief's intended victim was going to use the money in his pocket to pay for an operation to restore his son's sight and he had no other means of paying for the operation, he might well refuse to accede to the thief's threat. In this case the threat, although taken seriously, would not be capable of gaining the victim's compliance. A could still act on her threat to harm B, but she would be unable to exercise coercive power over him.

I have just outlined four conditions that are necessary for the exercise of coercive power.[13] When these conditions are satisfied, a situation exists in which it is "rational" for B to accede to the demand implicit in A's threat that he perform a certain action. In this context, "rational" means that only when these conditions are satisfied does it even make sense for B to accede to the threat; it does not mean that this course of action is the only one that B has a good reason to perform.

Coercive power always relies on the compliance of the subordinate agent with the threat made by the dominant agent: B must choose to let A's threat affect his behavior. While A may be able to harm B without B's compliance, A is able to exercise coercive power over B only through B's own decision to accede to A's threat. Coercive power cannot literally make an agent *do* anything. One who wishes to coerce someone can only make the consequences of doing things different from what they otherwise would have been for the agent; the victim of coercive power is nonetheless able to make choices about how to act in response to the threat that he faces. That is, he may choose to act in a confrontational rather than a submissive manner. The response to a coercive situation is not fully determined by the coercing agent; the consequences for the coerced agent of pursuing those responses are, however, fundamentally altered by the coercing agent. Here again, the idea of there being two components to human freedom is relevant. Although a situation of coercion constrains an agent's action-environment, it does not take away her ability to choose between the options the coercing agent presents her.

Understanding this aspect of a coercive situation gives the agent who is being coerced a reason to resist the coercion: By resisting, the coerced agent is able to maintain her own self-determination in a way that she cannot if she accedes to the threat made by the coercing agent. It therefore may be just as "rational" for the coerced agent to respond to the coercive situation by resisting as it is for her to be compliant.

One might object to this account of the nature of coercive power by pointing out that an exercise of coercive power can be based upon either the subordinate agent's or both agents' mistaken understanding of the ability of the dominant agent to affect the action-environment of the subordinate agent. For example, if the object concealed in her trench coat pocket with which a thief threatens her intended victim is really her finger and not a gun, but the intended victim believes that the object pointed at her is indeed a gun, then the thief's coercive exercise of power over the victim is based not upon the thief's actual ability to change the victim's action-environment, but upon the victim's false belief that this is the case. This shows, the objection maintains, that coercive power should not be defined in terms of the dominant agent's actual ability to control the subordinate agent's action-environment, but rather in terms of the subordinate agent's belief that she can do so.

This objection raises the issue of what I call the *Oz Phenomenon,* the ability of an agent to exercise power over other agents because these agents have false beliefs about the dominant agent's ability to change their action-environment. I use this name because the Wizard of Oz had power over the inhabitants of Oz as a result of their false belief about his ability to alter their action-environment by keeping the witches from harming them. The Oz Phenomenon is an important one, for it shows that agents are able to coerce other agents by acting upon their beliefs rather than by controlling their action-environment directly.

The existence of the Oz Phenomenon does not, however, affect the validity of my account of coercive power because the Oz Phenomenon is parasitic upon exercises of coercive power that have the character I have attributed to them—that is, the actual ability of the dominant agent to control the action-environment of the subordinate agent. Only because coercive power has such a structure can the Oz Phenomenon work to constitute relations of coercive power. Because the Oz Phenomenon depends upon the subordinate agent's understanding of "real" exercises of coercion, the existence of the Oz Phenomenon does not undercut the account of coercive power I have developed.

However, this objection does call attention to the fact that coercive power relations can be brought into existence by means of the subordinate agent's false understandings about the ability of the dominant agent to harm him. This is an important source of power for a dominant agent so long as her ability to realize her threat is not questioned.

My account of coercive power demonstrates the limitations of the view that social relationships are always constituted by agreements or understandings among the agents that make them up. In one sense, it is true that social agreements—that is, social practices—set the contexts within which agents act. As opposed to social theories that limit themselves to cognizing human behavior, my account moves from the beginning in the realm of human intentional actions. However, this does not mean that power is not itself a factor that can be wielded within a practice. As we have seen, a practice can itself be so constituted that one agent is able to determine the context within which another agent acts without the latter agent's being similarly able to determine the context of the former agent. This is what is meant by coercive social power.[14]

The Productivity of Coercion

At this point in the specification of different types of power, I shall compare force and coercion. The basic feature of coercion that I shall highlight is that in cases of coercion, as opposed to force, the dominant agent has the ability to use the subordinate agent's actions for his own benefit. I shall characterize this as the *productive* nature of coercive power.

To understand the productive nature of coercive power, recall my claim that force is not as extensive a social presence as is often assumed. Force exists only in its exercise. Although one may possess the "means of force", this only means that one has the ability to intervene in an agent's action-environment through the use of force. Moreover, force itself is, as noted, predominantly negative in that it can keep an agent from performing certain actions but cannot get an agent to *do* anything. Once an agent actually *acts*, force cannot be the only type of power that is present. When the possibility of the use of force grounds an agent's attempt to avoid its exercise, the action takes place in the logical space of coercive power rather than force. Unlike force, coercive power actually functions by getting an agent to *do* something. The logic of a threat is precisely its positing an action that an agent is able to forestall by acting in an appropriate manner.

This discussion allows us to see the two senses in which coercive power is productive. First, it *produces* actions by the subordinate agent who is seeking to keep a threatened action from being undertaken by the dominant agent. I have already spoken of this aspect of coercive power by stressing its "positive" form in contrast to force. Coercive power is productive, however, in a second sense as well: Because the subordinate agent performs certain actions, he can actually *produce* something that the dominant agent is able to appropriate. That is to say, coercive power results in the production of certain benefits that accrue to the dominant agent.

In this respect, an exercise of coercive power has a fundamentally different structure than an exercise of force. It does not require that the dominant agent do anything except make a threat in order to exercise such power and receive benefits from it. In the case of force, the dominant agent must actually do something to block the subordinate agent's actions. With exercises of force, an expenditure of energy by the dominant agent is required to alter the subordinate agent's action-environment. The exercise of coercive power, on the other hand, does not require any significant new action on the part of the dominant agent: If the dominant agent is in a position to make an effective threat, he can receive benefits as a result of the productive nature of coercion without having to do anything himself.[15]

This distinction between force and coercive power is one reason why force is not as pervasive a phenomenon in the social world as the threat of its exercise. The actual use of force requires that the dominant agent actually do something. This is simply not required when the use of force is only threatened. Although a dominant agent will often use force as a means of convincing the subordinate agent that his threat is one that he will actually realize if necessary, such uses of force are mainly instrumental—that is, a means of conveying an intention and not actually an attempt to change the subordinate agent's action-environment.

But although an exercise of coercive power differs from the use of force in regard to productivity, there is one respect in which they are similar: both occasion the existence of resistance. By *resistance* I mean the attempt by the subordinate agent to change her circumstances in regard to the dominant agent so as to diminish the dominant agent's power over her. Exercises of coercive power are as likely to produce resistance as exercises of force. The coerced agent, so long as she remains aware of her status as coerced, is aware that power is being exercised over her.[16] As such, she realizes that she is not free to pursue the actions that she would like. And this fact produces feelings of resentment and the desire to break free of the yoke of coercive power.

Coercive power is, like force, an "incomplete" type of power. Because coercive power occasions resistance to its exercise, an agent with coercive power has reason to seek a means to reduce such resistance. One way to do so is to obscure the nature of the relationship between herself and the subordinate agent. That is, a dominant agent has a reason to seek to develop misunderstandings among subordinate agents about whether they are actually being coerced.[17]

But this means that there is a tendency for dominant agents to seek to enlarge the various types of power that they have over an agent and to obscure the nature of the relationship between them. In order to see how this is possible, we shall need to investigate the next type of power, that of influence. Before doing so, however, I shall introduce an important *caveat* into this discussion of different types of power. In discussing the nature of power, I have retained the traditional formula "*A* has power over *B*". Using this formula isolates the two social agents in the power relationship from the more general social context within which they exist. Although such a separation is helpful for analytically distinguishing different forms of power, it gives a misleadingly static view of how social power is "distributed" among social agents. The existence of social power relationships among social agents is necessarily contested, depending upon the attitudes and actions of social agents external to the two agents in a power dyad.

To see this, consider the example of the environmental group's protest that I used to illustrate the nature of coercion. In discussing that example, I focused upon the local government and the environmental group, ignoring the presence of any other actors within the social field. This is certainly an abstraction, for there are many other actors there.

The actions of these other social agents have an effect on whether it makes sense to attribute to one agent power over the other. For example, if the government's decision to arrest the protesters would result in widespread disaffection from the government, disaffection that would result in the toppling of the government and the realization of the ends of the environmental group, then it would not make sense to say that the government really had power over the environmental group, all things considered. Although it could arrest the members of the group, this hardly amounts to power over them in light of the consequences of such actions.

When the environmental group ignores the government threats and decides to go through with its demonstration, the balance of power between government and demonstrators shifts. But the distribution of power between the two depends not only on their actions in regard to each other, but also on the effect these actions have on other groups in the society. If the environmental group, for instance, resists the government passively, it invites retaliation, and it may do so expressly in order to gain the sympathy and support of other groups that, so far, have not been involved in the conflict. The distribution of power between environmentalists and the government thus depends upon the reactions of third parties to the government's retaliation; a whole network of groups and individuals determines the distribution of power between any two agents.

This example allows us to see that the attribution of power to a social agent always presupposes the existence of a given social context. The attribution of power to the government is always made in light of an understanding of how agents external to the two central agents will act. The presumed action of these agents constitutes the context within which attributions of power are made. Since social contexts are always capable of changing, however, the existence of power relationships is always dependent upon certain assumptions about how the social context will continue to function. This is an important feature of power to which I will return in Chapter 7.

Influence and Its Forms

Influence is a type of power that fulfills the interest of the dominant agent in having his power over a subordinate agent misrepresented. The importance of influence as a distinct form of power lies in its role in relation to the other types of power that I have discussed. It extends those types of power into a more stable social situation, one that makes the subordinate agent misunderstand her own situation.

Influence is, however, a difficult concept to analyze because it includes a wide range of phenomena. At the one extreme, there are cases in which one agent simply supplies another agent with a piece of information that affects the decision that the latter makes about which course of action to pursue; at the other, there are cases of charismatic influence in which the charismatic individual is able to get another agent to do nearly anything that he wishes. Since the latter sort of example seems to be a clear case of the use of power whereas the former does not, one must distinguish cases of influence in which power is a factor from those in which it is not. In order to resolve this issue, I shall analyze the concept of influence in general before analyzing instances of influence that are also examples of power.

In general, the distinctive feature of influence is that it occurs through the acceptance by the subordinate agent of something that the dominant agent tells her. In moving from force through coercive power to influence, one moves from a non-discursive form to a purely discursive one. Influence is a pure form of communicative interaction, one in which no non-discursive action is involved. An agent *A* *influences* another agent *B* if and only if *A* communicatively interacts with *B* in such a way that, as a result, *B* alters his assessment of his action-environment in a fundamental manner. When a student comes to me, for example, and says that she is interested in pursuing a career in philosophy, I have an opportunity to influence her decision. I can do this in a number of ways. For example, if I think that it would be a mistake for her to pursue this option at all, given my assessment of her abilities and the job market, I may try to convince her that she would be better off choosing some other sort of career. If I succeed in doing that, I will have influenced her by convincing her that the action-alternative that she saw as most desirable, namely pursuing a career as a philosopher, was one that really was much less desirable than she had thought. By either showing her aspects of that alternative that she had not noticed or convincing her that she would not be able to follow it as easily as she had thought, I would cause her to reassess the desirability of that option.

The specific nature of influence will emerge from the juxtaposition of this situation with one in which I use coercive power. For example, if the student insisted on applying to graduate school and I threatened her by saying that, if she did so, I would write a bad letter of recommendation to those to which she did apply, but that if she did not I would help her pursue some other career option, I would be exercising coercive power rather than influence. This is because I would be using, as the basis of my threat, my ability to change the likelihood of her being able to pursue her chosen option. Although I would be attempting to *influence* the graduate schools not to accept her, I would actually be attempting to exercise *coercive power* over the student herself by changing her action-environment.

This example brings out an important aspect of influence, namely its role in the constitution of coercive power relations. Although this is a theme that requires more extensive treatment than I can give it in the present context, let me just call attention to the structure of the example I have just given. In it, coercive power is exercised through the use of influence. Because I have the ability to influence the graduate schools not to accept the student, I can exercise coercive power over her.

Influence can proceed either by affecting an agent's assessment of the options that she already sees as existing for her, as in the case I have just considered, or else by getting the agent to enlarge (or diminish) the set of action-alternatives within her assessment of her action-environment. To stick to the example of advising a student on a career choice, I might be able to influence the student not to pursue a career in philosophy by showing her that there was a program in journalism for which she would have a good chance of being accepted and that would better suit her talents and temperament. If she had never thought of this as a career that she could pursue, my mentioning it to her might influence her to take it seriously and eventually to decide to give up philosophy. In so doing, I would change her assessment of her action-environment by getting her to see the existence of an option that was not previously apparent. My influence would proceed from my ability to convince the student that there was an option for her career that she had not considered.

With this observation, we are brought back to the recognition that very different types of cases all fall under the scope of the concept of influence. As I mentioned, on the one extreme there are cases in which one agent simply brings something to the attention of another agent that causes the latter to alter her evaluation of her situation, but that she would have used on her own, had she had access to it. For example, I might influence a student's career choice by pointing out some statistics to which she did not have access. Had she had access to these statistics, she would have reached the same evaluation as she did as a result of my influencing her. In such cases, the influencing agent merely serves as a means of access to information, making no substantive contribution to the influenced agent's reassessment of her situation. The influenced agent processes the new information—and its impact on her action-environment—on her own. These are the sorts of cases in which the attribution of power to the influencing agent seems misguided. The reason for this is that we do not think that the changes brought about by the influencing agent in the influenced agent's action-environment amount to constraint. The influencing agent does not materially affect the influenced agent's assessment of her action-environment, since the information would be used by the influenced agent to the same effect regardless of how she received it. Since my definition of power-over requires that the dominant agent constrain the action-environment of the subordinate agent for the relation between them to be one in which power is present, cases of influence where this does not occur are simply not cases of the exercise of power.

Such cases contrast markedly with cases in which the contribution of the influencing agent is much more substantive: The charismatic political leader is able to influence his followers to perform actions simply by telling them to do so. In such cases the mere fact that the influencing agent says that the influenced agent should do something is sufficient to get her to do it; the influenced agent exhibits no independent rational processes of deliberation or assessment whatsoever. Because of her admiration for the political leader, the follower is unable to question his motives for doing anything and simply accedes to his wishes. Here, the influencing agent has substantive control of the influenced agent's assessment of her action-environment. Because the influenced agent's trust in the influencing agent is so extreme, she will act as he wishes, regardless of the wisdom of so doing; she has no independent will of her own, and her action is thus controlled by the influencing agent. In my terms, because the influenced agent makes her action-environment into a reflection of the desires of the influencing agent, her action-environment is constrained and the relation between them is one in which power is a factor.

Advertising is, of course, a central social phenomenon in which power in the form of influence is used. A company produces a product in order for people to consume it. To bring this about, the company needs to publicize the availability of the product and explain to consumers what benefits will accrue to them from using it. In so far as advertising performs this function, it seeks to influence consumers to use the product and is unproblematic. Problems with such a use of influence crop up when the advertisement goes beyond this information-providing function. For example, if the advertisement presents false information to consumers, such as suggesting to them that consumption of a certain product will lead to increased sexual attractiveness when this is not the case, or if the advertisement creates an anxiety in consumers that only the consumption of the product can alleviate, then the influence exercised by the advertiser over consumers becomes one in which power is being exercised.

In order to develop an understanding of the relation between influence and power, it will be useful to extend my typology to various different types of influence.[18] I shall limit myself to distinguishing three of them.

The first type of influence that I shall distinguish is that of *rational persuasion*. It is exemplified in the first scenario presented above: An agent is able to present another agent with information that gets that agent to reassess her understanding of her action-environment with the result that the agent changes her evaluation of it. The important characteristic of this form of influence is that the influenced agent retains her own critical faculties but is led to a reassessment of her understanding of her action-environment through the efforts of the influencing agent.

The central feature of this type of influence is that the influenced agent is treated by the influencing agent as capable of full self-determination. The influencing agent simply provides certain information or perspectives that help the influenced agent reach what the influencing agent thinks is a more adequate understanding of her situation. As such, this form of influence is not a form of power.

Such a form of influence is fundamentally different from a second one, which I will call *personal persuasion*. Personal persuasion is a general form of influence that includes charismatic influence. In this type of influence, the influenced agent's reassessment of her action-environment is not achieved by the influencing agent's presenting her with new substantive reasons and/or information. Instead, it is the mere perception of the desires of the influencing agent that accounts for the influenced agent's reassessment. The case of the charismatic political leader described above is an example of this type of influence.

The central feature of influence via personal persuasion is that the influenced agent does not make her choices on the basis of reasons that she can present in the form of a rational argument, but rather on the basis of the desires of the influencing agent. The basic motto of this form of influence is "Trust me!" The influencing agent is able to get the influenced agent to do what he wants simply on the basis of the personal relationship between them. This form of influence is one in which power is being exercised because the dominant agent constrains the subordinate agent's assessment of her action-alternatives. It is also a type of power that attains great political and social significance when it operates on the level of charismatic leadership.

A third type of influence, which I shall call *expertise,* can be thought of as falling halfway between these other two forms of influence. In an exercise of power based upon expertise, the influenced agent accepts the advice of the expert and bases her actions upon such advice. As in cases of personal persuasion, the influenced agent acts without being able to give a rationale for her action other than the claims made by the influencing agent; in this case, however, there is a presumption that the rationale could be supplied by the influenced agent if she were able to gain access to all the knowledge that the influencing agent has available to him. Although the achievement of such an explicit understanding of the rationale is not something that could even in principle be actualized in all the cases of expertise, it remains a regulative ideal for expert-based power relations.

Normally, when one thinks of influence based upon expertise, one thinks of a specific type of such influence that I call *distributive expertise.* In these cases, an expert possesses some specialized knowledge that allows her to tell the influenced agent how best to proceed in a certain situation. A doctor's advice to take a certain type of pill is an example of such a power relationship. Because a doctor has knowledge about how the pill will affect me, I accept his advice to take it.[19]

There is, however, a second type of expertise that will play a large role in my considerations of social power in the final chapter of this study. This type of expertise is a relation of *apprenticeship* in which a master—an agent possessed of certain knowledge or skill—is able to transmit that knowledge or skill to another agent, an apprentice, thus enabling the apprentice to act in ways previously unavailable to her. Teaching is an example of this type of expertise, for students come to have new knowledge or skills as a result of being taught.

This type of expertise grounds a power relationship in so far as the apprentice desires to possess the knowledge or skill possessed by the master and is willing to submit to his decisions in order to achieve this. When the apprentice is able to master the desired knowledge or skill only by means of a personal relationship to the master, the master comes to possess power over the apprentice.

Such a relationship is depicted in the film *The Karate Kid*. In that film, a young boy desires to learn karate and apprentices himself to an old man, a master of that skill, in order to do so. The film presents its view of how relations of apprenticeship embody power in a humorous way by having the karate master order the boy to perform a series of tasks that, though beneficial to the master, seem to both the boy and the audience to have absolutely no relation to the boy's learning karate. The boy's faith in the master is sorely tested, but remains a focus of this film's exploration of the nature of power relationships. In the end, the boy's faith is justified when it turns out that each task that he completed—for example, washing the master's car—involved the perfecting of a habitual motion necessary to the successful performance of karate.

This film demonstrates that a power relationship based on an agent's mastery of an area of knowledge or a skill involves the apprentice's trust in the perceptions of the master. Such relationships are essentially hierarchical in that the knowledge or skill that constitutes the basis of the relationship must be unequally possessed in order for the relationship to have any rationale at all. As a result of such a hierarchy, the master's judgments about the tasks that the apprentice must undertake may not be scrutable by the apprentice. He must submit himself to the master in order to gain the mastery of the knowledge or skill that he wishes to gain.

These three types of influence are not meant to be an exhaustive typology. I have simply aimed at giving a sense of the variety of different phenomena that fall under the concept of influence and to show that power is not always a factor in them.

The distinctive nature of influence as a type of power is something that Spinoza recognizes in his *Tractatus-Politicus*. In that work, Spinoza distinguishes among a variety of different types of power:

> One man has another in his power when he holds him in bonds; when he has disarmed him and deprived him of the means of self-defense or escape; when he has inspired him with fear; or when he has bound him so closely by a service that he would rather please his benefactor than him-

self, and rather be guided by his benefactor's judgment than by his own. The man who has another in his power in the first or second way holds his body only, not his mind; whereas he who controls another in the third or fourth way has made the mind as well as the body of the other subject to his right; but only while the fear or hope remain.[20]

In this passage, Spinoza makes a number of points relevant to our current discussion. The first is that influence requires that the influenced agent subordinate her judgment to that of the influencing agent. I have tried to capture this notion by claiming that those cases of influence in which the influencing agent affects the influenced agent's action-environment in a substantive manner are those in which power is involved.

Another important point that Spinoza makes in this passage is that influence is a more secure form of power, since the influenced agent willingly does what he does. In the case of coercion, on the other hand, as Spinoza points out, while the subordinate agent chooses to act as a result of his perception of the dominant agent's ability to harm him, he still would rather do otherwise. Spinoza's observation brings home the point that influence is a more stable form of power than coercive power; for, so long as the influenced agent does not have grounds to question the role of the influencing agent, he will willingly do all that is asked of him.

This fact about influence is one that Dennis Wrong highlights in his discussion of power.[21] In his typology of forms of power, the concept of authority functions in much the same way that the concept of influence functions in mine. One of the strengths of his analysis is that he sees that this type of power is not as likely to engender resistance as are force and coercion. Influence is therefore a type of power that serves to render the possession of other types of power more secure. Indeed, one political theorist goes so far as to talk of influence as "a 'hidden' kind of power".[22]

Manipulation

Although manipulation might seem to be a distinct type of power, I shall argue that this is not the case. In my view, manipulation is a specific form of influence. The distinction between manipulation and influence does not have to do with the type of power that is exercised over the subordinate agent, but involves the manner in which the dominant agent exercises that power. As a result, unlike instances of influence, manipulation always carries with it the presumption of being morally suspect.

There are two different species of manipulation, cognitive and emotional. In each case, an agent seeks to influence another agent by means that are morally dubious. In the case of *cognitive manipulation,* agent *A* manipulates *B* by influencing *B* for her own purposes or ends while keeping this fact concealed. When someone tries to get her roommate to leave town for the weekend by saying that the roommate needs a vacation, when she really wants the roommate to leave so that she can be alone, then she is manipulating her. Because the person tries to influence her roommate for purposes of her own while keeping this fact from her, the manipulation is cognitive.

Emotional manipulation, on the other hand, succeeds by appealing to an agent's emotions. An agent *A* emotionally manipulates an agent *B* by influencing *B* by means of an appeal to *B*'s emotions that keeps *B* from being able to make a fully rational decision. When a young daughter gets her father to buy her a horse by sitting on his lap and acting coquettishly, she is manipulating her father—that is, she gets her father to make a decision that is emotionally rather than rationally grounded. Another example of such emotional manipulation is a television commercial that shows pictures of starving babies, using a viewer's guilt as a means of getting him to donate money.

These two species of manipulation have in common the attempt to influence others by morally questionable means. In each case there is a basic moral principle of treating others fairly and truthfully that is being violated. They are cases of power because the subordinate agent's action-environment is being constrained by the actions of the dominant agent.

Normally, manipulation will succeed at some cost to the subordinate agent, although this need not be the case. For example, Edward Rochester's attempt to get Jane Eyre to fall in love with him by pretending that he is going to marry someone else is an example of a case of influence that is also a case of manipulation. It is influence because Rochester believes correctly that Jane Eyre will come to feel love for him if she sees him courting someone else. But it is also an instance of manipulation because he is trying to influence her and is keeping that attempt hidden from her view. This form of interaction, in which one agent tries to influence another agent while keeping the reasons for his attempt concealed, is what characterizes this type of manipulation as a form of influence.

This example shows that manipulation need not aim at harming the influenced agent, although it is true that it often does so. Rochester manipulates Jane Eyre's feelings in an attempt to help her rather than to harm her, to make her aware of her love for him, a love that will be requited once she has acknowledged its existence.

Despite the fact that an agent's manipulation of another may aim at benefiting that other agent, manipulation remains a morally suspect social practice. This is true for two reasons. The first is that one can never be sure that the influenced agent is not being treated as, in Kantian terms, a means rather than an end-in-itself. The instrumental use of another is morally suspect. The second reason that manipulation is morally suspect is that the possibility of self-deception is so great in such contexts. An agent can easily believe that his manipulation of another will result in her making a better choice than she would make in the absence of such manipulation, when this is not the case at all.

This analysis of the concept of manipulation makes it clear that manipulation is not simply a different type of power from influence; rather, to say of a case of influence that it is manipulative is to characterize the influencing agent's manner of achieving his influence. Any of the more particular forms of influence can be engaged in manipulatively. For this reason, manipulation is not a distinct type of power.

The Typology of Power

The typology of power presents power as an articulated structure. There are three aspects to the articulation of power, which I shall now summarize systematically.

The first aspect of the articulation of power is that the three types of power are internally related to one another. Each type of power has a certain "problem" in it that is solved by means of the "next" form: the "uneconomic" nature of force leads to the more "economic" form of coercive power, while the "resistance" generated by both of these types of power can be lessened by means of relations based on influence.

The second aspect of the articulation of power is that a given empirical power relation need not be an instance of only one type of power. The example of the young punk whose thumb is cut off by a gangster shows that force can be used in such a way as to simultaneously constitute a threat. Such an "instrumental" use of force entails the co-presence of force and coercion in the same action. This example does not show that power always has a mixed character, that an empirical instance of power will not fit neatly into an ideal typical scheme. Rather, it shows that the logic of power is such that more than one type of power can be present in a single action.

A third aspect of the articulation of power is that one type of power can be used to ground another. I illustrated this feature of power relationships while analyzing the nature of influence with an example in which a student was coerced in her career choice. As I remarked at the time, one interesting feature of that example is the fact that the ability to coerce such a student depends upon the ability to influence graduate schools. This means that one type of power can be based upon the existence of another type, that their empirical existence can be interdependent.

Once one reflects upon this example in a general light, one can see that it highlights a general feature of power. In the instance just mentioned, there are different audiences for the two exercises of power, but this need not be the case. I may be able to coerce you because I can threaten to use force against you. In such a case, you are the audience for two distinct types of power relations with me: The coercive relation between us is based upon the possibility of my using force on you.

The notion of a field can help us attain an appropriate understanding of the articulated nature of power. By thinking of power as a field whose lines of force are constituted by the various different types of power all being present simultaneously, we can avoid thinking about the forms of power in inappropriate ways. Instead, we shall focus on the diverse nature of the lines of force that constitute the field of power in its specificity.

This typology of power should not be thought about in terms of the idea of an ideal type as used by Max Weber. The idea of ideal types suggests that the types of power be seen as ideal examples of power relations, even though actual power relations will not be as neat and clear-cut as the typology suggests. In empirical reality, the suggestion would be, we cannot expect to meet with examples of such ideal types in their purity, but only in combination with other types. Personality psychology uses an ideal typology to suggest pure forms of personality structure that are not actually met with in reality. Nonetheless, actual human psychologies are thought of as composed of a mixture of the ideal types. Applying such a logic to types of power would mean, for example, that one should not expect to find clear cases in which influence but not coercion was used. Although it would be conceded that different types of power are analytically distinguishable, it would be maintained that empirical reality contains only mixed examples in which the ideal realities can be treated only as components of the actual situation.

But this manner of interpreting the typology of power is fundamentally inadequate. The notion of ideal types covers up the articulated nature of power by interpreting the complexity of actually existing power relationships as the result of the messiness of empirical reality as opposed to the clarity of theoretical analysis. As I have just argued, however, there is a specific logic to the articulated nature of power, one that makes power a more complex social reality than a simple interpretation of its typology would suggest. In understanding the nature of social power, it is therefore important to move beyond an interpretive scheme such as that of ideal types.

I shall conclude this chapter by presenting an example of a single action that exhibits all the types of power that I have delineated, thus giving a clear illustration of the articulation of power. In this case, power is being exercised simultaneously in regard to a number of different audiences, and the type of power that is exercised depends upon which subordinate agent or audience is being considered.

Consider a situation in which one country decides to bomb another country as a reaction to terrorism. In so doing, the first country actually exercises its power along a number of different dimensions. In the first place, in so far as its bombing harms the capacity of the other country to carry out further acts of terrorism, such an act is an instance of force. However, it is also clear that the bombing is not simply a single act with no consequences. It is an action that is intended to have effects on both the target nation's assessment of terrorism as an action-alternative and on the assessment of other nations as well. It is intended to make them realize that all terrorist acts will be met with in a similar fashion. In other words, this country is trying to get others to see that it will be willing to use force to retaliate against terrorist acts. In this respect the bombing resembles the scenario I presented from *The Pope of Greenwich Village:* It is an instrumental use of force that attempts to get certain nations to realize what the results of their actions will be and therefore to cease from supporting terrorist activities. Finally, the government of the bombing country is also attempting to influence its own populace, showing them that it is not willing to be intimidated by violent acts. In such a case it is interested in influencing public opinion in its favor.

This example completes my demonstration that power is a more complex social reality than its typology might suggest. The simple fact that a single action can impact upon different agents in different ways has allowed me to show how a single exercise of power by a social agent can articulate itself into a variety of forms of power in regard to different agents. One and the same action can constitute various types of exercises of power, depending on which subordinate agent is being considered. The articulated nature of power, a feature of power that allows it to appear in different guises to different agents, is thus one of the central aspects of the field theory of power.

6

Structures of Domination

IN DEVELOPING the idea of the articulation of power, I specifically abstracted from the uses to which such a structure could be put. In the present chapter, I shall take up this question by discussing the nature of domination, one of the most significant uses of power within society. The concept of domination furnishes the social theorist with a means for describing a particular use of power by one social agent over another. That is to say, there are systematic uses of power that constitute the domination of one agent by another and that social theory needs to be able to characterize. The result of this analysis will be to supplement the framework of concepts for describing power to include a new category, that of *uses* of power. Although, in this chapter, I shall discuss only one specific use of power—that is, domination—there are other uses of power that social theory needs to recognize. In particular, in Chapters 9 and 10 I shall argue that social theory needs to recognize a "positive" use of power, transformative power, in addition to domination, a "negative" use of it.

Let me make one important specification concerning the argument of this chapter. I shall demonstrate that the concept of domination has an important place in descriptions of power in society. In so doing, however, I shall not make any specific claims about the particular forms of such domination that characterize American society. In sticking to my project of developing an ontological understanding of power, I shall avoid defending any specific use of the concept of domination, such as its use to characterize gender relations in American society. Though particular types of domination that exist in our society form the background for my concern with this topic, the question of these more content-specific characterizations is beyond the scope of this study.

I am arguing, however, that the concept of a *use* of power is itself part of the framework of concepts necessary for understanding the nature of social power. This aspect of a power relationship must be distinguished from the specific mechanism(s) whereby such uses are realized. Only by means of a systematic distinction between the types and the uses of power will a theory of power achieve both enough generality and enough specificity to conceptualize such central social phenomena as domination and oppression.[1]

The specific argument of this chapter will be that there are two techniques of domination that social theory needs to acknowledge. The first, which I shall characterize as *domination from below,* begins with the use of force and articulates itself upon that. By means of an examination of Hegel's lordship-and-bondage dialectic, I shall show how this form of domination is achieved. I shall also show that Marx should be seen as making important supplementations to this theory. *Domination from above* is a form of domination based upon influence. I shall argue that Nietzsche theorizes about this form of domination. Each of the forms that domination takes is equally basic to understanding the nature of this use of power in society.

Analyzing "Domination"

The first step is to clarify the nature of the concept of domination. Max Weber is one social theorist who thinks that the concept of domination has an important role to play in social theory. Weber's reasons for making this claim, however, differ from mine. Weber argues that the concept of power is

sociologically amorphous. All thinkable qualities of a person and all thinkable constellations can place someone in a place where he can carry out his will in a given situation [that is, exercise power according to Weber's own definition]. The sociological concept of "domination" [*Herrschaft*] must therefore be a more precise one and can only mean the chance of finding submission to an *order.*[2]

Weber argues that the concept of domination is the appropriate one to use in social theory because "domination" has a more precise meaning than "power". His claim is that this precise meaning—the possibility of having one's orders obeyed—gives it an important place within social theory. For Weber, the concept of domination provides a means for understanding relationships of command and obedience, something that is necessary for any theory of society but that cannot be achieved by means of the more amorphous concept of power.[3]

Although I have argued that the concept of power can be given a precise meaning for social theory, I do not think that this means that social theory can do without the concept of domination. The sorts of issues that Weber wishes to conceptualize by means of that concept—for example, how one group can come to achieve rule over another group—are precisely the issues that the term "domination" can give us a means of analyzing. Although I do not believe that the concept of power is amorphous in Weber's sense, its generality does not give us a specific means of referring to the sorts of ongoing relationships that Weber discusses by means of the concept of domination and that form an important topic for a social theory of power.

It is important to realize, however, that the term "domination" has a different semantic value in English than it does in German. In English, the term "domination" is not one that has a common use in the sense we shall give it. Although we might speak, for example, of Bjorn Borg's *domination* of the game of tennis in the late seventies, in English "domination" does not have a common use as a means of describing generic social relationships. This is not the case in German. The term *Herrschaft* is a completely ordinary word meaning "rule" or "command", among other things. Weber's use of the word *Herrschaft* must be understood as reflecting this feature of ordinary German usage. Although the use of the term "domination" in English will not be able to rely on ordinary usage in this way, I shall still employ it, since social theory needs to have a means to conceptualize such relations. So I shall use "domination" as a term with a specific meaning in describing the relationship of a ruling group to a ruled group.

As I have said, it is necessary to distinguish domination from the various types of power that I discussed in the previous chapter. Those types of power were specific mechanisms whereby one agent could constrain the action-environment of other agents. When using the term "domination", I shall not, first of all, be referring to single interactions between two agents, to single exercises of power. I shall use the term "domination" to refer to the power that one social agent has over another in situations in which that power is exercised by the dominating social agent over the dominated social agent repeatedly, systematically, and to the detriment of the dominated agent. The concept of domination therefore refers to a specific manner of exercising power. Such an exercise of power must be one that conditions the relationship between two agents in a longstanding manner. "Domination" refers not to a single exercise of power but to a *relationship* between two social agents that is constituted by the existence of a power differential between them.

This shift from single exercise of power to ongoing social relationships that are constituted by the existence of a power differential among social agents is an important shift of focus that is achieved by means of the use of the term "domination". It allows a social theorist to change her focus from questions about what sorts of effects can be the basis of a legitimate employment of the concept of power to questions about the systematic nature of such effects in society.

But not every ongoing relationship between two social agents that involves a power differential is an example of domination. "Domination" also specifies the ends to which such power is exercised. A relationship between two agents is an instance of domination only if the dominated agent is specifically harmed through the relationship. That is, the concept of domination does not, *contra* Weber, refer to a specific type of power relationship, one grounded on obedience to commands. As I shall use it, the term "domination" specifies the use to which a power relationship is put—that is, the dominant agent exercises her power to the detriment of a subordinate agent.

Domination can be distinguished from the types of power I previously discussed by considering the question of the sorts of agents who can stand in the relation in question. The agents related in the forms of power could be either single human beings or collectivities made up of them. Just as it makes sense to say, "The United States coerced South Korea by threatening to cut off aid unless it agreed to hold free elections", it also makes sense to say, "The thief coerced me to hand over my wallet by threatening to kill me". The logic of my analysis of power-over was that either individual or group agents could be the relata in a social power relation.

Things are different in the case of social domination: The relata in relationships of domination are primarily social groups. The primary sense of social domination is one in which one group is said to dominate another. For example, men are often said to dominate women; white, blacks; straights, gays; capitalists, workers. In each case, one group is posited as the possessor of power over the other group. Relations of domination between individuals, such as Fred's of Mary, must be conceptualized as a result of the overall framework of group domination, in this case of men over women. In the absence of an overarching social structure of domination, it does not make sense to claim that one individual's domination of another is an instance of social domination.

This is not to say that it does not make sense to talk about a single individual dominating another individual. A wife can, for example, dominate her husband as a result of their psychological patterns. Similarly, Robinson Crusoe can be said to have dominated Friday. When the term "domination" is used within social theory, however, it refers primarily to the *social* phenomenon of one group dominating another. By qualifying the term "domination" with the adjective "social", I want to limit my consideration of general relations of domination to those that have such a social structure.

With these remarks in mind, I am now ready to specify my use of the term "domination" more precisely. I shall say that the power that one collective agent has over another is an instance of *social domination* if and only if that power is exercised by the dominating agent in a systematic manner at the expense of the dominated agent. This definition specifically limits the use of the term "domination" to characterize the relationship between collective social agents. It states that the attribution of "domination" to a social agent is based upon two separate claims. The first claim attributes to that agent power over another social agent. Since domination is a specific use made of power, it can be realized by means of the types of power I have previously distinguished. Indeed, there can be no domination without there being exercises of power through which such domination is constituted. As such, "domination" is a general term that needs to be given a more specific content in specific situations.

But the repeated use of power is not itself sufficient to characterize a situation as one in which domination exists; the power must be systematically used by one agent to the detriment of the other agent. Only when such a systematic structure can be demonstrated is there a situation in which domination exists. It is for this reason that I speak of domination as involving a power *relationship* that harms the subordinate agent.

My understanding of the concept of domination differs significantly from that put forward by Weber. As I have noted, Weber defines domination as involving the likelihood of an order's being followed. In my framework, such a definition makes domination into a specific type of power, one that straddles coercive power and influence. It is not simply a generic concept for these different types of power, however, since many forms of influence do not involve orders.

More importantly, Weber's definition, like my earlier ones, is neutral in regard to the aims for which such power is exercised. My definition of domination is thus a more specific understanding of domination than that which Weber employs.

This manner of characterizing domination gives rise to some fresh problems, however. First, there is the question of paternalism. Say that an agent has power over another agent and exercises that power in a systematic way, but does so for the benefit of the dominated agent. One example of such a relation is that of parents with their children. The problem is that my definition seems to rule out the possibility that paternalistic uses of power can also be dominating ones.

The first thing to note about this question is that it indirectly supports my contention that domination is a *use* and not a *type* of power. Paternalism is not a particular type of power, but a way of legitimating the use of power. For a relationship between two agents to be an instance of paternalism, it must be a hierarchical one. The precise form of such hierarchy is left unspecified by characterizing the relationship as paternalistic; all that is specified is that the power exercised in the relationship is intended to benefit the subordinate agent.

It certainly is true that parents can dominate their children, especially when they think they are really acting for the children's good. This does not mean, however, that paternalistic relationships are necessarily relationships of domination. They only become such when the dominating agent acts against, rather than for, the benefit of the dominated agent.

Paternalism can be used to legitimate relationships of domination. When one nation claims that it is invading another nation because the latter is not yet ready for independence, it is likely that the paternalistic justification serves as a cover for brute domination. This fact does not negate the countervailing fact that paternalistic relationships can, under specific circumstances, actually work for the benefit of the dominated agent.[4]

A second issue raised by my definition of domination is whether it is correct to say that relations of domination always exist at the expense of the dominated group. Can't there also be a relation of domination in which the dominated agent in some sense benefits from the relationship? In other words, it might be argued that some criterion other than harm to the dominated agent is needed by which to judge whether a relationship is one of domination.

This discussion raises the complex issue of how to assess whether a relationship between two agents benefits those agents. Clearly, a power relationship between two agents can benefit the subordinate agent in one respect while harming it in another. The subordinate agent, for example, might wind up being well fed but lacking a sense of independence and self-determination. Assessing the benefits and harms in a relationship is a difficult thing to do. Nonetheless, I do not think that these difficulties stand in the way of my conceptualization. Rather, they indicate the complexities involved in moving from the ontological level at which I am proceeding to the more specific task of applying these abstract concepts to social reality.

My definition of domination so far only discusses relations of domination between two social groups. I have also said that it makes sense to posit a relationship between two individual agents as one of domination when their individual relationship is dependent upon the general group relation of domination. I therefore shall specify a use of the term "domination" in which it can characterize a relationship between individual agents. I will say that a relationship between two *individual* agents *a* and *b* is an instance of *domination* if (1) *a* is a member of group *A* and *b* is a member of group *B*; (2) group *A* dominates group *B*; and (3) the domination relationship between *a* and *b* is an instance of the generic domination of *B* by *A*. The first two clauses state that two individual agents can stand in a relationship of domination to one another only if they do so in virtue of their being members of social groups that stand in a domination relationship with one another. The third clause specifies that the individual relationship between the two individual agents is a case of domination only if the relationship between the groups determines the dominating aspect of their relationship. It is meant to exclude claims that one individual agent dominates another on the basis of some factor other than those considered in the generic case of domination.

Lordship and Bondage: Hegel on Domination

Having explored the meaning of "domination", I am now ready to develop the two models of domination. The first, domination from below, is articulated by Hegel in his presentation of the lordship-bondage relationship in the *Phenomenology of Spirit*. Although Hegel's discussion of the lordship-bondage relationship is not his full-fledged theory of society, it contains important insights that are relevant to a theory of social domination. Indeed, I shall show that Hegel's characterization of the lordship-bondage relationship privileges coercion as the means whereby social domination is constituted. He does so because he sees the productive nature of coercion as the rationale behind social relations of domination.

Let me begin with a comment about Hegel's terminology. In characterizing the lordship-bondage relationship, Hegel uses personification. For example, he uses the term "the lord" in a manner that is ambiguous. On the one hand, he could be talking in a general way about individual social agents who are lords. On the other hand, "the lord" can be a way of referring to the class of lords and how they behave. As I have argued elsewhere in regard to Marx, the use of such a terminology can be seriously misleading.[5]

I shall interpret Hegel as using this form of discourse as a means of talking about the group of lords in a personified manner. The main problem that this causes is that it obscures the fact that relationships of domination do not exist primarily at an individual level, but only on the basis of relations among collective agents. It thus precludes Hegel from discussing issues that require reference to more complex relations among the individual social agents that compose the collective agents in a domination relationship. As I shall argue in the next chapter, such relations are crucial for understanding the full dynamics of relations of social domination.

Hegel's discussion of domination occurs through a contrast between two types of power relations, what he calls the "life-and-death struggle" and the "lordship-bondage relationship."[6] Hegel's manner of presenting these relations is to focus on two "consciousnesses" that are seeking to gain self-affirmation through their encounter with an- "other" consciousness. In the life-and-death struggle, the first consciousness has its certainty of itself threatened by the very existence of the other. As a result, in order to confirm its own existence, the consciousness decides that it must annihilate the other. The reciprocal nature of this relationship results in a struggle to the death between the two consciousnesses, with each one seeking to affirm itself by canceling— that is, killing—the other: "Thus the relation of the two self-conscious individuals is such that they prove themselves and each other through a life-and-death struggle."[7] As I pointed out in Chapter 3, the two consciousnesses engaged in the life-and-death struggle encounter each other on an external level, the level of force. The struggle between them remains one that contains no level of mutual acknowledgment other than that of the mutual decision to do battle.[8] Each is simply trying to destroy the other through the use of overt physical violence.

The lordship-bondage relationship stands in marked contrast to the life-and-death struggle. What constitutes this new form of relationship is the shared recognition between the lord and the bondsman that the former could kill the latter. That is, the factor that actually terminates the life-and-death struggle—the dominant consciousness's ability to annihilate the subordinate consciousness—is not itself exercised in the lordship-bondage relationship. It remains, however, a permanent possibility that determines the relationship between the two consciousnesses and constitutes the new form of relationship between them as one that involves coercive power.

> The lord relates himself mediately to the bondsman through a being that is independent, for it is just this which holds the bondsman in bondage; it is his chain from which he could not break free in the struggle, thus proving himself to be dependent, to possess his independence in thinghood.[9]

The fact that the lord has the ability to kill the bondsman causes the bondsman to fear that he will do so and thus to do the lord's bidding in an attempt to get the lord to refrain from so doing.

Hegel's discussion of the lordship-bondage relationship parallels my own discussion of coercive power, just as his discussion of the life-and-death struggle parallels mine of force. Thus, it is the *threat* of the lord's killing the bondsman that forms the basis of the bondsman's obedience to the lord. I claimed that a coercive power relation is constituted by just such threats. Similarly, the life-and-death struggle's *external* nature parallels my claim that, in exercises of force, the dominant agent restricts the ability of the subordinate agent to pursue the action-alternative that she would choose.

However, there is one important respect in which Hegel's discussion of the lordship-bondage relationship differs from my discussion of coercion: Hegel is describing a relationship based upon domination, an ongoing relationship between two social agents in which power exists in the form of domination. This discussion does not apply to specific interventions, but only to social relationships.

This emerges clearly from a consideration of the distinction between the life-and-death struggle and the lordship-bondage relationship. Hegel sees that force, unlike coercive power, cannot by itself constitute an ongoing relationship, but at most a struggle—that is, an occurrent, if somewhat long-term, event. Indeed, Hegel claims that the life-and-death struggle is superseded by the lordship-bondage relationship precisely because the life-and-death struggle can only realize itself through repeated instantiations. Once a consciousness has "won" the life-and-death struggle, according to Hegel, it is faced with the realization that the consciousness over whom it was victorious is no longer there to provide it with recognition. All that the consciousness can do to get such recognition is to seek another consciousness with whom to begin the struggle once again.[10] The struggle, as an occurrent event, is the locus of an exercise of force—indeed, of violence. In my terms, this means that force, while successfully able to restrict the actions of another agent, is unable to constitute an ongoing relationship of domination by itself; an ongoing relationship of domination requires a more complex ontological structure than is available at the level of force. As such, ongoing relations are analogous to relations of coercion in that they require awareness on the part of the subordinate agent of the dominant agent's ability to use force.

An adequate theory of social power needs to follow Hegel in according primacy to ongoing social relationships. Theorists who focus upon occurrent exercises of force, or, indeed, of coercive power, fail to see that there is an important distinction between occurrent exercises of power and relationships in which one agent has power over another. The behavioral tradition among power theorists—which has focused predominantly upon occurrent interventions in which power is exercised over an agent—underestimates the importance of power *relationships*. But ongoing relationships constituted by the *possibility* of the exercise of negative effects are a fundamental form by means of which social power is realized.

Our understanding of this issue will be fostered by considering how a relationship of domination differs from a single occurrent exercise of power at a basic ontological level. This will allow us to see how Hegel's analysis of relations of domination differs from the analysis of the simpler exercises of coercive power upon which I have previously concentrated.

To begin, consider what is necessary to transform a situation in which coercive power is exercised into one of ongoing social domination. An occurrent exercise of coercive power is based upon the recognition by the subordinate agent that the dominant agent is threatening to exercise a detrimental effect upon his welfare unless he does something that the dominant agent wishes. This recognition can be transformed into the basis for an ongoing relationship of social domination once the subordinate agent sees the ability of the dominant agent to harm him as a basic constituent of his ongoing situation. For if the subordinate agent understands the omnipresent possibility that the dominant agent might intervene in his situation, the dominant agent need no longer issue a threat in order to create the means to coerce the subordinate agent. Rather, her ability to harm the subordinate agent has been transformed into a structural feature of the subordinate agent's action-environment with the result that his action-environment is *structurally constrained*. Exceptional circumstances may cause the subordinate agent to reevaluate his acceptance of the dominant agent's ability to harm him as a part of his action-environment; nonetheless, in the normal course of events the power of the dominant agent has been accepted by the subordinate agent in the form of an *anticipatory reaction* that results in his acting as if a threat had been made.[11]

Hegel's discussion therefore shows that coercive power can come to occupy a fixed social structure of mutual understanding in which one agent reacts to the potentially harmful effects another agent can have on his welfare. The dominant agent need no longer make an actual threat, for his ability to affect the subordinate agent's action-environment is acknowledged by both agents as the basis of their relationship.[12] This fact about coercive power relationships, as William Connolly has pointed out, makes them both very useful to the dominant agent and also hard for the subordinate agent—as well as the social theorist—to detect.

The distinctive ontological character of relationships of domination points toward a second distinctive feature of such relationships: the fact that the dominant agent is able to receive an ongoing benefit from them. Hegel argues that the lord actually receives a benefit from the relationship as a result of the fact that the bondsman is put in a position where, in order not to face the serious negative consequences that the lord is able to inflict upon him, he must do the lord's bidding. In doing so, the bondsman actually produces things that can be either immediately beneficial to the lord or else appropriated by the lord for some form of mediated or delayed use. The dominant agent thus reaps significant material benefits from an ongoing relationship of domination.

I have already conceptualized this aspect of coercive power relations as their *productivity*. By the use of this term, I indicated the fact that the dominant agent in such relationships receives benefits for which he does not need to expend an equivalent amount of energy. Hegel's account of social domination shows that such domination can use this aspect of coercive power relations as the basis for its existence. But not only this: the productive nature of relations of domination provides the *rationale* for their existence. A social agent has an interest in occupying the dominant position in a social relationship of domination because such a position results in his receiving material benefits from the efforts made by the subordinate agent.[13] In an exercise of force, the ability of the subordinate agent to perform an action is simply hindered (or the agent is made to behave in a way that he does not wish). With domination, however, an agent can be made to *do* something that results in the dominant agent's reaping significant material benefits.

The productive nature of relations of domination based upon the ability of the dominant agent to coerce the subordinate agent explains why relations of domination play such an important role in the structuring of power in society. So long as a dominant group relies simply on relations of force, it may be able to secure its position as one of dominance. It is also able to use particular interventions of force to appropriate items possessed by the subordinate agents. Other than that, however, there is little productive use to which force can be put. When a dominant group wishes to receive systematic material benefits from its dominance, it needs to rely upon the efforts of the subordinate group itself. Once the dominant group has managed to create an ongoing relation of dominance in which the subordinate group is made to act in ways that benefit the dominant group, the relation between the two groups changes in fundamental ways. At this level, significant benefits accrue to the dominant group without the direct use of force.

Hegel's analysis of domination shows us how domination can come into existence on the basis of coercive power relations among social agents. When a collective agent is able to coerce another collective agent, then the basis exists for constituting an ongoing relationship of domination between the two agents. I have called this analysis of social domination one "from below" because it points out how domination comes into existence on the basis of a less complex form of power. By making this argument, Hegel illustrates one possible strategy that a group can use to achieve social domination of another group.

Before moving away from Hegel's analysis of domination, however, let me make one comment about it. I already mentioned that Hegel's analysis proceeds by means of a dyadic conceptualization in which he personifies both the "lord" and the "bondsman". Such dyadic logic, however, actually obscures the *social* nature of the phenomenon Hegel is interested in conceptualizing—that of domination. The technique of personification, interesting as it may be as a literary device, does not allow Hegel to refer to relationships among the members of either the dominant group or the subordinate group, or to more complex relations between the groups. As a result, the model of domination that he articulates needs to be supplemented, as I shall do in the following chapter, by a model that takes more account of the social structure of domination.

Marx and the Hegelian Conception

Having discussed Hegel's view of domination from below, I now would like to turn briefly to the work of Karl Marx. While it is illuminating to see that Marx shares this Hegelian conception of domination, I shall also show that Marx's view of domination contains an important addition to the theory of domination from below.

In order to see that Marx employed an Hegelian notion of domination, we need only consider the view of domination that Marx placed at the heart of his analysis of capitalist society.[14] According to Marx, the key concept for understanding the nature of capitalist society is surplus value. By producing products for the capitalist but receiving in return only a wage sufficient to reproduce themselves, Marx claimed, the workers in a capitalist society were producing surplus value that the capitalist was able to appropriate.[15]

When we consider such a claim from the point of view of the conception of domination that it presupposes, we can readily see that it is an attempt to extend Hegel's idea of the productivity of domination to a capitalist society. The basic point of this analysis is to show how the capitalist benefits from the coerced labor of the proletarian. In so doing, Marx is applying Hegel's theory of domination from below to a capitalist society.

Further reflection on Marx's theory of capitalist society, however, brings out certain weaknesses in Hegel's view for which Marx proposes a solution. For example, consider Marx's theory of class consciousness. That theory is intended by Marx as a theory of the process whereby the workers will come to a recognition of their situation and attempt to change it. But this theory raises two important issues that Hegel did not consider. The first is that of *resistance* to domination. This is an issue that is important in thinking about power, as I pointed out earlier in this study. Hegel is concerned to demonstrate that the bondsman achieves a more developed form of consciousness than the lord does. This claim is important for Hegel's purposes, since it furnishes the grounds for the next development in the story he is telling of the growth of consciousness. However, it results in an omission from his discussion of relations of domination. Marx's discussion of the situation of the worker in a capitalist society, dependent as it is upon Hegel's view of the lordship-bondage relationship, goes beyond Hegel in just this respect.

The question of resistance is an important one for any theory of domination to analyze. As long as the dominated group realizes that it is being dominated, it has an incentive to strive to avoid the continuance of such domination. Resistance is a natural correlation to power, as Foucault has stressed.[16]

In the last chapter, I pointed out that the phenomenon of resistance explained one aspect of the articulation of power, namely the interest that a dominant agent has in developing a coercive power relationship into one that is also based upon influence. So long as a dominant agent maintains a coercive relationship, there will be a tendency for the subordinate agent to resist and, thus, a need to use force to realize the threat upon which the dominating agent's coercive power rests. However, such exercises of force are costly in terms of resources, and hence the dominant agent has an interest in avoiding cases of resistance.

It is for this reason that dominant agents do not remain content with the possession of domination based upon force and coercive power alone. There is an inherent tendency for them to secure their position of dominance by developing misunderstandings among the dominated about what is happening to them. If it is possible somehow to convince the subordinate group that it is not being dominated, then an important ground for its resistance has been eroded.

This is the basis of both ideology and ideology critique. Since dominating agents have an interest in somehow convincing the dominated agents that they do not stand in relations of domination with them, they will attempt to develop various "ideologies"—that is, conceptual attempts to describe the situation of the dominated agents in such a way as to conceal their domination. If they are successful in doing this and in getting the subordinate agents to accept such descriptions, the chances of an overt movement of resistance coming into existence will be decreased.

Thus, the supplementation of coercive relations of domination by a form of ideology that obscures these relations parallels the movement of the articulation of power. Similarly, Marx's analysis of ideology parallels the argument that I made that influence is a form of power that diminishes the possibility of resistance to coercion.

There are, of course, a variety of strategies for formulating an ideological cover for domination. A well-known one is to claim that the domination relationship serves the interests of all, when it really benefits only the dominant group. This requires somehow persuading the dominated group to see themselves as beneficiaries of the domination that actually has them as its victims.

Another strategy for concealing domination relies more centrally on the nature of power itself. One feature of ongoing relations of domination that makes them easy to camouflage is the fact that they take on the appearance of natural relationships. That is, the alterations in the action-environment of the dominated agent may be perceived by that agent as unavoidable and necessary, in the same way that natural constraints are perceived. The role of the dominant agent in constituting such constraints is then obscured. As a result, ideology will often take the form of a *naturalizing* of the social relations of domination.

A dominant social agent who has managed to secure the means necessary to influence the subordinate agent whom he also has coercive power over is one who has achieved *hegemonic* control. "Hegemony" is a concept developed by Antonio Gramsci in order to characterize the very situation that I have just presented.[17] An agent's hegemonic power over another agent is realized by the fact that the dominant agent has achieved an articulated power distribution, one in which all the mechanisms of power are used to provide the agent with power over a subordinate agent.

I have now shown that Marx's understanding of capitalist society works within Hegel's conception of domination while also extending that analysis in an important direction. One of Marx's central insights is that social domination need not limit itself to employing a single type of power. As he saw, it is easier for a social group to maintain its domination by relying on the articulated nature of power in order to attain hegemony.

The Logic of "Good": Nietzsche on Domination

Nietzsche is as interested in domination as Hegel and Marx. Indeed, Nietzsche focuses on the nature of domination in a more single-minded manner than does Hegel. The various analyses that he undertakes in his writings all focus upon ways in which human beings dominate one another and even themselves.[18] For Nietzsche, domination is perhaps the fundamental fact of human life.

Nietzsche presents a very different theory of domination, however, one

that I characterize as *domination from above*. The reason for this is that influence, or more specifically manipulation, is the form of power that, in
Nietzsche's analysis, is used as the basis for domination. Nietzsche seeks to
show that one group's domination of another can come about simply through
its ability to get the members of the other group to conceive of themselves, or
the world, in a particular way. As such, this mode of domination does not
require any particular non-discursive abilities to be concentrated in the hands
of the dominant group. Their domination is able to occur precisely through the
medium of discourse.

It might be thought that, in treating Nietzsche as developing a theory of
domination, I am being unfair, for Nietzsche views power as a wider phenomenon than can be captured under the rubric of domination. Nietzsche's use
of the term "power" derives from Plato's. As I showed in Chapter 1, Plato
uses the term "power" as a general mark of being—that is, to signify that
general characteristic of things in virtue of which they exist. Such a usage is
also present in Nietzsche's notion of a *will to power,* through which he argues
that all the phenomena of existence can be explained through the idea that
things have an inherent amount of power that they seek to increase. Therefore,
Nietzsche's theory of power would need to be assimilated to the concept of
power-to and not power-over, as I am doing.

While I do not disagree with this interpretation of Nietzsche's thought, it
misconceives of how I shall use Nietzsche's ideas. I wish to show that it is
possible to take up one aspect of Nietzsche's thought and to use it as the basis
for a model of domination that differs in significant respects from the model of
domination from below. In so doing, I will simply bypass Nietzsche's more
general metaphysical view of power, in which he treats power as a positive
and productive phenomenon as well as a negative and repressive one. While
this gives a one-sided picture of Nietzsche's entire philosophy, I am not attempting to present a comprehensive picture of it here. I shall simply draw on
some Nietzschean themes in order to construct a model of domination from
above.

To understand Nietzsche's analysis of domination, let us begin with his
analysis of the way in which the term "good" functions within appraisals.
Nietzsche is trying to point out that the term "good" does not follow a single
logic as most ethicists up to his time had assumed. The logic that was supposed to hold for the term "good" can be outlined by means of the following
example: To say of a knife that it is a good knife is to say of it that it is able to
fulfill its function well. Knives, being human creations, exist in order to fulfill
a human purpose, namely that of cutting things. The logic of the term "good"
is thus tied to a teleological understanding of things.

Now, when we turn from the realm of human products to human beings themselves, there is a question about how to apply this view of the term "good". Although it may hold true for human artifacts, how is it possible to analyze appraisals of human beings and their actions in such a manner?

Consider the judgment "Jennifer is a good student." How are we to un-pack the logic of this occurrence of the term "good"? Corresponding to the previous analysis, one could say that there are certain forms of behavior that students should perform. Such things as attending class, doing one's assign-ments, and showing respect for the teacher are forms of behavior that a stu-dent who is "fulfilling her function" does, just as a knife that is fulfilling its function cuts well. A good student is one who performs these functions well, who fulfills her role in an exemplary manner.

But students are people and not knives. As a result, one needs to find a means of justifying the claim that there are certain forms of behavior that are characteristic of students who are "fulfilling their function". In the case of knives, it is possible to justify the ascription of a purpose to them because knives are the products of human activity. Because knives are created by hu-man beings, human beings are justified in saying what their purpose is. As a result, ascribing goodness to a knife that fulfills its function well makes sense, since knives are human creations that are intended to fulfill human purposes.

This understanding of the logic of "good" allows us to see why Nietzsche attributed such importance to the "death of God". So long as the human being was seen as a divine creation, then the evaluation of human actions on the basis of divine purposes made sense: The actions of human beings could be judged analogously to the behavior of artifacts created by human beings. People were good in so far as they, like all artifacts, fulfilled the purposes of their artificer.

Once God "died", however, there was no clear way in which to identify the purposes of the artificer of human beings. In the absence of a creator of human beings, there is no apparent way to legitimate the idea that human be-ings have a certain function in terms of which their actions can be evaluated. For Nietzsche, the "death" of God marks a crisis in the Western understand-ing of human beings and their lives.

Thus, Nietzsche has developed an analysis of evaluative statements that shows that they presuppose a teleological conception of the items judged. All evaluative judgments are made from the perspective of the ability of an item to fulfill its function. In fact, judgments using the term "good" without qualifi-cation merely conceal the fact that the term "good" always means "good for the following end".

What does this analysis say about the claim that a good student performs certain sorts of actions? Nietzsche's revolutionary move is to claim that, despite the "death" of God, such claims have an implicit teleology—that is, make reference to some end. His claim is that such ends are not revealed in the grammatical form of the judgment, which actually conceals the judgment's implicit teleology. All evaluations are made from a point of view, but this fact is normally concealed by the judgment's objective form. That is to say, when "good" is attributed to a human action, this is because that action fits *someone's* purposes, even though the judgment itself does not make reference to those purposes.

In the example of the good student, the evaluation of the student is made from the perspective of a teacher.[19] The behaviors that are posited as specifying the functions of a student are ones that make the student an easy one for the teacher to have in the classroom. The evaluation is based upon the pliability of the student, not characteristics that would necessarily benefit the student herself.

The crucial insight that Nietzsche's understanding of the term "good" allows him to see is that the term can be used in various different ways depending upon the perspective from which it is deployed. It is this idea that Nietzsche uses as the basis of his model of domination from above.

Domination from above is characterized by Nietzsche as the *priestly valuation*. In *The Genealogy of Morals,*[20] Nietzsche presents his observations on the priestly valuation as a development of a more basic form of valuation, the *aristocratic valuation,* in which relations of force play a basic role. Nietzsche encapsulates the difference between these two valuations by claiming that the noble valuation is based on the good/bad distinction while the priestly valuation is based upon the good/evil distinction.

In the good/bad distinction, the term "good" functions from the perspective of the strong as a means of affirming their own self-evaluation. "All truly noble morality", Nietzsche tells us, "grows out of triumphant self-affirmation."[21] He speaks of the "aristocratic value equations good/noble/powerful/beautiful/happy/favored-of-the-gods."[22] In this "strong" valuation, the characteristics of one's own group are posited as good, worthy of emulation. "Bad" is then used as a term of contrast to characterize the behavior of those who fail to live up to the noble ideal. "Bad", Nietzsche says, functions in the aristocratic valuation as "a by-product, a complementary color, almost an afterthought."[23]

In the good/evil distinction, however, the negative rather than the positive term of the dichotomy functions as the primary one. Once again, there is a concealed perspective from which such valuations are made, only this time it is the perspective of the priests, the weak. In the priestly valuation, certain forms of behavior and ways of thinking are characterized as evil, things to be avoided. "Slave ethics, on the other hand," Nietzsche tells us, "begins by saying *no* to an 'outside', an 'other', a non-self, and that *no* is its creative act." [24] Such a valuation has its origin in the attempt to limit a certain set of behaviors and beliefs. It begins by creating a negative evaluation of this form of life, a form of life it seeks to control. The crucial feature of this valuation, for Nietzsche, is that the same form of life that the noble valuation refers to by the term "good" occupies the referent of the priestly valuation's "evil". The priestly valuation represents for Nietzsche both a development out of and a reversal of the noble valuation. Through it, a group denies the validity of the behavior of another group.

The reason that the priestly valuation is able to constitute a form of domination is that it becomes accepted by the very agents whom the priests are seeking to dominate. Because this valuation is formulated in terms of an objective characteristic of actions, those actions being judged evil, the strong can be convinced by the priests that they ought to accept such valuations as having universal validity. When the strong come to accept this view, they have been duped by the priests, who are now able to dominate them.

Nietzsche's analysis of the priestly valuation thus presents a model of domination from above. Nietzsche has demonstrated that it is possible for one group to dominate another group simply by means of ideas, by getting that group to think about themselves in a manner that allows them to be subjugated. Such a form of domination is able to succeed because the true nature of the ideas by which it occurs is concealed in a form of language that has the appearance of objectivity. His analysis of the use of the term "good" is intended to demonstrate that, despite the appearance of objectivity, such a term functions subjectively in that its use is only justified from a certain perspective. Since this perspectival aspect of the judgment is concealed, however, the subordinate group views the judgments as valid independently of the perspective from which they are made. As a result, a group can come to think of itself in terms created by the perspective of another group without realizing it. It is this particular mechanism that Nietzsche highlights as the origin of domination.

Nietzsche wants to claim more than simply that domination has its origin in the use of a concealed perspective in making evaluative judgments. He claims that *all* ostensibly objective judgments function in this way. Truth, for Nietzsche, is simply a particular perspective that has gained ascendancy, just as knowledge is simply a form of power.

The first aspect of this claim is that all knowledge is a form of valuation. By this, Nietzsche argues that there is no such thing as truth, conceived of as a perspectiveless view of reality. [25] Criticizing Kant's idea of the thing in-itself, Nietzsche argues that all knowledge is human knowledge, and hence asserted from a position, a perspective.

But once Nietzsche has managed to assimilate knowledge to evaluation, he is able to use his own analysis of the function of evaluations to claim that all knowledge functions to enhance the position of the agent from whose perspective it is made.[26] For Nietzsche, knowledge is power not because it allows the agent who possesses it to do something, but because it implicitly asserts the validity of the (concealed) perspective from which it is made.

Nietzsche's analysis of evaluative judgments led him to the broad skeptical claim that all ostensibly objective judgments are simply forms of power—that is, attempts to legislate to others a way of seeing the world. The problems of articulating such a view in a self-consistent manner have long been known. That is, it seems as if Nietzsche's view, if true, cannot be stated. The statement "All judgments are perspectival" is itself a judgment and hence must itself be described in terms of the very claim it asserts. But this would invalidate the seemingly objective sweep of the statement.

The universality of Nietzsche's claim is also something that is open to doubt. That is, one might want to assert that knowledge is not always power, since there are both forms of social interaction between human beings other than attempts to gain power over them and forms of objective judgment other than attempts to assert the superiority of one's own point of view. For scientific knowledge to be possible at all, Nietzsche's view of judgment must be false.

Fortunately, one need not accept Nietzsche's entire view of knowledge in order to develop a model of domination based on his point of view. All that is necessary is that one accept the idea that a valuation can function as a means for attaining power, though its role will not be perceptible by those over whom it is exercised. On the surface, a valuation is simply a claim that some form of behavior is good, bad, or indifferent. Such a claim purports to register an objective property of something, an action, let us say. So when we say, "Stealing is bad", for example, we are making an objective claim about such action: It is bad and should therefore be avoided.

Nietzsche argues that the function of such a valuation is to get someone who wants to steal not to. In my terminology, the valuation functions as the means of getting a social agent to alter his action-environment in such a way that he will no longer pursue the course of action that he originally desired to follow. The power involved in such an interaction is obscured, however, for the valuation presents itself in the guise of an objective truth, information that is simply provided to the agent whose subordination is being sought.

According to Nietzsche, then, a valuation is a means that a social group can use to gain power over another group even when that latter group seems to be in a position to dominate the former. Indeed, the "story" that Nietzsche tells in the first essay of *Genealogy of Morals* is precisely the story of how a social group—the priests—can come to achieve dominance over another group—the nobles—who seem to occupy the superior position in terms of power.

The noble valuation is, for Nietzsche, the natural discursive counterpart to a society based upon force relations. The strong are those who are able to do what they choose and who can simply overcome the weak when they wish. The weak are objects to be used by the strong, or else pitied for their lack of strength. In cases where they interfere with the actions of the strong, they are simply crushed.

In the priestly valuation, power exists in a different form—that of influence—for the strong are dominated by the weak because the weak are able to convince the strong that certain ways of behaving are not appropriate. By getting the strong to accept the idea that the forms of behavior that were characteristic of their way of life are evil, the priests are able to dominate them by getting them to reject such forms of behavior as unacceptable. It is influence that constitutes the power of the priestly caste and that enables them to dominate the strong.

In the analysis of the priestly valuation, Nietzsche is thus calling to our attention a situation of domination in which brute strength plays no role. The power of the priests in this valuation is constituted by their discursive abilities, their ability to develop conceptual distinctions that come to be accepted as definitive by all members of a society, including those who are thereby harmed.

Nietzsche's fundamental insight into domination is that it need not be founded on relations of force at any level. Neither the actual exercise of force nor the threat of its use is necessary to constitute social domination.[27] What Nietzsche saw as one of the most crucial discoveries of human beings—a discovery he unfortunately sometimes attributed to the Jews—was that they could use the minds of other human beings as the chains for their own servitude. Because people's beliefs have a constitutive effect on what they do and allow to be done, domination can be constituted within the realm of belief alone.

One result of Nietzsche's analysis of priestly power is that it demonstrates that influence is an important means for the constitution of relations of domination precisely because it works in a way that is so difficult to detect. It is simply not apparent to the strong that, under the influence of the priests, power has been exercised upon them. Because the power of the priests masquerades as a form of truth, the strong are unable to detect the presence of a "regime of power" as constituting their own "knowledge", their own "truth". The positivity constituted by such a form of power makes it hard to detect.[28]

The Nietzschean account of domination from above thus provides a more fundamental characterization of how influence can work than the account that I discussed in the previous chapter. Because the influence that Nietzsche is discussing takes place at the most basic level of the constitution of a human being's understanding of the world, it need not be limited to the restructuring of options already given to an agent. Such domination works by first making social agents aware of the options that they face as having a certain character. It is a use of power, since it affects an agent's understanding of his action-environment; but it is not interventional, because it does not so much restructure an agent's action-environment as constitute his awareness of it in the first place.

In concluding my discussion of Nietzsche, let me guard against one possible misinterpretation of his views. In discussing Hegel's view of domination, I mentioned that it led naturally to a view of ideology as an extension of the means whereby a social group achieves its domination. That is, the realm of discourse could be seen to play an important role in domination from below, for by misrepresenting the nature of its situation to the subordinate group, the dominant group would decrease the likelihood of resistance and/or revolt.

Nietzsche's account of domination from above is fundamentally different from such a view of the nature of ideology. The Hegelian-Marxian view of ideology posits ideas as having a secondary role to play in the structuring of domination. Only when there is a primary structure of domination does it make sense for ideology to have a role in maintaining such a structure. Nietzsche, however, attributes a fundamental and basic role to the realm of ideas or discourse in the constitution of domination. The view of itself that the subordinate group has is, according to Nietzsche, itself a basic means of domination. The distinctiveness of Nietzsche's approach is that it sees such elements of discourse as the primary tools whereby one social group is able to dominate another.

Toward a Theory of Domination

The central aim of this chapter is to demonstrate that a theory of social power needs to include an account of the uses to which power can be put, an account that will itself employ the concept of domination. In part, this is because the concept of domination provides a means of referring to long-term and structural uses of power, which are important aspects of the working of power within society.

In developing my argument, I have shown that Hegel and Nietzsche characterize domination in different ways. Hegel's theory of domination from below characterizes domination as primarily a phenomenon based upon the ability of one social group to affect the welfare of another social group adversely. Nietzsche's account of domination from above posits domination as constituted by the ability of a dominant group to get a subordinate group to accept negative self-valuations that further the interests of the dominant group. There is a certain irony in this particular juxtaposition, for it is the great idealist Hegel who offers a *materialist* conception of domination, while the anti-idealist Nietzsche presents a *symbolic* conception that focuses on the realm of ideas.

Given the difference between these two models of domination, it might be thought that social theory needs to opt for one of the two as the correct one. On the contrary, the desire to articulate a single model as the only appropriate model for understanding domination as a social phenomenon is mistaken. Social theorists should avail themselves of both models. The real mistake lies in thinking that any single account of domination is sufficient to explain all its heterogeneous forms.

This mistake is encouraged by the views of Hegel and Nietzsche themselves. Although each of them recognizes the possibility of using force to structure a society, both seek to show that there is an alternative means for constituting domination in a society, namely through the use of the particular mechanisms of domination that I have designated as the material and the symbolic conceptions. However, in making their argument, neither Nietzsche nor Hegel distinguishes the general concept of domination in a systematic way from the specific mechanism that each sees as *the* means whereby domination can be constituted. As a result, each of them makes a tacit identification of domination in general with a specific mechanism of domination.[29]

My own account of domination has been based upon the very distinction that both Hegel and Nietzsche ignore. I have claimed that domination is a specific use of power, one that harms the subordinate group but requires specific mechanisms for its instantiation. Nothing in what I have said, however, requires that domination be identified with a specific mechanism or even that any mechanism be seen as the basic one.

On the contrary, by recognizing the fact that society itself is made up of individuals who are members of various groups and thus stand in multiple relations to members of other groups, we will see that society need not be conceptualized in the unitary fashion theorists often do. The social world is more complex and even contradictory than its conceptualization by social theorists. Various social groups overlap with one another, giving rise to dynamic tensions that characterize the structure of society itself. But strategies for attaining social dominance need have no more unity than society itself. To seek to find the basic model that explains social domination is to embark on a hunt for a phantasm. There are various strategies for achieving dominance that a social group can avail itself of. Hegel and Nietzsche highlight two such strategies. To seek to reduce them to a single model is to reduce the complexity of the sources of domination.

Thus, even though Hegel and Nietzsche propose different accounts of *the* basis of domination, this need not concern us. Once we accept the idea that different instances of domination may have different *bases,* we will see that the Nietzschean and the Hegelian accounts can both contribute to our understanding of the varying means whereby domination may be constituted.

Let me conclude this chapter with a reminder. My analysis of relations of domination is part of a broader program, that of introducing different uses of power into the vocabulary of social theory. A use of power differs from a type of power in that it is not a particular mechanism in which power exists, but has a particular end in view for that employment of power. Domination is one such use of power, but there are others. In particular, there is a transformative use of power—that is, a use of power that seeks to transform the very relationship within which it is exercised. This is a use of power that has not been adequately recognized by most social theorists, and I will explore its nature later in this study.

Appendix: Foucault on Domination

Perhaps the most interesting contemporary theorist of power and domination is Michel Foucault. I have not yet discussed his theory because it straddles the two conceptions that I have isolated, making important contributions to both of them. Let me now turn to his view.

Michel Foucault is often regarded as inaugurating a totally new discourse about power. In one sense, this claim has some justification, in that Foucault's studies of the development of social institutions and scientific discourses from the Renaissance to the present show the workings of power in a powerful and unsettling manner. However, in another sense Foucault is, as he himself often acknowledges, working firmly within the Nietzschean tradition.

We can see that this is the case by considering the following claim that Foucault makes about the relation between power and truth: "There can be no possible exercise of power without a certain economy of discourses of truth which operate through and on the basis of this association. We are subject to the production of truth through power and we cannot exercise power except through the production of truth." [30] By conceptualizing power and truth as standing in a necessary relation to one another, Foucault places himself firmly in the Nietzschean camp. For Foucault, as for Nietzsche, social domination requires a particular form of truth, of "knowledge", without which it could not exist. But equally importantly, a particular form of knowledge or truth can only be conceived of in relation to a particular structure of domination.

Foucault has made many important contributions to our understanding of the nature of power and domination. As I shall argue in the following chapter, Foucault's stress upon the particular interactions among human beings through which domination is accomplished marks an important corrective to theories of domination, such as the Hegelian, that are articulated at a group level. Further, his claim that power is both repressive and constituting is an important corrective to views of power that see it simply as a form of social domination.

Nonetheless, one aspect of Foucault's conceptualization of power is problematic. He tends to *subjectify* power, to treat it as an agent capable of having its own aims, strategies, and the like. This aspect of Foucault's thought is apparent in the following passage in which he is discussing the transition to the characteristically modern form of power:

> Power would no longer be dealing simply with legal subjects over whom the ultimate dominion was death, but with living beings, and *the mastery it would be able to exercise over them* would have to be applied at the level of life itself; it was the taking charge of life, more than the threat of death, that gave power *its access* to the body.[31]

In passages such as this one, Foucault attributes to *power* the structure of human agency—that is, the capability of performing actions with strategic intent.

Such usage is highly problematic. It is a return to a metaphysical stance in that it posits a supra-human subject in the manner of Hegel's positing of *Geist* as necessary for explaining the nature of human social development. It is not even clear, however, what Foucault's understanding of the composition of power is, what causes it to "act" in the manner that it does.

By positing power as a quasi-subject, Foucault is able to attribute dynamism to it. But this simply obscures the actual nature of what is happening, making human beings subject to the development of an entity whose structure we cannot fathom, let alone control. The mysticism inherent in Foucault's hypostasis of power is a serious flaw in his conceptual framework and the theory of power he seeks to develop.

This is not to say that Foucault does not have interesting new insights into the workings of social domination. It is simply to say that couching these insights within his particular conception of power is a fundamental flaw that obscures the genuinely novel insights it contains.

As I said, Foucault's position in regard to social domination is Nietzschean—that is, he believes that social domination proceeds most basically through the medium of thought, discourse, knowledge, although he sees such discourse as situated in a way that Nietzsche did not. The fundamental subjects of Foucault's analyses are the structures of human knowledge and thought, and how they function to make possible regimes of power that are equally important for the possibility of the development of such knowledge itself.

Foucault's fundamental thesis—taken from Nietzsche but put in starker terms—is that every item of knowledge is equally a means for attaining power. As I have argued, it is possible to use such a thesis as a means for understanding the nature of social domination without accepting the universality of the claim itself. That is to say, Foucault's contribution to the theory of domination is that it focuses upon the development of more subtle, complex, and material strategies for social domination than those which were previously available through the use of the Hegelian model. By placing Foucault's insights into this context, we can learn from his analyses without succumbing to the metaphysics of power on which they are based.

Foucault's contributions to the theory of domination are thus not limited to the Nietzschean view. His analysis of the role of power in the constitution of the human being shows a fundamental lacuna in the Hegelian-Marxian view. A central point of Foucault's description of the workings of contemporary disciplinary power is that such power constitutes the human being in a manner that allows it to occupy certain social positions in society. The Hegelian-Marxian view, with its emphasis on coercion and ideology, fails to provide a sufficiently material analysis of the means whereby human beings are constituted by a system of domination as able to act in that system. As a result of Foucault's analysis, the Hegelian-Marxian model can be seen to require a fundamental supplementation. In the following chapters, I will return to his view of power a number of times in order to avail myself of some of his key insights into the nature of power and domination.

7

Situated Social Power

IN DEVELOPING the field theory of power, I have criticized various assumptions made by theorists in both the Anglo-American and Continental traditions about the nature of power. In this chapter, I shall focus upon another mistaken assumption made by many power theorists, the assumption that power is dyadic. According to this assumption, power is "located" within a dyad consisting of a dominant agent and a subordinate agent over whom he wields power. The salient feature of this conception of power is that it localizes power to a sphere of existence made up of the two social agents who constitute the central actors in the power relation itself. The power that exists between them can then be understood by simply considering their relationship without reference to their wider social context.

This model is a feature of the discourse of many of the social theorists whom I have discussed, even though they often do not specifically acknowledge it. Brian Fay, on the other hand, argues that a critical social theory must work with a dyadic conception of power. His argument for this view is that only the dyadic conception of power gives both the dominant and the subordinate agents a degree of responsibility for the existence of the power relation between them:

> Something as crucial in social life as power must involve the activity of those being led or commanded as much as those leading or commanding. Power must arise out of the interaction of the powerful and powerless, with both sides contributing something necessary for its existence. *Power must be dyadic.*[1]

Fay argues that only the dyadic conception of power does justice to the fact that power arises out of the interaction of two parties—the powerful and the powerless. Without a dyadic conception of power, Fay implies, the role of the disempowered would not be recognized, making it impossible to articulate strategies by which they can seek to change the power relationships within society. As opposed to a model that conceives of power as something that can be possessed by a dominant agent, Fay's dyadic conception stresses the relational nature of power, the fact that power is always the outcome of a social relationship.

While Fay is right to stress the role of the disempowered in constituting the very relations in which they lack power, it is a mistake to see this fact as legitimating the dyadic conception of power. The problem with the dyadic conception of power is that it abstracts from an important aspect of power relations, namely the fact that they come into being as a result of the actions of agents who do not themselves figure explicitly in the power dyad itself. As I shall argue, in the central relationships that involve social power, it is precisely the role of "social others" that needs to be highlighted if one is interested in both understanding and criticizing such power relationships. Those social theorists who, like Fay, ignore these "peripheral" social agents fail to provide a model of power that can fulfill the task they are interested in, namely that of illuminating strategies for social change.

In this chapter, I shall develop a conception of power—the *situated conception of power*—that rectifies this shortcoming of the dyadic conception. The situated conception of power, while acknowledging the role that the disempowered play in the constitution of power relations, nonetheless also conceptualizes the role of "peripheral social others". By calling this account of power "situated", I stress the fact that the power dyad is itself *situated* in the context of other social relations through which it is actually constituted as a power relationship.

The situated conception of power is an important aspect of the field theory of power. By seeing the power that the dominant agent has over the subordinate agent as the result of the actions of peripheral social agents, the situated conception of power extends the idea of a social field to another aspect of power: It treats an agent's power over another agent as a result of the social field within which the two agents are themselves located. Only in the context of a social field constituted by agents external to the power dyad is that dyad itself constituted as a power dyad.

Grading and the Student-Teacher Relationship

As a first step in my argument that the situated conception of power illuminates some fundamental aspects of power that have been overlooked by many social theorists, I shall analyze the specific power relation that exists between a teacher and a student. I have chosen this example to highlight the nature of situated power for a number of reasons. Foremost among them is the familiarity and simplicity of the idea that teachers exercise power over their students. Although this idea is quite obvious, its very self-evidence allows us to see the need for using the situated conception of power in order to analyze it. In later sections of this chapter, I shall go on to apply the situated conception of power to other, more controversial examples.

The teacher-student relationship is extremely complex and is constituted by a multiplicity of overlapping and conflicting tendencies. In looking at it, I shall not attempt to develop a theoretical model that describes the actual structure of power in that relationship but shall focus solely upon the role that grading plays in its constitution as a power relationship.[2]

While it can be argued that evaluation is necessary to the practice of teaching—for it is the means whereby the teacher is able to communicate to the student the latter's success in acquiring knowledge or skills—grading does not have such a status; it is simply a particular means whereby such evaluation is accomplished. Within American education, assigning a student a grade has become the general way in which a teacher evaluates the student's performance.[3] It involves giving a particular "mark" to a student, a mark that places that student's accomplishments in some comparative relation to the accomplishments of other students. Thus, while grading is the specific form that evaluation takes within American higher education and not a universal feature of teaching itself, it is also a feature of the student-teacher relationship that helps constitute it as a power relationship. The question that I shall pose, then, is this: How is a teacher constituted as having power over her students in virtue of the fact that she grades them?

Let us consider how the dyadic conception of power would analyze a teacher's power over her students. Fay presents the following definition of power: "A exercises power with respect to B when A does x a causal outcome of which is that B does y which B would not have done without the occurrence of x".[4] According to this definition, an agent exercises power over another agent only when the dominant agent does something that results in a change in what the subordinate agent does. A teacher's power over her student is seen as the result of actions that she performs. For example, if a student was not doing the work required of him, his teacher could attempt to get him to do the work by threatening to lower his grade significantly if he did not work harder, or by assigning him an extra paper that he would have to do to pass the course. In such a case, the teacher would be trying to get the student to work harder by threatening him with a lower grade or even failure if he failed to comply with her demands.

While the dyadic conception of power may be able to give an account of how the teacher exercises power in such disciplinary situations, it is not able to give an account of a more basic aspect of the power inherent in the teacher-student relationship. Students routinely act as they do in a classroom because of the power that teachers have, even though teachers themselves do not do anything special to cause students to alter their actions. The mere fact that a teacher will grade her students gives her power over them.

The point I am making is that the power that a teacher has as a result of grading her students is not simply *interventional*—that is, something that occurs as a result of actions that a teacher performs; a teacher's power over her students is *structural*, a feature of the structure of their relationship that is constituted by the fact that the teacher evaluates the performance of her students by means of a grade. Fay's definition does not acknowledge such structural aspects of power relations; the ongoing structuring of a student's behavior by the fact that his teacher will grade him cannot be accommodated within Fay's definition.[5]

This example suggests that a more comprehensive conception of power is required, one that recognizes not only particular interventions as instances of the presence of power in society but also ongoing structural features of social relationships. The situated conception of power recognizes power as a factor in ongoing social relationships, the sorts of situations in which, according to the dyadic conception, a dominant agent does not exercise power at all.[6]

According to the situated conception of power, one needs to move beyond the classroom itself in order to gain an adequate understanding of the power of a grade, for the teacher's power over the student is constituted by the actions of social agents who are *peripheral* to the central dyad. The question that needs to be clarified is precisely how the actions of these social others constitute the relationship between the central agents as a power relationship.

In order to explicate the role that agents external to the power dyad play in the constitution of a situated power relationship, I shall ask why a student is harmed by receiving a grade that he perceives to be low.[7] There are, of course, many reasons why a student might be harmed by receiving such a grade. A student who, for example, thought that she had written a good paper might be hurt because she would take that low grade as signifying the teacher's belief that she had not succeeded in so doing. Another student might be hurt because she wanted to please her teacher and took the low grade as meaning that she had not done so.

For the purposes of my discussion, I shall "bracket" all the reasons why a student might be harmed by a low grade and ask whether—leaving to one side all the effects that can be localized to the dyadic relationship itself—there is not another important dimension to the harm done to a student by a low grade.

To see that this is so, consider the following situations in which a low grade comes to have an adverse effect upon a student's welfare. A student's parents might punish him for receiving a low grade; an honors society might not admit a student with a low grade; a principal might expel a student for receiving a low grade; a law school might use the low grade as a means to weed out the student; a firm might reject the student's application because of the low grade: all these are examples of agents external to the power dyad whose actions are dependent upon the grade and who harm the student because he received a low one.

In all of these examples, it is obvious that the grade itself, being by nature a sign, does not have an adverse effect on the student's well-being. Rather, the grade's negative effect is constituted by the way in which social agents peripheral to the student-teacher relationship react to it.[8] A student's well-being is affected by the grade only through the mediation of human beings situated outside the classroom, who use the grade as a sign that results in their administering "harm" to the student—for example, by denying him access to the opportunity to further his education. To use a familiar example, a student who wishes to attend medical school but who fails organic chemistry will have that option foreclosed.

Although these facts are familiar enough, they cannot be accommodated within the dyadic conception of power. The situated conception of power, on the other hand, acknowledges the fact that power relationships are constituted by the presence of social agents who are peripheral to the central power dyad and whose treatment of the disempowered agent constrains his action-environment, that is, constitute the dyad as a power relationship. It posits a structure of *social mediation* that is essential to the constitution of social power relationships, for, without the "cooperation" of social "others" with the "intent" of the teacher's grading, the student would not be harmed by receiving a low grade.[9] Only because these others do cooperate with the teacher's intent does the student have an interest in receiving a high grade from her teacher, a grade that will result in others' having a positive assessment of her abilities and achievement, thus allowing her access to the item over which they have control. It is the presence of these others, acting as the conduits through which the teacher's act is transformed into a set of social realities constraining the student's access to various things, that constitutes the relationship between the student and the teacher as one involving social power.[10]

This is not to say that a student who receives what he takes to be a low grade from a teacher does not feel hurt. My account merely claims that one aspect of the hurt that the student experiences when he receives the "low" grade should be seen to be an anticipation of the actual harm that the grade will do him. In this sense, I want to suggest that social theorists need to recognize that an individual's experience of the world has an explicitly social content in that an agent's actual subjective experience is a reflection of the social structure of his world.[11]

The account that the situated conception of power gives of a teacher's power over a student can be made more persuasive by the fact that, if a student can be sure of never encountering an individual who will use a low grade as a basis for her treatment of the student, the fact of grading will not result in the teacher's having power over the student. In actual social situations where parental authority has broken down and young people have little hope of being in a position where a grade might function as a means of access to a decent job, discipline has become a major educational problem. One reason is that the power of the teacher has been eroded by the fact that the dyadic relationship between the student and the teacher is no longer situated upon a field of social relationships that amount to a constraint of the student's action-environment.[12]

The example of the teacher-student relationship, then, shows that agents peripheral to the power dyad play a constitutive role in the formation of a social power relationship between two social agents. In such cases, an agent's power over another is determined by the use that the peripheral agents make of the two agents' actions and decisions. The *differential structure of orientation* that the peripheral agents have in regard to the dominant and subordinate agents is the crux of the social power that the dominant agent "possesses". The actions of other social agents constitute a broad social field that both structures and conveys power between the two agents who form the central dyad in a situated power relationship.

Advantages of the Situated Conception

Although power has often been seen as dependent solely upon the actions of the dominant and subordinate agents, such is not the case according to the situated conception of power. Situated power relationships are not constituted by threats that a dominant agent makes to a subordinate agent, but make it possible for the dominant agent in such a relationship to make an effective threat to a subordinate agent in the first place. When, to choose a slightly different example, a teacher threatens a student by saying that he will lower his grade unless he has sexual relations with him, the effectiveness of such a threat can only be understood against the background of an already established situated power relationship, one that is itself not constituted by such a threat. It is the background field constituted by such relations that I have analyzed by means of the concept of situated power. Situated power relations are structural in nature, and thus are more independent of the particular volitions and decisions of individual social agents than can be accounted for by using the dyadic model of power.

The situated conception of power also denies the claim that power is really a form of social agreement or consent among social agents.[13] Though the subordinate agent certainly *submits* to a situated power relation, such submission cannot be adequately characterized by the notion of an agreement. Both parties to an agreement must have roughly equal ability to affect each other. But this is precisely what is not the case in relationships of situated social power. The subordinate agent faces a situated power relationship as a given over which he can have little effect but which will have a significant effect upon him. He encounters such situations much as he does natural necessities, as things to which he must submit in order to realize his own desires and intentions.

While discussing the nature of coercive power in Chapter 5, I pointed out that all attributions of power to an agent depend on the context. The case under consideration was the attempt by police to coerce an environmental group into refraining from holding a demonstration. The question of who had power over whom, I argued, depended upon the ways in which other social agents reacted to the actions of the two central agents. I shall call this the *contextuality of power attributions*.

In order to have a clear understanding of the situated conception of power, it is important to distinguish it from the contextuality of power attributions. From the perspective of the contextuality of power attributions, the entire power debate has focused upon a mistakenly abstract conception of power in so far as it has treated power as something that resides in social agents independently of the broader social context. The contextuality of power attributions shows that power does not work in this abstract way. We attribute power to an agent only when there are no countervailing social factors that would keep her from exercising her power should she choose to. This is a point that David Hume makes in the following quotation:

> But according to common notions a man has no power where very considerable motives lie betwixt him and the satisfaction of his desires, and determine him to forbear what he wishes to perform. I do not think I have fallen into my enemies [sic] power, when I see him pass me in the streets with a sword by his side, while I am unprovided of any weapon. I know that the fear of the civil magistrate is as strong a restraint as any of iron, and that I am in as perfect safety as if he were chain'd or imprison'd. But

when a person acquires such an authority over me, that not only there is
no external obstacle to his actions; but also that he may punish or reward
me as he pleases, without any dread of punishment in his turn, I then
attribute a full power to him, and consider myself as his subject or
vassal.[14]

Hume points out that an inequality that allows one agent to harm another without being harmed by that agent is not in itself sufficient to constitute the relationship between them as a power relationship. The presence of the magistrate
functions in Hume's example as an equalizer keeping the armed agent from
being able to harm the unarmed agent with impunity. The relationship between the two agents is not a power relationship precisely because of the effect
that the social context has on their dyadic relationship.

The contextuality of power attributions is certainly an important point that
any theory of social power needs to acknowledge. Nonetheless, the situated
conception of power, in that it claims that there are certain relationships of
power that would not be relationships of power were it not for the social context, asserts the converse of this point. According to the contextuality of
power attributions, power is attributable to an agent only when there are not
social factors that would keep her from exercising her ability to affect another
agent. Only in the absence of such countervening social factors is a difference
in abilities or possessions sufficient to constitute a power relationship between
the two agents.

The situated conception of power operates at a different level of analysis.
It claims that certain power relationships come into existence only by means
of the actions of social agents who simultaneously empower and disempower
other social agents by means of their differential responses to them. It thus
posits a particular structure of social mediation external to the power dyad that
is essential to the constitution of that dyad as a power relationship. In a different context, Hume recognizes the importance of such structures of social mediation: "The mutual dependence of men is so great in all societies that scarce
any human action is entirely complete in itself, or is performed without some
reference to the actions of others, which are requisite to make it answer fully
the intentions of the agent." [15] The situated conception of power is a manner of
understanding the nature of power relationships that involves such a view of
human action. Its specific claim is that social power relationships require a
social field that goes beyond the two central agents.

The situated conception of power thus agrees with the contextuality of
power attributions in stressing the importance of the social context in constituting the power relationship between social agents. However, it makes a

more specific claim about how power relationships are constituted. It asserts that many relationships of social power are constituted *in the first instance* by the way in which peripheral social agents treat both the dominant and the subordinate agents. As such, it claims that a particular type of social context can constitute a power relationship between two social agents. The situated conception of power differs from the contextual view in that it posits a particular form of social power relationship as important for understanding the nature of power in contemporary society; it does not simply make a general point about the importance of the social context in assessing who has power over whom. The situated conception of power therefore functions at a more basic ontological level than the contextuality of power attributions, positing a specific structure of social relationship as the basis of social power.

The Concept of a Social Alignment

In developing the situated conception of power, I have argued that the relationship between the two agents who form the power dyad is constituted by a ground of peripheral social relationships. Not any set of peripheral social relationships, however, is sufficient to constitute a relationship between two agents as a power relationship. It is therefore necessary to develop a more specific model of the structure of social relationships through which situated power relationships are constituted.

The concept that I shall use to refer to the specific structure of social mediation through which situated power relationships are constituted is that of a *social alignment*. *Webster's* defines the term "align" in the following manner: "to bring into line; to array on the side of or against a party or cause; to be or come into correct relative position". "Alignment" is then defined as "the act or state of being aligned; esp. the proper positioning of parts in relation to one another".[16] By using the term "alignment" to refer to the structure of social relationships that are necessary for constituting a situated power relationship, I am emphasizing the "relative positioning" of social others that is necessary for the constitution of a situated power relationship.

In order to explain my use of this term, let me consider two contexts in which the word "alignment" normally occurs. Nations are spoken of as being *aligned* with one of the two superpowers or as being *non-aligned*. In this use, the term indicates that each superpower has a certain set of policies around which the aligned nations orient themselves. The superpower is a focus for the activities and policies of its aligned nations. In this use, the concept of alignment indicates a center for the *orientation* of the actions and positions of other nations.

The second use of the term "alignment" is one that has to do with cars. We speak of the *alignment* of the front wheels of a car—that is, a structure in which the front wheels are parallel with one another and perpendicular to the body of the car. In this use, the concept refers to a geometrical distribution of the parts, a *coordination* of two parts of the car that enables the entire car to run smoothly.

By using the term "alignment" to refer to the structure of peripheral social agents through which a situated power relationship is constituted, I am drawing on both of these ordinary uses. The behavior of the agents external to the power dyad can be seen as *oriented* around the actions of the two central agents, for it is their actions that the peripheral agents use to structure their treatment of the subordinate agent. Furthermore, their *coordinated* actions are needed to create a smoothly functioning power relationship, even though they are not the central location of the relationship itself.

A situated power relationship between two social agents is thus constituted by the presence of peripheral social agents in the form of a *social alignment*. A field of social agents can constitute an alignment in regard to a social agent if and only if, first of all, their actions in regard to that agent are coordinated in a specific manner. To be an alignment, however, the coordinated practices of these social agents need to be comprehensive enough that the social agent facing the alignment encounters that alignment as having control over certain things that she might either need or desire. In cases where this coordination of the peripheral society agents exists and is used to determine an agent's access to certain desirable items, these peripheral social agents constitute a social alignment.

The concept of a social alignment thus provides a way of understanding the "field" that constitutes a situated power relationship *as* a power relationship. In the grading example, I argued that students face a whole set of possible consequences that are contingent upon the grades they receive from their teachers. I am now claiming that this set of contingencies is best conceived of by means of the concept of a social alignment, for the contingencies consist in the differential treatment that the subordinate agent will receive from others. Because these social others *align* their treatment of the subordinate agent around her own actions as well as those of the dominant agent, the relationship between these two agents is constituted as a social power relationship.

A social alignment is thus a quasi-monopolistic structure through which individuals gain access to things that they might wish to have. As such, it constitutes a constraint on the action-environment of such individuals. I earlier mentioned the question of getting into medical school. Because such things as the opportunity to study medicine are desirable and controlled by the grading alignment, the grading alignment is able to function as a social alignment.

Let me note in passing that alignments need not be fixed institutional structures. To see this, consider a group of businesses that decides to boycott all the products of a certain country. In that case, the country is being treated in the same manner by all these social agents (i.e., the businesses), so that their action of coordinating their purchases constitutes one crucial aspect of an alignment. If the businesses are an important, non-replaceable outlet for the products of that country, then they have a second characteristic that is necessary for them to function as a social alignment: They control an important item that the country desires, namely a market for its goods. If they have this sort of monopolistic control over the purchase of these products, then the businesses form an alignment by coordinating their purchases in a systematic manner. By boycotting the goods of that country, they are able to create a situated power relationship with it.

This example shows that alignments are not limited to permanent and fixed modes of social interaction; they can come into existence for specific purposes and for limited amounts of time. In such cases, alignments may function in an interventional rather than a systematic manner.

My discussion of the nature of a social alignment shows that situated social power is not easily constituted: An entire set of social practices has to be coordinated in certain very specific ways in order for such power to exist. If the "backups"—that is, aligned social practices—are not in place, there will be a means for the subordinate agent to escape the power that the dominant agent has over her.

I shall refer to this aspect of a situated power relationship as its *heterogeneity*. By that term I indicate the fact that situated power does not reside exclusively in a single site or institution of society. The situated conception of power shows that social power is a heterogeneous presence that spreads across an entire set of agents and practices, although its exercise depends upon the actions of the dominant agent. Such heterogeneity is constituted by a complex coordination among agents located in diverse sites and institutions, all of whose presence in a social alignment is necessary to constitute a situated power relationship.

This general account of the role of alignments in the constitution of situated social power relationships will be strengthened by considering an example of how, in the absence of such an alignment, the power of an agent will be severely limited. Consider a situation in which a city passes a law that requires businesses to meet new pollution standards. The law states that businesses have to make certain investments in their physical plants in order to conform to the new code. Suppose further that a large firm threatens to move out of the city if it is forced to comply with the new code. As a result of this threat, the city allows the firm's plants to remain in their present condition and to disregard the newly passed law.

In this example, the local government is not able to use its power to get a large corporation to comply with its wishes. We can understand why once we realize that the two alignments are competing with one another for power. The governmental alignment acts through a variety of social institutions, including the legislature and the police. It seeks to force the corporation to accept its own demands as binding on its actions. If it had been successful, the governmental alignment would have had power over the corporation. The corporation, on the other hand, employs many of the government's citizens in its productive activities. It also generally complies with governmental regulations and is a source of governmental income. Because the corporation is able to relocate, it can threaten to take an action that would adversely affect the local government. Not only would such an action cause unemployment and loss of essential revenues; it might even cause voter unrest and lead to an adverse electoral result. Because of these possible results, the business's threat is likely to succeed and keep the local government from enforcing stricter pollution requirements than are generally in force in other locations to which the corporation could move.

My analysis makes it clear that the reason that the local government is unable to succeed in its attempt to get the corporation to comply with the law is that it lacks a broad enough governmental alignment to back up its efforts. Although the local government has a judicial and police branch with which to enforce its legislative decisions, the corporation's ability to relocate gives it a simple means of avoiding compliance with those strategies and tactics. Only if other local governments were prepared to back up the decisions of the first government would that government's coercive power be truly effective in relation to large, relatively mobile corporations. That is, the local governments would have to have some mechanism for creating an alignment in regard to decisions made about regulating corporate practices. From such a point of view, we can see the role played by more comprehensive governmental structures: They play precisely the role of an alignment by coordinating the decisions of more local governments.

This scenario also shows a serious problem with the demand made by both conservatives and progressives for local government control. The problem with such an idea is not simply that local governments are more corrupt or susceptible to extra-political pressure, as many have suggested, for such problems are, at least in principle, soluble. The real problem is the lack of an alignment structure.

Some Consequences for Social Theory

In order to illustrate how social theory will benefit from adopting the situated conception of power, I shall outline four specific applications of the conception to problems in social theory. First, I shall show that the situated conception of power provides the means for understanding institutional power and expertise. I shall then demonstrate that it gives an account of how "macro" phenomena like the male domination of women come to be factors at the "micro" level of individual social interactions. I shall also show how the relationship between a capitalist and a worker can be analyzed by means of the situated conception of power. Finally, I shall present the conception's explanation of processes of "subjection" —that is, of how individual social agents are constituted by the presence of power in society.

INSTITUTIONAL POWER AND EXPERTISE

In order to show that the situated conception of power provides a clear manner of conceptualizing the power that agents have within social institutions, I shall consider the example of a judge. In so doing, I shall show that the account of power that I developed in the context of the teacher-student relationship can be generalized so as provide a means of understanding the structure of institutional power.

Clearly, a judge has power over a prisoner in that his decision about the prisoner's guilt or innocence, as well as about the severity of the punishment, has a significant effect on the prisoner's well being. If a judge declares a prisoner to be guilty, then the prisoner is placed in prison; if a judge declares him innocent, then he is freed.[17] This aspect of the judge-prisoner relationship makes it similar to the teacher-student relationship that I explored earlier in that the dominant agent makes a decision that affects the well being of the subordinate agent.

The conception of a situated power relationship allows me to explain how the judge's power over the prisoner is constituted. The judge's act of declaring guilt or innocence, or of pronouncing sentence, is used by other agents to determine the manner in which they will treat the prisoner. The various agents who compose the judicial and penal systems—from lawyers and bailiffs to police and prison guards—all structure their relation to the prisoner around the pronouncement of the judge. It is this structure of differential relation that constitutes the power that the judge has over the prisoner.

This example shows that positions of power within specific social institutions can be explained by means of the situated conception of power. Such positions can be seen as a sort of limiting case of this conception of power, in which the social alignment that constitutes the power is a single social institution and the social practices located within it.

The example of the judge also shows how the situated conception of power makes sense of the idea that "expertise" is a prevalent form of power in contemporary society, one that has many pernicious results. Although many social theorists have objected to the rise of experts in contemporary society, they have failed to provide a sufficiently material (i.e., social) analysis of what such expertise amounts to. The situated model of power shows that the rise of expertise in contemporary society corresponds to the development of a specific social structure that allows the expert to become a wielder of power.

Once we recognize the existence of a situated power relationship "behind" the power of an expert, we can see that the normal legitimation of such expertise obscures the structure of power that constitutes expertise as a specific form of social practice. When thinking about why an expert is given power, we tend to focus upon the dyadic relationship between the expert and the social agent over whom he has power. Because the expert has more knowledge than other social agents, we assume that the expert's power is legitimately held. Thus, a teacher is given the power to grade the student because of a belief that the teacher is an expert in virtue of her possession of a certain amount of esoteric knowledge. As a result of this expertise, it is thought that the teacher has the ability to discriminate among different levels of performance on the part of students. The teacher's assigning of grades is taken to be a rational means of assessing the students' abilities. Similarly, in the case of the judge, his expert knowledge in judicial matters is the justification for placing him in a situated power relationship with those accused of criminal offences.

But although the expert's possession of knowledge is normally seen as legitimating his possession of power, the situated conception of power allows us to see that there is no necessary connection between the expert knowledge possessed by the empowered agent and the structure of the power relationship itself. While the expert may *be* an authority about certain subject matters, this authority is distinguishable from the authority she comes to *have* as a result of being situated as an empowered agent. Although the normal understanding of experts makes it seem that the knowledge that the expert has makes the power structure in which she takes part inevitable, the situated conception of power shows that the power that accrues to the expert in virtue of her esoteric knowledge is a result of the use of her expert knowledge as the ground of a situated power relationship. It thus shows that the normal manner of legitimating such relationships is invalid, since it fails to explain why the possession of esoteric knowledge legitimates the creation of the specific social structure of expertise.

SITUATED POWER AND DOMINATION

Another advantage of the situated conception of power is that it explains how domination, which is usually conceptualized as a "macro" feature of a society, impacts upon the lives of individuals at the "micro" level. I shall focus upon sexism in order to show how the situated conception of power helps explain certain of its features.

In making this argument, I shall examine a specific male attitude. Although many men acknowledge the domination of women in all contemporary societies, these same men will often deny that they play any role in such domination. Not only do they not experience themselves as dominators; they claim that they do not themselves act in ways that dominate women.

Of course, feminists have argued that the fact that men have these feelings does not contradict the fact of male domination. Pointing, for example, to statistical inequalities in pay, they maintain that there is a structure of male domination despite what many men may feel about themselves.

But such a response does not explain why men feel the way that they do. One way of accounting for these feelings is to say that men simply have false consciousness. One would argue that, despite what men happen to believe, they actually dominate women. They do not recognize this fact because their consciousnesses do not reflect social reality in an accurate manner.

The perils of using the idea of false consciousness are clear from the history of the Marxist use of this concept.[18] It is therefore not an adequate means of understanding the view that many men have about their own roles in male domination.

The situated conception of power, however, provides an alternative means for understanding how the following two claims can both be true: that contemporary society is male-dominated and that, nonetheless, many men do not experience themselves as dominators. The situated conception of power explains this by distinguishing between the social field for specific power relationships and the power dyad itself.

Let us consider a relationship between a husband and a wife where the husband sees himself as not dominating his wife. We need to understand why it makes perfectly good sense to claim that the husband does dominate the wife in this relationship, despite his desire not to, as a result of the sexist nature of the society in which he lives.

To begin with, in claiming that society is sexist, one is claiming, among other things, that women are treated differently from men. In particular, within our society women have less access to many things that are normally deemed important for living a fulfilled life. There is a whole series of economic facts that mean that women have a much harder time gaining access to social goods than do men. For example, it is generally acknowledged that women have more limited opportunities on the labor market than do men. When they do get jobs, their pay is equal to only 60 percent of that which men receive. There are also problems with sexual harassment in jobs. Further, banks and other financial institutions tend to be more stringent in loan requirements for women. Single women, not having husbands to use as references, have a harder time getting loans. Considerations such as these point to a social structure that entails that women have more difficulty gaining access to certain sorts of goods than do men.

In the terms that I have developed, all of these facts amount to the claim that there is a "gender" alignment through which women are treated differently from men. That is, various social institutions and practices—from banks to businesses—use a woman's gender as a basis for their treatment of her.

Now the gender alignment, although peripheral to the nature of a particular marriage, constitutes the social field for the relationship between a husband and wife. The situated conception of power shows why, despite the husband's best intentions, that relationship will be one in which he has power over her. For when a wife considers the benefits of her relationship to her husband, she will not only be considering what that particular man is like as a husband but the alternatives that she would have to face were she not married to him. Limiting ourselves to strictly economic factors, we can see that her economic situation will be very different depending upon whether she is married. By choosing marriage, she will receive many benefits because of her relationship to her husband. As a result, she gains something from the marriage and thus has a reason both to enter into it and to stay in it that transcends the particular nature of the marriage itself. It is this set of reasons, reasons that focus on the gender alignment, that constitute the marriage relation as a form of power in our current society. The power that husbands have is not the result of their own particular intentions, though they may choose to use their power to enhance their own status in the family; that power is the result of the situated nature of the marriage relationship itself. The general social disposition to treat women differently from men—a disposition that I have explored very superficially—functions as an alignment that constitutes the husband's power over his wife and their relationship as an example of situated power.

The situated conception of power thus provides a clear way of understanding the power that accrues to individuals when they occupy certain social roles and the power that others lose when they occupy other ones. To be a husband or a wife, a student or a teacher, is to occupy a particular social role in virtue of which one's power is constituted. The situated conception of power explains how individuals come to have a social being that transcends their own individual existence.

It is worth noting that there are features of the husband-wife relationship that are different from those in the teacher-student one. A husband does not, for example, grade his wife as a teacher does her students. Nonetheless, the situated model of power demonstrates certain important similarities in the two relationships, similarities that might not be noticed in the absence of the model. The central similarity is that a woman's access to things that she desires depends on her relationship with a particular man, her husband, just as a student's access depends on her relationship with her teacher. Just as a teacher works to differentiate among her students on the basis of abilities, a husband is also "marking" a woman as acceptable by marrying her. This badge of respectability functions like a grade in so far as it allows married women access to different sorts of things than non-married women have.

Of course, not all gender domination can be explained by the situated model of power. The ways in which women think about themselves and their possibilities is not something that the situated model of power is attempting to explain. It does, however, show that power is exercised within particular social relationships that do not themselves seem to be the locus of power: Because of the presence of a social field in the form of a social alignment, the central dyad is made into a power relationship. As a result, the situated conception of power provides social theorists with an important means of analyzing the nature of social domination.

THE POWER OF THE CAPITALIST

I would now like to show the usefulness of the notion of situated power by exploring the relationship between capital and labor. Of course, this notion has been the focus of extended analysis by both liberal theorists and Marxists. It is my contention, however, that the concept of situated power provides a clear means of legitimating the claim that capitalists have power over the workers whom they employ.

The analysis of the power components of the capitalist-laborer relation combines aspects of the two types of alignments I have just discussed. In the first place, a single firm is a social institution in which the capitalist has power over the worker in a manner analogous to that in which the judge has power over the prisoner. The decisions of the capitalist in regard, for example, to hiring and firing are taken by the other agents within the firm as determinative of their own practices. The laborer is hired, given work, paid, and so on as a result of the capitalist's decision to hire him. Within a single firm, the capitalist has a position of situated power over the worker.

However, there is more to this analysis than the fact that, within the single firm in which the worker is employed, the capitalist has power. A second feature of the capitalist's power over the worker depends upon the limited set of options that the worker has for living a life in which he will be able to achieve certain goals he has for himself and for his family without retaining the job that has been given to him by the capitalist.[19] I would now like to show how the model of situated power explains this aspect of the relation between the capitalist and the worker.

To do this, let me outline two aspects of the capitalist alignment that will allow us to see the way that it constitutes the capitalist's relation to the laborer as one involving situated power. The first aspect of the alignment consists in other firms. A capitalist has power over a worker in his firm because there are no easily available employment options open to the worker. There are two reasons for this. The first is that, in some types of employment, being fired is a bad mark that other employers use as a reason not to hire a worker. The analogy to grading is obvious. The second is that the relatively high unemployment levels present in a capitalist society make a worker unsure of his chances of finding new employment. Marx himself conceptualized this aspect of the capitalist mode of production as the "reserve army of the proletariat" and argued for its structural necessity in maintaining capitalism. My analysis also sees this aspect of the economy as having an important role in constituting the capitalist's power over his worker.

The second aspect of the capitalist alignment that needs to be borne in mind is the lack of welfare options. Since I have defined an agent's power over another agent as his alteration of the action-environment of that agent, a capitalist's power over a worker would be greatly diminished if there were state-financed means whereby a worker could meet many of his needs and desires. It is important to the maintenance of the capitalist's power that the worker not be able to rely on such options. But this means that the welfare options that are available to the worker must be such that he will not see them as fully acceptable alternatives to employment. And this, in turn, entails that the government not fund them in ways that would make them acceptable alternatives. This analysis shows that many institutions other than firms themselves play a role in the capitalist alignment, that alignment through which a capitalist is empowered in relation to workers.[20] Thus, when a wage offer is made by a capitalist to a worker, the presence of the capitalist alignment structures the options that the worker is able to consider in deciding whether to accept it. The worker's action-alternatives have the structure that they do in virtue of the presence of the various facets of the capitalist alignment that result in the capitalist's having power over the worker.

By focusing attention on the role that social alignments play in the maintenance of a power relationship, I have shown how the appearance of freedom in the relationship between the worker and the capitalist—which has been emphasized by liberal theory—conceals a deeper level at which power is exercised. Only because the options facing the worker have the structure that they do will the worker be "willing" to work for the wage he does in the conditions that he faces. This structure of alternatives is precisely what the concept of a social alignment refers to.

SUBJECTION AND SITUATED POWER

The situated conception of power also makes an important contribution to our understanding of the very basic levels at which power operates in society. Foucault has spoken of *processes of subjection* in order to indicate that the same processes that form the individual as a "subject" of consciousness also form that individual as "subjected" to power.[21] The situated conception of power provides a means of understanding Foucault's view as part of a general theory of power in society.

In order to understand such processes, I shall focus upon power relationships that have two specific features. The first is that the subordinate agent has some desire for the items over which the alignment has control. The second is that the agent is able to affect how the dominant agent will act in regard to her. When these two features are present in a power relationship, the structure of that relationship becomes much more intentional. If, for example, a teacher decided arbitrarily on whether to give a student a good grade, then, although it would still be true that the teacher had power over the student, such power would not ground a power relationship in which the student could affect how she would be treated. Only when the subordinate agent has some effect on the dominant agent's actions will the dominant agent's power have some effect on the subordinate agent's conduct or understanding.

These two features explain how such power relationships result in a process of subjection. To see this, consider the teacher-student relationship once more. First, note that the teacher-student relationship is one that is characterized by the two additional features I just outlined. A student's access to certain items—for example, jobs—is at least partially determined by the grading alignment. It is also true that a student has a great deal of influence upon how a teacher grades her. By working harder, she will usually be able to produce better papers and examinations, the sorts of things that form the basis for the teacher's evaluation. Indeed, the "point" of the power relationship is precisely to get the student to adopt such a strategy. The power of the teacher is not arbitrary; it seeks to elicit actions on the part of students that affect how they will be judged by the teacher. Insofar as a student performs the sorts of actions that the teacher seeks to have her perform, like studying and writing, she will do things that make it likely that she will receive a better grade from the teacher than she would have received had she not performed such actions.

The situated power relationship between a student and a teacher thus results in the student's adopting certain courses of action in her attempt to affect the teacher's grading of her. For a student facing a teacher, the teacher's power is located in his ability to affect her future. As a result, she will do things that the teacher wants.

This means that the result of the existence of such a power relationship is that the subordinate agent comes to adopt long-term strategies of action that are predicated upon the existence of such power relations. He will adopt certain courses of action for the instrumental value they have in allowing him to realize his other purposes. But this process is precisely one of subjection—that is, the creation of the human agent as having desires that are adopted as his own as a result of his interaction with a power structure over which he has no control.

The crucial thing to recognize is that the presence of power relationships causes human beings to make choices that determine the sorts of skills and abilities they will come to have. As a result, since the formation of skills and abilities is a fundamental aspect of the constitution of character, human beings come to be the sorts of beings that they are as a result of the presence of power relationships. The situated conception of power thus provides a clear way of understanding how power does this by affecting the constitution of human beings at the level of desire, skill, and ability.

This analysis demonstrates that situated power relationships have one important similarity to the structure of coercive power relationships: They get subordinate agents to do things that they would not be likely to do in the absence of the power relationships. The central difference between coercive and situated power is that it does not take a threat on the part of the dominant agent to constitute a situated power relationship, as it does in the case of coercion. Unlike coercion, a situated power relationship is constituted as a structural feature of the relationship between the dominant and the subordinate agent that appears to be independent of their individual volitions. Situated power appears to the subordinate agent as a fact about his situation that he must reckon with if he wishes to fulfill his desires.

Conclusion

The basic contention of the situated conception of power is that a power dyad forms only one of two important elements in most relationships of social power. The other element in such relationships is a social alignment, a structure of peripheral social agents that controls and distributes certain items in society. It is the presence of such a social alignment that constitutes the relationship between two social agents as one that involves social power.

Acknowledging the importance of alignments in the constitution of situated social power results in a very different picture of social power than that which is conveyed simply by focusing on the two agents who form the central dyad in a power relationship. While the place and moment of the exercise of power may well be localizable to such a dyad, this is not the case for the power relationship itself. The dyad within which power is exercised is but the point of focus of a vast field of social forces that determine the nature of such an exercise. By failing to acknowledge the existence of such a social field and its role in the constitution of a power relationship, many power theorists have failed to articulate a model of social power that adequately conceptualizes the complex structure of social practices comprising the presence of power in the social world. The situated conception of social power rectifies this shortcoming by developing a clear picture of how such relationships are actually constituted in society.

In general, then, the concept of situated power demonstrates that power is a much more pervasive feature of the social world than liberal theory maintains. By seeing the importance of social alignments in creating a set of alternatives that an individual normally encounters as given, we are able to see the importance of power relationships in structuring and reproducing society as a whole. It gives us grounds to reject the liberal notion that power is only a peripheral phenomenon in modern societies, most of whose structures operate through the consent of those involved, and allows us to see how central a presence power is in those very societies.

8

Toward a Dynamic Conception of Social Power

THROUGHOUT THIS book, I have criticized certain basic assumptions that many social theorists have made in their attempt to understand social power. The first element in this argument involved my claim that power could not be adequately conceptualized by theories that did not place it within the context of intentional human actions. My own use of the concept of an agent's action-environment in the definition of power attempted to demonstrate that power is located within the sphere of intentional concepts in that the possible targets of a power relationship between two agents include an agent's understanding of her situation.

The situated conception of power continued my criticism of objectivizing theories of power, theories that treat power as an objective feature of the social world. By stressing the role that peripheral social agents play in the constitution of certain power relationships, the situated conception of power accentuates the social nature of power, the fact that power relationships are an effect generated by a particular structure in a social field. By denying that power is something whose existence can be judged by focusing simply upon the two central agents in a power dyad, the situated conception of power marks an even more fundamental departure from models that treat power as simply an objective feature of the social world.

The view of power that I have advanced so far in this study thus makes two fundamental breaks with much of the thinking about power within Anglo-American social theory. In this chapter, I shall argue that one further break is needed if an adequate conception of power is to be achieved. This break entails replacing the idea that power is essentially a static phenomenon—one

163

that does not require a temporal dimension—with a dynamic view of power that explicitly incorporates temporal factors.

The assumption that power is static is not one that is explicitly stated in the conceptions of power put forward in the power debate. Nonetheless, it is one that is involved in treating power as some-Thing that can be possessed by a social agent. If power is a Thing that is possessible by a social agent and if such possession is treated as an objective fact about that agent, then power is conceptualized in an essentially static manner.

But power needs to be conceptualized as a *dynamic* phenomenon, one that has temporal as well as static aspects to its existence and is therefore always "in motion". Questions like "Who has power in society?" tend to treat power in an objectivizing manner by seeing it as a static phenomenon that can be located in a given social space. Although the situated conception of power challenges the idea that the social location of a power relationship is as easy to determine as some social theorists have maintained, it does not specifically reject the spatial orientation of these theories.

To treat power as dynamic is to treat its temporal dimension as equally as important as its spatial dimension. It is to treat power as something that does not simply exist as a static social presence, but as something that is continually being reconstituted and/or altered by means of the actions and understandings of social agents. A dynamic conception of power acknowledges that power is a particular type of ongoing social process, not simply a static social distribution.

I shall argue for the need to take a dynamic view of social power as follows. I shall begin by outlining the basic parameters of a dynamic conception of power by means of a discussion of Marx's view of social (re)production. I shall then return to the idea of situated social power and show how a dynamic understanding of power can be used to develop a more complete picture of the nature of situated power relationships as ongoing social relationships. By introducing such ideas as countering and alternative alignments, I shall flesh out the basic picture of power that the situated conception presents. In conclusion, I shall show that a dynamic conception of power makes intelligible the nature of new social movements by showing that their aim is a fundamental realignment of social power.

Power and Temporality

In criticizing the views of power articulated by social theorists within the power debate, I pointed out that such views tend to focus upon particular interventions as the appropriate sort of place within which to locate power as a social reality. At that point, I claimed that this was a mistake, for power is not simply *relational*—that is, something that relates human beings to one another in particular interventions; power, I argued, exists in *relationships*—it has a primary location in the ongoing, habitual ways in which human beings relate to one another.

One of the strengths of the situated conception of power is that it acknowledges that power exists primarily in social relationships and not in isolated exercises. It posits a particular ontological structure of human social relationships as constituting situated power relationships and, in so doing, explicitly posits ongoing social relationships as the primary locus of power in society. When relationships rather than events become the focus of a theory of power, it becomes clear that power is not a piece of property that can simply be physically possessed by its owner.[1] As the situated conception of power correctly recognizes, an agent's power over another agent is a result of the structure of a broad social network.

I would now like to emphasize the inherently dynamic nature of this view. In treating ongoing relationships as the primary locus of social power, the situated conception of power focuses on a dynamic temporal process by means of which power relationships are constituted in the social world. Although I will develop this feature of situated power relationships more fully later in this chapter, temporality is already implicit in a situated power relationship when aligned social agents orient their own acts around a *prior* action by the dominant agent. Because of this structure of social mediation, situated power relationships have an essentially temporal aspect that is not acknowledged by alternative conceptions of social power.

Conceptualizing power as the result of social agents' ongoing actions causes the temporal dimension of such actions to become a point of focus. One needs to ask such questions as the following "What is responsible for the 'ongoing' nature of such social relationships?" "What keeps social agents acting in the ways that they do?" "What accounts for the changes in their behavior?" Once temporality is introduced into the account of power, power relationships are conceptualized as inherently changing and changeable aspects of society.

An adequate conception of power, therefore, must have a means for acknowledging the dynamic nature of power as a social relationship. What this means, however, is that power relationships, if they are to continue to exist, must constantly be *reproduced* by the actions of social agents. Once power is recognized as having its basis in the manner in which social agents interact with one another, its reality is seen to lie in the ongoing nature of such interactions. Power, like all social relationships, is dynamic, not static. It can be a constant feature of the social world because it can constantly (re)produce itself. A dynamic theory of power must focus upon such processes of (re)production.[2]

Marx was the first social theorist to raise explicitly the question of dynamics within social theory. He does this by means of the concept of (re)production. This concept is used within Marx's theory of capitalism to describe the dynamic process by means of which capitalist social relations are able to continue to exist. One of Marx's achievements as a social theorist is to recognize the need to incorporate temporal processes within his social ontology.

Marx treats the question of how a social system maintains its own existence as one of the basic questions to be asked about it. In articulating a structural model of capitalist society, he seeks to answer this question for capitalism. Marx's fundamental insight about the nature of social systems is that they have both structural and dynamic aspects—indeed, that their dynamics is what makes their structure possible.

Questions concerning the (re)production of the capitalist mode of production are, for Marx, distinct from historical questions about its genesis. "(Re)production" is a concept that functions to highlight certain questions about the maintenance of the productive system that are independent of questions about its historical evolution from another mode of production. "(Re)production" is an aspect of the currently ongoing social relationships of production and not merely an historical or future-oriented aspect of a society. The temporality of the present of a social system includes an orientation to the future because that system can exist only by reproducing itself.

Marx's view of a society as an ongoing set of social relationships that need to reproduce themselves marks a watershed in social theory, one to which social theorists need to pay more attention. Anthony Giddens, for example, has attempted to convince other social theorists of its importance in the guise of the idea of the *duality of structure*.[3] By means of this idea, he seeks to get social theorists to acknowledge Marx's insight that the very actions that are the result of a social structure function so as to reproduce the structure that makes those actions possible in the first place.

I shall use the term *interactive nominalism*[4] to characterize Marx's view that social structures are nothing other than the ongoing actions of human social agents. While this may seem to be a truism, one that no social theorist would contest, it has important implications for the development of social theory itself. In particular, it entails that questions about the development and maintenance of a social system should be framed within the structural account of that system. But this means that social theory should consist of *dynamic* theories, theories that refrain from treating the structural aspect of a social system as something that can be adequately understood without incorporating a dynamic perspective.

One reason Marx's insight into the dynamic character of social processes has not received sufficient recognition is that he uses the concept of (re)production to conceptualize this aspect of social relations. Jürgen Habermas, for example, criticizes Marx's use of what he calls "the productive paradigm" in developing his critique of capitalist society.[5] In so doing, Habermas fails to see that Marx's use of the concept of (re)production does more than simply characterize the human being as a creature whose fundamental life activity is labor, a view that Habermas claims reduces all human activity to the attempt to control nature through means-end rationality. As I have just argued, Marx uses the concept of (re)production in order to establish his view of both the human being and human society as products of human actions whose very existence requires the ongoing activity of human agents.

In this respect, Marx's view of the human being and society resembles Aristotle's. In the *Nichomachean Ethics*, Aristotle introduces the idea of a virtue as a state of character that is achieved by the human being through repeated actions. Marx applies this basic ontological point to the entire social structure, by treating that structure as constituted by ongoing social relationships among human beings that are regularized in certain specific ways.

Marx's use of the concept of (re)production also seems to prejudge the question of how the dynamics of a social process will be resolved. As such, it does not seem to be an adequate concept to use as the basis of a "process" view of human society. After all, social systems develop in different ways. Sometimes they progress; at other times they atrophy. The concept of (re)production seems to imply a static temporal process whereby a society keeps pace with itself.

Such an understanding of the concept is misguided. Marx's use of it is tied to a particular problem, that of finding a way to critically describe the capitalist mode of production. In so far as "(re)production" is seen to conceptualize a fundamental aspect of how the capitalist mode of production seeks to keep itself in existence, it does not prejudge the question of how the capitalist system as a whole will fare. Marx has abstracted from such issues in order to understand the internal dynamics of the system. Indeed, he believes and goes on to argue that the system is inherently unstable in various ways.[6]

We need not concern ourselves with these aspects of his theory, however. I simply wish to point out that the concept of (re)production, although it grounds Marx's crucial insight into the dynamic nature of social systems, has problematic aspects. Taking "(re)production" as the fundamental category for thinking about the dynamic aspect of social reality is problematic because it may support the idea that social agents contribute to the dynamics of society only by *reproducing,* and never by *countering* the existing social relationships. The concept of (re)production may function as a way of reifying the temporal aspects of social relationships.

Therefore, in order to employ a conceptual framework that leaves open the possibility of alternative futures, I shall use the concept "dynamic" in order to conceptualize the temporal aspect of social systems. I shall therefore develop a *dynamic* conception of power—that is, a conception of power that explains how power as a social phenomenon exists as an ongoing but changing feature of society.

The idea that a dynamic theory of social power needs to develop, then, is that power, because it is the result of the ongoing actions of human beings interacting with one another and with their non-human environment, is always the result of human beings acting in particular ways. As such, it is not an "objective" feature of the social environment in the sense that human beings could not, by acting differently, alter it. In this sense, I shall claim that power is always contestable—that is, that power relationships are a site of constant and ongoing social contest.

One social theorist who has thematized the dynamic nature of social power is Michel Foucault. Foucault argues that power is not a static social presence. For example, he states:

> Where there is power, there is resistance, and yet, or rather consequently, this resistance is never in a position of exteriority to power. . . . Their [i.e., power relationships'] existence depends upon a multiplicity of points of resistance: these play the role of adversary, target, support, or handle in power relations. These points of resistance are everywhere in the power network.[7]

Although Foucault recognizes the dynamic aspect of power relationships by means of the concept of resistance, that concept is neither broad enough nor specific enough to provide an adequate basis for cognizing the dynamic nature of social power. The concepts that I develop in order to provide a dynamic account of social power will therefore depart in key respects from those that Foucault uses.

A dynamic account of power needs to recognize a number of different axes. In the last chapter, I already discussed one of these—the idea of subjection, the question of how a society can develop social agents into beings capable of holding positions within its structure. If the power relationships in a society are to transcend merely personal relationships, there must be a means for constituting human beings as occupants of social roles.

A dynamic theory of power also must focus upon the question of how the power relations that hold at a given moment in time can be maintained. Temporally speaking, the social present is brought into existence by a past and contributes toward the bringing about of a future. Thus, the "present" of social power relationships is one that contains the traces of the past and the seeds of the future. My ability to act today as I do is both the result of my acting as I did in the past and also contributes to my ability to act (differently, perhaps) in the future. This aspect of the temporality of human social action also needs to be captured within a dynamic conception of power.

Finally, there is the question of struggle—that is, the possibility that subordinate agents will seek to change the terrain of power that they face. This is the aspect of power that Foucault conceptualizes by means of his notion of resistance. It means that power relationships, as a result of the ongoing actions of human beings, must be constantly reconstituted, but that their reconstitution is never simply a matter of their simple reproduction. A dynamic theory of power needs to develop a means of talking about the contested reproduction of power relationships in society.

These then are the basic questions of social dynamics that an adequately dynamic view of power needs to provide means of answering. In the remainder of this chapter, I shall show how focusing on the dynamics of a situated power relationship results in developing a fuller understanding of the nature of those relationships.

Constraints on the Dominant Agent

I shall begin my presentation of a dynamic conception of power by looking at the position of the dominant agent. According to the situated conception of power, the power of the dominant agent is constituted by the presence of aligned social agents who use an aspect of his relationship to the subordinate agent as a criterion for the subordinate agent's access to certain items, access that they control. Because this conception proceeds in terms of a dominant and a subordinate agent, it might suggest that the dominant agent is empowered to act in regard to the subordinate agent in any manner in which he sees fit.

But although the dominant agent in a situated power relationship has power over the subordinate agent, this does not generally mean that he can exercise that power without any restraint. Rather, since a situated power relationship is itself constituted by the ongoing actions of the aligned social agents, in order to maintain his power the dominant agent in such a relationship must act in a way that does not disturb the ongoing patterns of actions that these agents engage in. The *present* actions of a dominant agent count on the *future* actions of the aligned agents being similar to their *past* actions. But this faith in a future whose path can be charted entails that the dominant agent not act in a way that challenges the allegiance of his aligned agents, for only through their actions can that future be made actual.

The ontological structure of a situated power relationship therefore entails a dynamic that results in the power of the dominant agent being exercised within a certain horizon.[8] Because his power is the result of the aligned agents' treating the subordinate agent in a certain manner, that power can be maintained only through the continued cooperation of the aligned agents. A dominant agent in a situated power relationship therefore needs to exercise his power in a manner that will not result in the failure of the aligned social agents to continue to empower him.

This feature of situated power relationships results in a number of different tendencies that restrict the power of the dominant agent. All of them depend on his need to keep the cooperation of the aligned social agents. In particular, there are two important limitations on the power of the dominant agent: the scope of issues over which he has control and the manner in which he exercises his power.

The scope of issues over which the dominant agent is able to make decisions is limited by the aligned agents. In general, aligned social agents empower him to make only certain sorts of decisions concerning a subordinate agent. The social alignment functions as a sort of transmitter, transmitting to the subordinate agent the effects of the dominant agent's decisions. In order for the alignment to do this, however, those decisions have to be seen as legitimate by the agents within the alignment at least to the extent that they will not simply refuse to continue acting as they are expected to. For if the aligned social agents fail to act in this manner, they will disempower the dominant agent. A police officer, for example, may refuse to enforce a law that she feels is ridiculous and unfair by simply turning her back when she sees the law being broken. This type of constraint on the dominant agent's exercise of his power exists within the alignment that constitutes the dominant agent's power in the first place and, as such, is a constraint on his power.

Although this feature of a power relationship can be thought of as a structural limitation on the power of the dominant agent, its existence is due to the dynamic aspect of power relationships. Because the dominant agent needs to maintain the cooperation of the aligned agents in order to maintain his power *in the future*, his decisions must be made in light of that need.

This limitation of the dominant agent's power is, however, itself not abso-lute: Like all aspects of social reality, it can become subject to conflict. A dominant agent can seek to enlarge the scope of decisions over which he has control. For example, a dictator who has seized control of his government may try to assume as much power as possible. He may decide, for example, to dissolve the legislative branch of government in order to enlarge the scope of his own power. Such an example shows that the scope of an agent's power is itself something that the dominant agent is able to enlarge; the crucial point to remember is that such an enlargement always contains within itself the possi-bility of backfiring in that it calls into question the ongoing allegiance of the aligned social agents.

I will therefore say that a dominant agent in a situated power relationship operates within a horizon of possibilities that is oriented toward the aligned social agents. While this horizon does not strictly limit what a dominant agent might be able to do, it does cause him to act in light of the importance that the aligned social agents play in constituting his power. This horizon functions as a limit on the ability of the dominant agent to do what he wishes without fear of negative consequences.

A second limitation on the dominant agent's power involves his treatment of the subordinate agent. Aligned social agents will only remain aligned with the actions of the dominant agent so long as he follows certain implicit rules of conduct. If he violates them, the aligned agents may no longer support his power by acting in the way that they have acted in the past.

A simple example of this process occurs when a group of gang members holds one gang member so that the leader can punish him for disobedience. If the leader exceeds the degree of violence that is tacitly acceptable to the gang members, they may challenge his actions, thus disrupting the normal structure of his empowerment. A more complex example involves the use of force by the police in apprehending a criminal. There are limits set on the amount of force that a police officer can use in doing this. When an officer exceeds these limits without a clear justification, then the use of force will jeopardize the arrest that she has made. In such a case, the legal system has institutionalized this feature of situated power relationships in such a way that the actual power of the police is limited by this requirement.

In order to see the implications of this idea, I would like to look at a more complex situation, namely that of non-violent political protest. Consider a case in which the non-violent protester uses her body to block the normal paths of access to some physical site—say a weapons manufacturing plant—that she sees as objectionable and to which she wishes to call public attention. By taking this action, she forces the police either to allow her to stage her blockade, thus disrupting the normal course of business, or to take some action to remove her physically. When the police use force in response to such protests, many social agents who normally allow the police to go about their business may become very upset and begin to put political pressure on their government to do something about how the demonstrator was treated as well as about the fundamental problem that her protest addressed. In such cases, the normal governmental alignment may be made to exert pressure on the police and on the owners of the objectionable site. The protester has, in this case, caused the aligned governmental agents to depart from their normal role because the police have used an excess of force, causing the general public to become engaged in the cause about which the protest was staged.

This example shows that, although a social alignment may empower a social agent in regard to another social agent, such empowerment always has tacit riders to the effect that the dominant agent must abide by certain standards of conduct. Although a dominant agent is always free to challenge the limits implicitly set on his conduct by the alignment, such challenges carry with them the possibility of alienating the aligned agents and thus undermining the power relationship.

By looking at the power of the dominant agent from a dynamic point of view, we have seen that his power is itself so constituted that it is a possible site of ongoing social struggle. The power that the dominant agent has is his only because of the cooperation of aligned social agents. They can try, in certain circumstances, to disalign themselves, just as he can try to broaden the range of issues over which they will align themselves with him. Power, as a dynamic social reality, can always be a field of social struggle, though not always simply between the dominant and the subordinate agents themselves. Aligned social agents may be the agents of social change, as the case of political protest that I just presented illustrates.

As a result of this feature, the situated view of power provides greater insight into the dynamics of social change than views such as the dyadic one. We have just seen that a power relationship may be altered as a result of actions undertaken by the agents ouside the central dyad. Agents who are peripheral to a given situated power relationship may, because of their own broader power relations with the aligned social agents, influence the alteration of the power in that relationship. In the case I just outlined, the general public's becoming involved in the police's treatment of a protester can result in the governmental alignment's changing its view about what the police can do and even about the issue over which the protest was staged. In such a case, the alteration of power is a result of agents' becoming interested in how a particular power relationship is exercised and thus moving into an aligned relationship with the protester. The situated conception of power, viewed in a dynamic manner, allows us to see social change as having a more mediated logic than views that focus only upon two social actors struggling against one another. Social change is a *social* process, one that needs to be understood in terms of the sort of dynamic model I have just outlined.

The power of the dominant agent in a situated power relationship, then, operates within a horizon based upon the need to maintain the allegiance of a social alignment. As a result, the dominant agent will normally act in such a way as to maximize her chances of keeping the cooperation of the aligned agents. In normal situations, this will result in a maintenance of the power relationship as it was; in revolutionary situations, however, the dominant agent can seek to enlarge the scope of her power or the subordinate agent can seek to alter the cooperative structure of a social alignment.

The Power of the Subordinate Agent

Having considered how the dynamic nature of social power affects the dominant agent's position, I shall now consider the parallel question with respect to the subordinate agent. What I wish to explore is how the acknowledgment of the dynamic nature of power results in an altered understanding of the subordinate agent's lack of power in a situated power relationship. This is an issue that I broached in discussing the horizon of concerns that limits the dominant agent's power by showing how a subordinate agent is able to alter the power which a dominant agent has over her.

A dynamic view results in a more fluid understanding of the nature of power: The subordinate agent is never absolutely disempowered, but only relatively so. She is disempowered with respect to a given dominant agent only as a result of the ongoing actions of the aligned social agents. But these ongoing actions are themselves subject to change for a variety of reasons. So just as the dominant agent's actions are subject to the problematic of maintaining power by maintaining the allegiance of the aligned agents, the subordinate agent is always in the position of being able to challenge the aligned agents' complicity in her disempowerment. The dynamic nature of power means that the dominated are always able to seek ways of challenging their domination.

Possessions of power by one agent are always potentially able to be *countered*. This means that there are ways in which subordinate agents can seek to achieve power over the dominant agent that would allow them to counter his power.

This point has often been glimpsed in an obscure manner by theorists of social power when they have claimed that the interesting question, from the point of view of the theory of power, is not whether an agent has power *simpliciter,* but whether that agent has power, *all things considered.*[9] For if the power that an agent has is counterbalanced by the power that another agent has, that agent will be in a very different situation than is suggested simply by saying that she has power. My claim is simply that such countering of the power of the dominant agent by the subordinate agent is always possible within a social power relationship.

In order to see this, consider the example of labor unions. Employers have power over their workers at least in part because employers form an alignment in regard to a worker at one employer's firm. A worker in a particular firm is a subordinate agent relative to his employer because there exists a set of aligned agents—namely other employers, the government, and so on—who treat that agent on the basis of his relationship to his employer. This set of aligned agents is one that I shall refer to as the employment alignment.

From this point of view, labor unions function to change this basic pattern of power by constructing a *countering alignment.* The presence of a labor union creates an alignment that is able to counter an employer's power over his employees by not allowing his decisions to impact upon a given employee without further consequences. A single employee, who without a union would simply be dependent upon an employer's decisions, now has power over his employer in so far as the members of the labor union are willing to use the relationship of the employee to the employer as a factor in how they will treat the employer. Since the employees in a union may decide to strike because a worker was treated unfairly, that worker has counter-power over his employer.

This countering alignment of the union fundamentally alters the constellation of power in the firm or industry because the employer is no longer able to affect the action-environment of a worker without having his own action-environment affected. For example, the fact that the union members may call a strike as a result of the employer's firing a given worker means that the employer is not simply a dominant agent in regard to his individual workers. Because the workers have organized into an alignment, they will be able to re-align the power situation in the workplace. The existence of a countering alignment gives a subordinate agent a degree of reciprocal power over the dominant agent.

But this means that an agent's power over another agent cannot simply be discerned by focusing on a single alignment; there may be a countering alignment that functions as a horizon within which the dominant agent is able to exercise her power. Countering alignments are a means through which the power of a dominant agent within a power relationship can be constrained. As such, they once again demonstrate the dynamic nature of social power relationships as social phenomena that are always at least potentially subject to change.

Alternative Alignments and Social Change

One aspect of the temporality of social relationships is that they need not remain the same over time; there is always a possibility of altering them. I shall now show how this fact entails the possibility of constructing *alternative social alignments* as a means by which subordinate social agents can change the power relationships within which they find themselves.

An alignment is an *alternative* to a given alignment for a social agent if and only if that alignment gives the agent an alternative means of access to the same items that she could have access to through the original alignment (or similar ones). The old-boy network is, in this sense, an alternative to the grading alignment. It allows certain agents to avoid the power of the dominant agent in the grading alignment by giving them an alternative means of access to jobs, an item that is available to social agents primarily through the grading alignment. Since an agent who has access to a job through such a means will not have to rely on the teacher's evaluation in the same way as agents who do not have such an option, the old-boy network fundamentally alters the power relationship between a student who has access to it and her teacher.

If one thinks about the classroom, it is clear that a variety of alternative alignments are present there. Aside from the old-boy network, there is also the fact that some students may have a special skill that will give them access to a job independently of how well they perform in the classroom. Athletes are an example of such a group. As anyone who has taught them knows, their ability to command well-paying and prestigious jobs in professional sports lets them stand in a fundamentally different relation to their teacher than do other students.[10]

These examples should make it clear that the existence of alternative alignments in a given social site results in a fundamental modification of the power of the dominant agent in that site. Because of the existence of an alternative alignment, an agent who might otherwise be subordinated to the power of the dominant agent is able to slip out of the net that the primary alignment seems to cast. An alternative alignment achieves this effect through an agent's action-environment. I argued earlier that an agent is able to exercise power over another agent by altering the latter's action-environment. This is precisely the role that an alignment plays in a situated power relationship: It empowers one agent by making another agent's action-environment dependent upon the dominant agent in some regard. An alternative alignment, on the other hand, seeks to give the subordinate agent a means of achieving her goals without the interference of the dominant alignment, thus restoring the action-environment to an equivalent of its original state. Alternative alignments function so as to undo the effects of the dominant alignment on an agent's action-environment.

Given this fact about alternative alignments, subordinate agents may actively seek to create such alignments as part of a strategy for altering the power situation that they face. In fact, the goals of many of the new social movements that have achieved such prominence in the last decades can best be understood in this light.[11] A primary goal of such movements has been the construction of social alignments that are alternative to those which have been seen as fundamentally oppressive.

For example, consider the variety of particular institutions and practices that can be classed together under the rubric of alternative medicine. I have in mind such things as the holistic health movement and alternative therapies. This movement has resulted in a fundamental realignment of a doctor's power over his patients. Prior to the existence of the alignment constituted by these institutions, an individual doctor had power over his patients because there were no other means of attaining access to certain expert skills that doctors have. Since the medical establishment, functioning as an alignment, attempted to make the patterns of medical care available to patients uniform in accordance with its own standards, patients could not turn to other practitioners in hopes of receiving alternative methods of treatment. Doctors were able to dictate the options that a patient had for receiving treatment.

The existence of alternative medical practices has meant that patients are no longer in a situation in which only one type of medical relationship and treatment is available to them. Since patients are able to choose among a variety of modes of treatment, individual doctors are placed in a situation in which they are more accountable to the desires of their individual patients. With the forging of an alternative alignment, the power inherent in the doctor-patient relationship has been fundamentally transformed despite the fact that there has been no alteration in the basic skills that doctors possess.[12]

This example shows that alternative alignments decrease the hierarchical structure of power that a given power relationship has. By providing a subordinate agent with a variety of alternative means of satisfying her desires, alternative alignments force the dominant agent who has an interest in continuing a power relationship to change the basic structure of his power.

There are many other examples of social movements that have sought to create alternative alignments as a means to achieve their ends. One such example concerns feminist presses. Many feminist writers and academics came to see that it was not possible for them to publish their work given the constitution of established presses. Pre-publication reviewers would examine their work and decide that it did not come up to the standards of traditional scholarship and/or writing. Indeed, this is not surprising, since these standards were part of what such feminist writers and scholars were challenging.

The point of interest to my argument is that such feminists found themselves face to face with a social alignment: The editors and reviewers were part of a social structure that restricted the feminists' access to the printed word. One strategy that was used to counter this alignment was the establishment of feminist presses—that is, presses that were run by feminists and committed to publishing the work that feminist writers could not get published elsewhere. Their establishment created an alternative alignment. The traditional publishing alignment, rather than being able to make feminists conform to traditional canons of writing, found itself outflanked as the feminist publishing alignment gave feminist writers the well-deserved opportunity to have their writing published.

The traditional presses did not remain untouched by this development: In order to keep from being perceived as oppressive by the majority, they had to make a move to incorporate the sort of writing they had been instrumental in excluding. In other words, the creation of the alternative alignment and the ensuing period of competition also resulted in a change in the character of the dominant alignment. Traditional publishing houses, faced with the rising popularity of alternative feminist presses, attempted to incorporate feminist works into their own offerings so as not to lose their market dominance.

For many other social movements, alternative alignments are part of the strategy for challenging the power of a dominant alignment and achieving their own goals. The alternative energy movement, the health food movement, and many others have achieved some success in altering the alignment structures they have challenged; other movements have not.

These examples point to the usefulness of the dynamic conception of power as a means for understanding the strategies and goals of new social movements. These movements have sought to alter the power relationships within which social agents find themselves as a means toward giving these agents a greater degree of control over their lives. Using the dynamic conception of power allows us to see that these movements have attempted to achieve their goals in large part through the creation of alternative alignments, social stuctures that both in themselves and through their effects alter the basic power of dominant alignments.

If alternative alignments, countering alignments, and the possibility that an agent may decide to forego the items available to her through various power relations are included in the broad social context of a situated power relationship, it becomes clear that social power, despite its ubiquitous presence in the social world, is by no means a monolithic structure. There is room for individuals to maneuver within the constraints imposed upon them by power relationships. By relying on given structures of alignments to counter the power of a dominant agent within a central alignment, and also by forging new alignments, social agents are able to achieve a greater degree of control over their lives, to receive the items they desire through channels alternative to those present in the central alignment, and to achieve a degree of independence from the power constituted by such an alignment.

The Power of a Teacher Reconsidered

I introduced the situated conception of power with a discussion of the power that a teacher has over her students in virtue of the fact that she grades them. At that time, I mentioned that this account abstracted from many other aspects of the relationship between a student and a teacher. Having discussed certain of these aspects, I would like to amplify my description in light of the dynamic conception of social power.

I shall argue that the teacher's power over her students, which she has in virtue of the fact of grading and the grading alignment, is itself situated in a field of hierarchical practices that constitutes a constraint on the teacher's ability to use her personal discretion to grade the student. So, although the teacher is the agent in whom power is localized through her act of grading, she also functions as a social delegate and not simply as a free agent. She is constrained by the alignment, just as she is empowered by it.

This becomes apparent once the practice of grading is seen to be situated in the larger context of an educational institution. Two sets of demands are made on such institutions. The first is from the institution's clients, or, as I shall assume in this case, the parents of the clients. They pay the institution's fees, and in return they expect that their children will receive an education that will enable them to gain entrance into certain sorts of careers. That is, they expect that, as a result of the teaching that their children receive (assuming that they do well), their children will have preferential access to certain sorts of job possibilities. For example, the average father or mother who sends a daughter to an expensive private college or university expects that this will result in the daughter's having access to the better-paying or higher-status jobs in society. If a collegiate institution is unable to provide this service, it will no longer find clients.[13] From a social perspective, this is a central service provided by the institution.

Thus, a collegiate institution is faced with a demand that is constitutive of its providing its students with an education: that the diploma amount to an entrance ticket into specific sorts of job or educational opportunities for its clients. But the very same institutions that function as the grading alignment are the institutions that a college's students need to have access to. Indeed, this "circularity" is constitutive of the power that is distributed within this alignment.

The question that faces a college or university is how to satisfy this demand. In order to ensure the viability of such an alignment, the college must, among other things, be able to assure these aligned institutions that the grade point average of a student is a reasonably reliable criterion to use in deciding whether a student will be the sort of person those institutions desire to admit. It must be able to assure those institutions that its "products" can be judged by criteria that are used to judge the products of other, similar institutions.[14]

This means that a very specific sort of demand is made upon grading policies. Although this demand does not fully determine the specific manner in which a given teacher grades, it does constrain the institution to provide grades that will have the social meaning that they are assumed to have. If an institution fails to do this, it will be failing to meet the demands of its clients and will wind up not being able to provide the service for which it is being paid. In the long run, this will cause a crisis in the institution.

So a teacher, although in one sense having the power to grade students, in another sense must exercise that power in accordance with principles dictated by the nature of the social institution of which he is a part. Although he may be able, in specific instances, to depart from the institution's criteria, his grading policy is not fully under his own control. The institution itself has an interest in controlling the grading policies of its members. Through its administrative officers or senior members, it scrutinizes the grading practices of its teachers in order to ensure that the institution is providing its clients with the sort of product that it claims to be providing.

A consideration of the larger social context within which an educational institution is located shows that the context places constraints on the way in which power can be exercised. The use of the grade by the aligned social sites, as I have noted, both empowers and constrains the dominant agent. The college may choose to use a teacher's grading policy as a factor in deciding whether to continue his employment. In such cases, the single practice of grading comes to function in two intersecting practices within the overall alignment: The teacher stands in a position of power in regard to her students in virtue of grading, but she is also in the position of a subordinate agent in regard to her employment and hence must submit to the power of others.

This discussion shows why it is important to supplement the situated conception of power with a dynamic one. My initial discussion gave the impression that, since the dominant agent in a situated power relationship determined who had and had not met the criteria for success, he had power over the subordinate agent in the relationship. This picture of the power relationship does, in fact, represent the way in which power normally presents itself to someone in such a situation—as concentrated in the hands of a single agent who makes the decision as to whether (or how well) the person has met the criteria of the institution. Once power is seen as a dynamic feature of social relations, however, it becomes apparent that this picture ignores the dominant agent's own position within a complex social network and the way in which it constrains her ability to use her power according to her own lights. In a sense, then, the dominant agent acts as a sort of "designated agent" for the alignment in general.

Of course, there will be disagreement about what policy an individual agent ought to adopt in order to fulfill the needs of the institution. There is scope for individual initiative in deciding on an appropriate policy. However, the individual policy decisions of agents who have social power are all made within the horizon provided by these general considerations. They must use that power in a manner that is deemed acceptable by the agents within the aligned social institutions in order for the alignment to continue to function as it does.[15]

In the previous section of this chapter, I argued that a teacher's power is also limited by alternative alignments present in the classroom. The old-boy network, inherited wealth, and the possibility of acquiring a job through the possession of a specialized skill are all factors that can be conceptualized as alignments alternative to the grading alignment. But there is another factor that affects the power of a teacher: the presence of a countering alignment based on the fact that a student's evaluation may be used as a factor in determining the future employment of her teacher. If the teacher is aware of this fact, his power to grade the student will, to a certain extent, be determined by the *reciprocal power* that the student possesses over him in virtue of the presence of the countering alignment. Since a single teacher's power over a student through grading is usually not, in American education, very great, the fact that a single student's evaluation of the teacher will not by itself have much effect does not undermine the theoretical importance of her power. An agent's power over another agent has to be seen in the context of other aspects of the relationship between the two agents that result in a reassessment of the extent of the one agent's dominance over the other.

When all of these factors are taken account of, it becomes apparent that a teacher's power over her students is much more limited than my discussion in the previous chapter suggested. By viewing that relationship with the conceptual tools provided by the dynamic conception of power, I have been able to show that a teacher's exercise of power over her students exists with a limiting horizon. Even a power relationship that is as obvious as this one appears to be turns out to have a much more complex structure than I earlier acknowledged. The actual nature of the social power relationship between a teacher and her students can only be understood when the complex dynamics of power relationships is used as a guide.[16]

Conclusion

In this chapter, I have introduced the idea of a dynamic conception of power. According to this idea, power, like any social phenomenon, must be conceptualized dynamically—that is, as something that is always being (re)produced by the very actions in which it is being exercised. More specifically, I have shown that the situated conception of power has an inherently dynamic component that allows us to have a more fluid view of power relationships than we previously had. Because the power that inheres in the power dyad is (re)produced by the actions of the aligned social agents, there is always the possibility that the social field that they constitute will change, resulting in a fundamental alteration of the power dyad itself. On such a view, a picture emerges in which society is the site of continual struggles over power. The dynamic conception of power thus represents a crucial corrective to the static and objectivizing accounts of social power that have been influential within social theory.

9

Transformative Power

ONE OF the aims of this study has been to show the importance of the concept of domination for a theory of social power. I have consistently maintained, nonetheless, that the concept of power-over should not be identified with that of domination and have criticized such theorists as Hannah Arendt and Nancy Hartsock for denying this. There are uses of power-over that do not amount to the domination of the subordinate agent by the dominant one.[1] These uses of power-over can be designated as "positive" in that they serve to benefit the agent over whom they are exercised.

The one positive form of power which I have so far discussed in this study is paternalism. A relationship of power-over between two agents is paternalistic when the dominant agent uses his power to benefit an agent who is not fully capable of rational determination of his actions. Parenting is often cited as one example of a power relationship that is paternalistic. Parents make judgments about what is best for their children and use their power over their children to enforce these decisions. Such a use of power-over is paternalistic in that the children are assumed to be incapable of fully determining what is best for themselves. The parents' actions are legitimated as allowing their child to pursue activities that will benefit her despite her denial that this is the case. Because the child is deemed incapable of accurately judging her own long-range interests, the parents, believing themselves more capable of doing so, use their power in order to benefit her.

There are many other sorts of relationships that are paternalistic in structure, including treatment of the retarded and those with severe psychological disturbances. In each case, the paternalistic use of power-over is legitimated as based upon the subordinate agent's inability to judge his own interests rationally. Although the paternalistic use of power-over has many serious problems associated with it,[2] it is, nonetheless, one use of power-over that is not *ipso facto* dominating.

In this chapter, I shall discuss another positive use of power-over. The *transformative* use of power differs from paternalism in certain fundamental ways. In a transformative use of power, a dominant agent also exercises power over a subordinate agent for the latter's benefit. In doing so, however, the dominant agent's aim is not simply to act for the benefit of the subordinate agent; rather, the dominant agent attempts to exercise his power in such a way that the subordinate agent learns certain skills that undercut the power differential between her and the dominant agent. The transformative use of power is a use of power that seeks to bring about its own obsolescence by means of the empowerment of the subordinate agent.

Social theorists have not always given explicit recognition to the transformative use of power. Although mainstream social theorists have often discussed phenomena associated with it, recent feminist social theorists were the first to conceive of these phenomena as involving a specific use of power. These theorists, whom I shall call "feminist theorists of power", have argued that an adequate conception of power must recognize power's two "faces", whereas most social theorists have given explicit recognition only to the first face of power, that of domination. The feminist theorists of power claim that the second face, the transformative use of power, has been neglected by social theorists, including previous feminist theorists.

Although the feminist theorists of power have distinguished these two faces of power in an attempt to counter the view of motherhood that was articulated by earlier feminst theorists, the distinction between a dominating and a transformative use of power is one that has general significance for social theory. Specifically, recognition of the transformative use of power provides the means for a fundamental break with theories of power that see power-over as only a negative force in social relations. The concept of a transformative use of power provides a means of conceptualizing a positive use of power that shows power's importance as a constitutive force in human social relations.

But while the discussion within recent feminist theory of this notion highlights an important aspect of power that has not been adequately treated by earlier feminist and social theorists, I shall argue that its use by feminist theorists has certain crucial weaknesses. Because of their reliance on the practice of mothering as the "location" of the transformative use of power, such theorists have neglected the presence of this use of power in other social practices, while also tending to idealize the mothering practice itself. Once it is freed from the objectionable assumptions with which it has been connected within feminist theory, the notion of the transformative use of power will occupy an important place in an account of the nature of social power.

Mothering and Male Domination

One of the primary tasks of feminist theory is uncovering and thematizing the nature and extent of male domination within contemporary society. Indeed, such a task seems nearly coextensive with the idea of feminist theory itself. After all, a feminist must have some conception of the objectionable structures that she aims at eradicating; the concept of male domination seems to indicate the nature of those structures.

Feminists have taken various tacks in exposing and theorizing about the nature of male domination. In an encyclopaedic work, Alison Jaggar has presented three forms of feminism: liberal feminism, radical feminism, and socialist feminism.[3] While each of these forms of feminist theory has male domination as the object of its analysis, each provides a fundamentally different account of such domination and its relation to other forms of social domination. In addition, feminist women of color have contributed another voice to this discussion by showing the need for feminist theory to acknowledge the oppression of women of other races and ethnicities.[4]

It is tempting to think of the task of analyzing male domination as one that was accomplished by the "first wave" of feminist theorizing. To do so, however, is a mistake. The ways in which male dominance is achieved are complex and subtle, with the result that an adequate theory of such domination is still being developed. Feminist theorists continue to do important work on this topic. For example, in a series of essays,[5] Marilyn Frye has provided new insight into the workings of male domination. She argues that the type of power that males possess needs to be conceived of in ways that feminists have not previously done. Similarly, other feminist theorists have attempted to understand the relation between male domination and other forms of domination in society.[6] The ongoing nature of the work they have undertaken reveals the scope of the twin tasks of uncovering male domination and formulating an adequate theory of its workings.

In the course of developing a critique of male domination, feminist theorists focus upon the social practice of mothering. Their aim in so doing is to show that consigning women to the tasks of mothering plays a crucial role in the constitution of male-dominated society. As one feminist puts it:

First-wave feminists as varied as Kate Millet, Betty Friedan, Juliet Mitchell, and Shulamith Firestone all shared at least one common task:

to desanctify the family and demystify motherhood. . . . Far from being
an idyllic haven in a heartless world, the family appeared to . . . subordinate and oppress women on a daily basis.[7]

Such feminist theorists argue that women have been generally relegated to the
family and the practice of mothering within male-dominated society. As a
result of their assignment to the task of mothering the young, such theorists
argue, women have been kept from positions of power within society. In order
to combat this sexist practice, women are to reject their role as mothers and to
seek a place within more powerful social locations.

For the sake of convenience, I shall call theorists who adopt some form of
this position "feminist theorists of domination". For them, the role of mother
is one that reflects the second-class status of women within male-dominated
society, and one to which women have been directed by male-dominated
society. They tend to see mothering itself as by and large a negative social
practice and, located as it is within the nuclear family, a specific site of the
social oppression of women, one in which women are complicit in their own
domination.

Reevaluating Mothering

The feminist theorists of power are reacting to the negative valuation of
mothering put forward by the theorists of domination.[8] Although the feminist
theorists of power accept many of the points that the theorists of domination
have made about the need to think critically about women's role as mothers
within male-dominated society, they argue that it is a mistake to see mothering
in exclusively negative terms. For the feminist theorists of power, mothering
is also a social practice that women have shaped for themselves and that em-
bodies some of the values that women are striving to realize within society as
a whole through the abolition of male dominance. They argue that the view of
the theorists of domination is one-sided, concealing the positive aspects of the
practice of mothering.

The feminist theorists of power argue that the position of women as child-
rearers within male-dominated society is one through which women attain
power, albeit of a different type from that recognized by theories of male
domination. In their writings, they reject the idea that power is simply a
means that human beings employ for the domination of other human beings.
Instead, they posit a use of power that is linked to a positive capacity that
human beings have. These theorists claim that women, in virtue of the fact

that they are the primary caretakers of human beings, possess a special type of power that I, following their lead, entitle the *transformative use of power.*

The claim that women in a male-dominated society nonetheless have power has sometimes been expressed by feminist theorists of power by using the distinction between power-to and power-over. Recall that power-to specifies an ability that a person has, as when a person is said to have the power to accomplish a certain task. An artist, for example, can be spoken of as someone having creative power. By way of contrast, the concept of power-over is taken by such theorists to entail the domination of one human being over another.

Some feminist theorists of power have used the power-to/power-over dichotomy to criticize feminist theorists of domination for neglecting the Janus-faced nature of power in their claims that the position of women in male-dominated societies is one of powerlessness. These theorists of power characterize their own theoretical stance as one that recognizes both faces of power. They then argue that feminist theory needs to recognize the fact that women, even in male-dominated societies, have power-to—that is, are in a social position that relies upon many female capacities that need to be valorized. In other words, they claim that, although women are not socially dominant—they lack power-over—they do have special skills and abilities that have been ignored or devalued by traditional valuations but that enable them to act in important and valuable ways—they have power-to. These feminist theorists think of their project as that of uncovering and valorizing these powers-to in the practices that women have traditionally performed, in opposition to the feminist theorists of domination who see such practices as a source of female oppression.

This manner of presenting their claims has serious problems. Using the distinction between power-to and power-over does not make the point about power and its use within the practice of mothering that the feminist theorists of power wish to make. The type of power that they have isolated and theorized about is not one that is reducible to a particular set of capacities that women possess and to which other feminist theorists have been blind, although that is indeed part of the story. While it is important for women to create a positive valuation of their own abilities, one that denies the adequacy of negative valuations of mothering made from a male perspective, important issues are obscured by this use of the power-to/power-over dichotomy. The use of power that is being described in these accounts is one that involves the *power* that women have *over* other social agents; however, it is a use of power-over for a purpose other than that of social *domination.* This is the crucial distinction that I believe the feminist theorists of power are attempting to articulate, although their own employment of the power-to/power-over dichotomy distorts the nature of their claims.

There are two reasons why feminist theorists of power may be reluctant to use the concept of power-over to describe the position of women in male-dominated society. First, it seems contradictory to describe the position of women in male-dominated society as one in which they both lack and have power-over. To argue that women really do have power-over, even in a male-dominated society, would seem to undercut the important insights of feminist theorists of domination concerning women's lack of power in such societies.

Seeing the issue in these terms is, however, a mistake. Since attributions of power to an agent are always made in reference to a specific audience and predicate only a particular type of power of that agent, as the field theory of power has shown, it makes sense to say that women lack one type of power-over but possess another one, or that they lack power-over in regard to certain agents but possess it in regard to others. Once an objectified understanding of power is overcome, the seemingly contradictory claim that women both have and lack power-over in male-dominated society can be be seen to contain an important insight into the nature of the roles that women have occupied in such societies.

The power theorists may, in addition, be hesitant to use the concept of power-over to designate the power of women because of an identification of power-over with domination. I have pointed out that both Arendt and Hartsock make such an identification. Since feminist theorists conceive of the feminist project as entailing the transcendence of domination, the identification of power-over with domination makes it incoherent to attribute some form of domination to women.

As I have argued, it is a mistake to see all power-over as a form of domination. In fact, the central point that the feminist theorists of power are making is that power over another human being can be used for the benefit of that person rather than to dominate her. Once one accepts the claim that power over another human being is not necessarily a form of domination, there is no reason to deny the fact that the social positions that women have often occupied in male-dominated society involve their having power over other human beings. Rather than being used to dominate another human being, such power is being used to help another person reach a more autonomous stance, and it is constituted by such a goal.

With this observation in mind, let us see how the idea of a transformative use of power has been developed within the writings of recent feminist theorists. Jean Baker Miller was the first theorist to present such a use of power.

Beginning with a conception of power as "the capacity to produce change", she argues that there is a specific form of power that has been characteristic of women's lives.

> One instance [of women's effectiveness] is in women's traditional role, where they have used their powers to foster the growth of others— certainly children, but also many other people. This might be called using one's power to empower another—increasing the other's resources, capabilities, effectiveness, and ability to act.[10]

Miller's claim is that women have a different model of power than men, one in which one person's possession of power does not exist through the diminishing of someone else's.[11] Under this feminist conception of power, one seeks to empower another, be it one's child, a friend, or a lover. Miller explicitly links this sense of power to the idea of capacity or power-to, although she also claims that this power-to is inherently relational, a claim that contradicts its definition as simply an ability.

Miller's own terminology thus tends to obscure the important point that she is making about women's use of power. She claims that women have traditionally engaged in social practices whose aim has been the empowerment of other human beings rather than their domination. That is, Miller highlights women's engagement in social practices whose aim has been the constitution of human beings as social agents capable of autonomous action. According to Miller, women have had a fundamentally different mode of relating to other human beings than have men. Whereas men have used their power over others in order to dominate them and thus to enhance their own welfare, in their predominant social roles women have used their relation to others as a means of benefiting those others.

This is an important idea with many significant consequences. For example, consider the Hobbesian idea taken up by Hegel that one human being necessarily initially encounters another human being as a threat to its own existence.[12] Miller's claim allows us to see as specifically male this view of the encounter with another human being. Miller's view implies that such a conception of human social relations is male, for women do not see others as primarily a threat to their own existence. For women, relationship to others provides an opportunity to empower or transform the other—that is, an opportunity for a person to use her own abilities in order to enhance the capabilities of another human being. While this relationship may involve a type of power-over, it is one in which such power is used to enhance rather than demean the life of another human being.

Nancy Hartsock gives a more extensive description of a sense of power linked to women and their roles in male-dominated society. Her argument is that women generally have a different experience of power than do men, and this gives them a different standpoint from which to understand the nature of power.

> The female experiences not simply of mothering (but more broadly the general education of girls for mothering, and the experience of being mothered by a person of one's own gender) is one in which power over another is gradually transformed by both the powerholder and the being over whom power is exercised into autonomy and (ideally) mutual respect. The power of the mother over the child, and the sensual and erotic relation with the child, issue (in healthy relations) in the creation of an independent and autonomous being. Thus, the point of having power over another is to liberate the other rather than dominate or even kill her [as is the case, she claims, in male views of power].[13]

Hartsock's claim—that women have a different sense of power from men—is similar to that made by Miller. Relying on Nancy Chodorow's idea that the gender of the primary caretaker has central importance for the development of young children,[14] Hartsock argues that women experience power centrally through their role as nurturers, and that for them it is centered on helping rather than harming the person over whom it is exercised. As in Miller's account, Hartsock focuses upon a use of power that is linked to a project of making the other an independent being, rather than subjecting him or her to one's will. Hartsock's account of women's use of this type of power is more limited than Miller's: She restricts it to the context of mothering relations rather than nurturing relations generally. Unlike Baker, however, Hartsock does not theorize this relationship by means of the concept of power-to; indeed, she explicitly claims that such relationships begin as hierarchical ones, but change their form as the subordinate agent in the relationship develops into a more autonomous being.

Hartsock's account confirms my criticism of the attempt to conceptualize women's power in terms of the power-over/power-to dichotomy. As Hartsock points out, caretaking relationships involve exercising power over those who are taken care of, but such care attempts to create a being for whom such care is no longer needed. It is therefore insufficient to use the power-over/power-to dichotomy to distinguish this use of power from domination. The transformative use of power is characteristic of a social relationship that involves a complex mixing of power-over and power-to.

The final feminist theorist whom I shall cite to show the emergence within feminist theory of the concept of transformative power is Eléanor H. Kuykendall. In her commentary on Luce Irigaray's "And the One Doesn't Stir without the Other", Kuykendall argues that Irigaray posits the existence of a transformative use of power.

> Two principles, at least, are necessary to the development of a feminist ethic of nurturance. The first is that *power* exercised by the nurturer toward the nurtured (as by mother toward child) be not merely *dominant* or controlling, but primarily healing, creative, and *transformative*. The second principle, which complements the first, is that the relationship between the nurturer and the nurtured be not merely symmetrical, but at least potentially mutual and *reciprocal*.[15]

Kuykendall sees Irigaray as making two claims about the nature of the power relationship that exists between a mother and her child.[16] The first is that the mother seeks to benefit the child rather than to control her. This sort of conception of a transformative power relationship has been developed by other feminist theorists. The second point, however, is one that has not been articulated as clearly by other theorists, although Hartsock mentions it: The power relationship between the two must constitute itself as self-transcending—that is, as bringing about a situation in which it will no longer be necessary. The mother, to be a truly nurturant mother and thus to exercise power in a transformative way, must seek to develop her child into a full-fledged person, the sort of individual for whom such a one-directional power relationship is no longer appropriate. Transformative power seeks to transform the child into an adult and thus to bring itself into obsolescence. Once the relationship has been successfully implemented and used, it will gradually bring about its own dissolution into a more egalitarian relationship between the two agents.

Irigaray's characterization of transformative power is central to understanding its nature. Her claim shows that the transformative use of power has a very different basis from male-validated forms of power, for it does not adopt the strategy of enlargement as a means of keeping itself in place;[17] indeed, it seeks to eliminate the necessity for its own existence. The task of such power will be fulfilled when the grounds for its existence are no longer there.

The idea that transformative power relationships envision their own supersession is a unique contribution to the theory of power. The self-transcending nature of a transformative use of power clearly marks it off from other uses of power. To see this, consider the difference between a transformative use of power and a normal case of influence. Although both are exercised in order to make another agent accept what one wants her to accept, the transformative use of power does so for a different purpose and in a different manner. Often, an agent who exercises influence over another agent seeks to keep his influence over that other intact, ready to be used in other contexts. But this is just what transformative power seeks to avoid: It seeks to impose itself upon another in order that such interventions in the life of the other may become no longer necessary.

In developing their conception of power, feminist theorists of power have valorized forms of social practice that have been both traditionally relegated to women within male-dominated society and treated by that society as lacking importance and value.[18] They have shown that there is an important source of value hidden beneath the traditional valuation of women's activities, one that can be used both to strengthen women's self-valuation and to transform the nature of male social domains. The idea is not simply to point out the hypocritical nature of the traditional valuation—which demanded of women a certain mode of being and then denigrated them for exhibiting it—but to show that there are positive aspects of power embodied in women's roles as nurturers.

In looking at mothering, these theorists have stressed important aspects of that social role. At first, the child is a helpless creature who must receive care in order to remain alive. The relation between a mother and her child involves power because of this brute fact, feminists claim: Mothers have to use power because of the helplessness of their infants at birth.

There is more to the mother-child relation than this, however, for in the course of taking care of a child, the goal of the care changes from simply keeping the child alive to enabling the child to achieve independence. Mothers need to use power over their children because only through the use of power can a child be created as a truly social creature. Children have to be formed into adults through the decisions and commands of their parents. In such basic tasks as toilet training, parents use power over their children to get them to conform to certain social standards. But such use of power is not merely the disciplining of the child for the sake of acceptability, as might be thought when power-over is seen solely as a means of domination. Since the child emerges as an independent creature by means of such discipline, this use of power-over has a positive function in terms of the individual's life. In the transformative use of power, the goals of social acceptability and individual autonomy work hand in hand to creat a socially viable and individually mature human being.

We are now in a position to see how the transformative use of power differs from paternalism, another "positive" form of power. One of the primary characteristics of the transformative use of power is that it seeks its own elimination. One of the problematic features of paternalism is that it has a tendency to keep the subordinate agent in a state of dependency on the dominant, paternalistic agent. Because the dominant agent takes over many aspects of the subordinate agent's life, there is a tendency for such agents to fail to develop in ways that they might in the absence of paternalism.

A primary difference between paternalism and transformative power, then, is that whereas paternalistic relations have an inherent drive for stability, transformative ones are inherently dynamic. They view the subordinate agent as a developing creature whose course of development can be enhanced by the very relationship to the dominant agent.

Transformative Power and Social Theory

I shall now show that the idea of a transformative use of power has broader significance than is clear from the context within which it was developed. In particular, the idea of a transformative use of power refers to an aspect of power that has not received adequate recognition within social theory in general.

As I have argued, the feminist theorists of power are critical of a conception of power that sees it as inherently a form of domination. They believe that such a view—which was as characteristic of earlier forms of feminist theory as it was in certain branches of mainstream social theory—encourages the idea that the exercise of power is inherently suspect, thereby causing people to try to avoid using power in their relations with others. While this idea may have some validity so long as power is conceptualized on the model of simple domination of others, it is a mistake to abrogate all practices in which power is involved because of a theoretical commitment to the avoidance of domineering and manipulative relationships with others. Indeed, attempts to avoid exercising power may themselves be self-defeating and harmful. Attention to traditional maternal practices has allowed these theorists to see that power can be a positive force in interpersonal relationships.

The standpoint of the feminist theorists of power therefore provides a means of criticizing those social theorists who conceive of power in purely negative terms. Consider, for example, the work of Michel Foucault.[19] Although Foucault's rich studies of the rise of new "regimes of power" in the modern world provide many new and challenging insights into the nature of power, there is one respect in which his account remains within the perspective challenged by the feminist theorists of power. Foucault presents power as a negative social presence whose reach into the depths of our own being can be only partially resisted. He rejects a view of power as repressive and presents his own view as one that attributes to power a constitutive role in the shaping of human beings. Such a view of power demonstrates, according to Foucault, that the reach of power is deeper than theorists have previously recognized, for power actually shapes the human being in accord with its own autonomous designs.

We are meant to get a disturbing message from Foucault's portrait of power. We are supposed to see ourselves as victims of immense strategies of power through which we are constituted as the sorts of beings that we are, but which we cannot step outside of and control. The ability of power to constitute us is meant to startle us, to make us see ourselves as controlled by forces alien to us.

Reflection upon the work of the feminist theorists of power places such claims in a very different light. Their work allows us to see that not all uses of power have a negative and alienating effect upon the creature over whom power is used; indeed, it allows us to see that power is a necessary and positive feature of social relations that allows human beings to attain a degree of sovereignty and control over their lives. One need only think of a child who is not given any maternal attention in order to receive a different image of how power, when used in a caring and loving manner, can serve to develop rather than restrict a creature's growth. By articulating the distinction between a dominating and a transformative use of power, feminist theorists of power allow us to see Foucault's discussions of the growth of power in modernity as dependent upon an inadequate conception of power itself.[20]

Aside from being a critical weapon, the concept of the transformative use of power can also function in an important way within a feminist theory of social transformation. In this regard, it is important to remember that feminist theory is a practical theory in the sense that it is constituted by a practical commitment to the elimination of male domination. As such, one of its goals is the articulation of an adequate theory of the social transformation whereby male domination can be eliminated.

The concept of the transformative use of power provides feminists with a model for the social relations they should have with one another within the various organizations that constitute the women's movement. By stressing the importance of the transformative use of power within such organizations, feminists are able to articulate a model of how to interact with one another even in situations of confrontation. Because the "other" within a relation of transformative power must be seen as a human being whose own independence must be fostered, this concept gives feminists a way of thinking about hierarchical social relations that goes beyond their assimilation to forms of domination. As a result, feminists have often attempted to structure their own political practices in such a way as to embody nurturant practices within them.

This discussion shows that the concept of a transformative use of power has general implications for social theory once it is seen to be more than simply a new way of understanding the nature of maternal practice. The idea of a transformative use of power posits a form of social hierarchy through which dependent beings can be treated in a manner that allows them to achieve independence.

Criticisms of the Feminist Theorists of Power

I shall now consider in more detail the actual claims of the feminist theorists of power concerning the transformative use of power. I shall argue that, despite its general usefulness, the view of transformative power put forward by these theorists suffers from a number of central flaws that need to be eradicated before that notion can come to occupy its appropriate place within a general theory of social power.

I shall begin by making one clarification in the concept of transformative power itself. It is not always clear from the writings of the theorists of power whether they intend "transformative power" to refer to a distinctive type of power or a specific use of it. It is important to realize that transformative power does not constitute a distinctive type of power, different from those which I have so far distinguished; rather, transformative power is a specific use of those types of power, one constituted by the desire to empower the agent over whom it is exercised. Because of its distinctive aim, transformative power has different characteristics from power used to dominate other social agents. Nonetheless, it is a use of power that employs such types of power as influence, force, and coercive power. The distinction between transformative and dominating uses of power is made at a different level from the distinctions among the various types of power mentioned in Chapter 5.

This is not to say, however, that any particular exercise of power can be used in a transformative manner. A transformative use of power, although it involves exercising power over a social agent, seeks to empower that agent by developing that agent's capabilities more fully. There are certainly types of power that contradict this goal and that cannot therefore be used transformatively. For example, when a dominant agent influences another agent by convincing her that she is not smart enough to form an independent opinion about something, such an exercise of power contradicts the fundamental goal of a transformative use of power. By diminishing an agent's sense of what she can rightly expect of herself, one can exercise power over her; such a use of power cannot, however, function transformatively. So, although transformative power requires more specific mechanisms for its use, not any mechanism for exercising power can be used in a transformative manner.

I shall now turn to the problematic aspects of the account of transformative power found in the writings of the feminist theorists of power. As I have argued, the feminist theorists of power have, for the most part, achieved their insights into the transformative use of power by focusing upon women's role as mothers. But while this focus is both the source of and the inspiration behind their analysis, it is also one of its weaknesses.

There are really two related weaknesses of the feminist theories of power, both of which stem from the manner in which they conceptualize women as mothers. First, they idealize the role of the mother in mothering relations and fail to see the possibility of domination within such a social practice. Second, they tend to privilege mothering as the only practice in which nurturance takes place. Both of these problems result from an overemphasis on mothering as a social practice that is the distinctive province of women. This one-sided emphasis must be corrected if the claims concerning the transformative use of power are to be given their rightful place within social theory.

Looking at the work of Sara Ruddick will allow me to show that the feminist theorists of power idealize the mothering relationship. Ruddick is a theorist who also accords women a special role in society, but she does not use the concept of power to describe that role. As I shall argue, however, Ruddick presents a more complex picture of maternal practice whose insights need to be incorporated into the view of transformative power articulated by the feminist theorists of power.

Ruddick takes a somewhat different tack in attempting to valorize certain aspects of the work that women have traditionally done and the skills they have thereby developed. Rather than using a discourse of power, Ruddick attributes to mothers a distinctive approach to the world: "My point is that out of maternal practices distinctive ways of conceptualizing, ordering, and valuing arise." [21] Ruddick claims that the specific tasks that women have been called upon to perform in male-dominated societies have resulted in a specifically *maternal mode of being*. She develops the structure of this mode of being by claiming that "maternal practice is governed by (at least) three interests in satisfying these demands for preservation, growth, and acceptability [of children]." [22] She sees women as operating under three imperatives that specify how they must order their practices in order to fulfill their charge of raising and socializing children: Their children must continue to live, develop emotionally and intellectually, and come to fit into society in ways that the society deems acceptable. Maternal practice, Ruddick claims, is shaped by these demands in a manner analogous to the way in which human knowledge is shaped by specific human interests, according to Habermas.[23]

Ruddick's evaluation of the complex attitude toward the world and set of social practices that she calls "maternal thinking" is thus laudatory while nonetheless containing critical elements. On the one hand, she seeks to legitimize mothers' interests in preservation and growth as giving rise to a distinctive way in which women exist in the world as caretakers. Drawing on Heidegger's use of *care* as the fundamental structure of humanness, she valorizes the caretaking capacities that women have traditionally developed and sees them as giving rise to a specific way of being human, one that realizes the potential of the species in a positive way.[24] On the other hand, she sees one aspect of maternal practice—the interest in acceptability—as coming about through a need to accommodate maternal thinking to the realities of a world shaped by male power (i.e., domination) and as thus causing a rupture in that way of being.

> Out of maternal powerlessness, in response to a society whose values it does not determine, maternal thinking has often and largely opted for inauthenticity and the "good" of others. . . . This attitude [unlike those based on preservation and growth] is not a caretaker's response to the natural exigencies of child tending, but a subordinate's reaction to a social reality essentially characterized by the domination and subordination of persons.[25]

Here Ruddick acknowledges the fact that women's power exists in a context determined by males and claims that this has an important impact on the shape that maternal practice takes. As a result of this situation, she says, women have often failed to recognize the true potential of their maternal mode of being, opting instead for cooperation and complicity with a social power that is external to them but that is able to determine the nature of their practice.

Like the feminist theorists of power, Ruddick finds in the tasks and experiences of mothering a source for an alternative set of values. Although she does not use an alternative conception of power to ground her claims, she sees maternal values as being at odds with the idea of power as domination. She goes on to argue that maternal thinking can be a powerful corrective to the structure of power in modern society: "We must work to bring a *transformed* maternal thought [i.e., one that has been purged of its inauthenticity] in the public realm, to make the preservation and growth of *all* children a work of public conscience and legislation."[26] Rejecting Chodorow's claim that having men share equally in parenting responsibilities will result in a dramatic shift in the patterns of individuals' psychology, Ruddick asserts that more wide-ranging changes are needed for maternal thinking to realize its potential to alter the structure of the social world. Maternal thinking can play a role in bringing about fundamental social change, but only if it is expanded beyond its traditional realm into a vehicle for the formation of public policy.

Ruddick's account of a specific manner of being in the world that she calls "maternal thinking" thus has much in common with the views of the feminist theorists of power. Like them, Ruddick wants to revise the traditional valuation of maternal practices and to show that women have had many skills and abilities that have not been recognized by either male social theorists or the feminist theorists of domination. She sees this reevaluation as allowing for a revitalization of the public sphere by the introduction into it of new values that are already constitutive of maternal practice.

The distinctive feature of Ruddick's account, however, is that she sees maternal practice as inherently divided against itself as a result of its being situated in a world whose fundamental structures have been shaped by a male-dominated form of power. As a result, she takes a more critical and less ideal-istic view of maternal practice, distinguishing those aspects of it that are the result of an accommodation with the status quo and those that are derived from a truly alternative social practice.

Feminist theorists of power have tended to ignore the importance of this wider social context in presenting their view of transformative power. I be-lieve that Ruddick is right and that the feminist theorists of power need to incorporate this insight in order to achieve an adequate model of transforma-tive power. Transformative power cannot simply be modeled on the existent practice of mothering, for this practice is a divided one, with characteristics that result from the use of transformative power to empower a dependent so-cial agent and other characteristics that result from the situation of this prac-tice within a larger social setting shaped by practices of male domination.

The failure to acknowledge the importance of the larger social setting is not the only respect in which the feminist theorists of power idealize the mother-child relation. They have also failed to see that the self-transcending nature of transformative power is a source of significant problems for its use. Power, to be used in a truly transformative way, must be used with the goal of making the other into a being with enough independence and autonomy so that she no longer needs to be in a power relation with the dominant agent. The problem that this presents for the dominant agent is that the satisfactions that she has received from the relationship will have to change through time if she is to continue to nourish and care for her charge. This is, however, a diffi-cult thing for human beings to accustom themselves to; we seem to be destined to savor our pleasures in forms that we are used to. As a result, there is a temptation for the dominant agent to seek to keep the subordinate agent from growing and developing in a way that transcends that form of relationship.

Recent psychoanalytic research on the nature of narcissism has recognized how problematic the parent-child relationship really is.[27] In psychoanalytic terms, a narcissistic parent is one who is unable to maintain the relation with her child as one that seeks to provide for the child's needs; instead, she seeks to gratify her own needs by means of the child. Recent work has shown that such forms of parenting are much more common than had been previously acknowledged. Such parenting creates children who are themselves burdened by narcissistic character disorders, since they have been raised in a manner that did not allow them to distinguish sufficiently between their own needs and those of their parents. As a result, these "grown-up children", bearing the scars of their upbringing, are unable to exercise their power over their own children in a manner that will allow those children to develop into sufficiently autonomous beings.

The importance of this idea can be seen when we consider exactly how to specify the nature of a parent's nurturance of a child. Although we generally identify nurturance with an attitude of caring and concern that governs the basic interactions between a parent and a child, the perspective provided by psychoanalytic theory changes our view in a somewhat unintuitive manner. For example, a nurturant parent in the ordinary sense might not allow her child to engage in such activities as roughhousing with other children because she is worried that the child might get hurt. By showing concern, however, such a parent might actually harm a child's development, causing her to become obsessively worried about playing with friends. From the point of view of psychoanalytic theory, adequate mothering means allowing the child to achieve autonomy, something that cannot be measured by the attitude that governs the parent's interactions with the child.

The recent psychoanalytic literature on narcissism thus shows that parenting is an extremely charged and volatile relationship that is not adequately conceptualized through the concept of the transformative use of power alone. Although feminist theorists of power are right to point to childrearing as a locus of the use of power, their assertion that such power is used in a transformative manner belies the complex psychological reality of the relationship between parent and child. Although this relation may have the development of an autonomous being as its goal, it is so fraught with problems for both agents within it that it cannot simply be held up as an ideal that can be realized without problems. Consideration of the actual psychological reality of the parent-child relationship demonstrates that the transformative use of power can very easily turn into domination. The feminist theorists of power need to come to terms with the psychological facts involved in a transformative use of power in order for this concept to come to play the more central role in social theory that it needs to.[28]

The second weakness in the use of the concept of transformative power by feminist theorists of power as noted above, is a tendency to privilege mothering as the only practice in which nurturance takes place. Although the feminist theorists of power have demonstrated the existence of nurturant practices within a site in which the theorists of domination saw only domination, they need to move beyond the context of their discoveries to recognize other sites and practices within which women, as well as men, have exercised power in a transformative manner. Nurturant relationships exist, of course, in other social practices, and the idea of a transformative use of power can play an important role in understanding them as well. Teaching, therapy, and political organizing are examples of social roles within which nurturant practices play a central role. But almost any relationship with another human being is one in which nurturance rather than domination can be exercised. By remaining tied to mothering as the primary practice to use in conceptualizing the nature of transformative power, feminist theorists of power have created the misleading impression that such power exists only there and that women are the only social agents who are capable of such a use of power. An adequate conception of the transformative use of power needs to move beyond such claims.

I want to distingush my criticism of the feminist theorists of power from another one that is often made of them, namely that they are pro-family in too simplistic a manner. Such a claim is made, for example, by Mary G. Dietz when she characterizes the sort of feminist theorist whom I have been discussing as a " 'pro-family' feminist".[29] By talking about mothering, the feminist theorists of power are not referring primarily to the social site of the family, but rather to the social practice of mothering. It is the social practice that forms the object of a positive evaluation rather than the institutional site of the family. Although Dietz is correct in objecting to the privileging of maternal practices as the only ones in which women have exercised their distinctive capacities, she is wrong to use the concept of the family as the means of making her critique.

Conclusion

In this chapter I have documented the emergence within feminist theory of the concept of a transformative use of power. Although such a concept was developed as a means of responding to the negative valuation of the role of mother within feminist theory itself, I have shown the usefulness of such a concept for social theory in general. The idea of a transformative use of power gives us a means for arguing that power can be a useful and important aspect of a social structure.

I have also argued, however, that the account of transformative power found within the feminist theorists of power has certain defects. My aim in so doing has been to point the way toward the articulation of a concept of transformative power that, while dependent upon the claims of the feminist theorists of power, is freed from the limitations of their views. The task of the next chapter will be to show how this can be done.

10

Transformative Power and Social Domination

IN THE previous chapter, I discussed the emergence of the idea of a transformative use of power within the discourse of feminist theorists. In order to demonstrate the full significance for social theory of this idea, I shall present it in a more general context that the feminist theorists of power have. First, at a descriptive level, I shall show that, in his early dialogues, Plato presents a picture of Socrates attempting to develop transformative power relationships with his discourse partners. I will argue that the model of transformative power that emerges from a careful look at Socrates' elenchic interrogation of his interlocutors is free of certain of the limitations that are present in the picture of such relationships presented by the feminist theorists of power. This view of a transformative power relationship supplements that developed by the feminist theorists of power in certain important ways and places it in an appropriate context to be assimilated by social theory.

I shall then explain why such positive uses of power are difficult to achieve and why they have not been recognized by social theorists. I shall argue that situated power relationships are often superposed upon transformative power relationships, so that the dominant agent no longer uses his power over the subordinate agent in order to empower that agent; instead, a concern with social acceptability comes to the fore. As a result, the very existence of transformative power relationships within the social practices of contemporary society becomes hard to detect.

Understanding Socrates

In the early dialogues, Plato paints a portrait of Socrates, whose inter-actions with his fellow citizens involve a mode of interrogation known as *elenchus*. The aim of an elenchic interrogation is primarily negative in that it seeks to show that a certain claim to knowledge cannot be sustained in the face of persistent questioning.

The interesting thing about Socrates' practice of elenchic interrogation is that it has a profound effect on his discourse partners. Indeed, I shall argue that Socrates' practice of elenchic interrogation is an example of the trans-formative use of power, the use of power to empower another human being. Although not all of Socrates' interlocutors come to recognize this intent as lying behind his practice, Socrates consistently attempts to get them to enter into a transformative power relationship with him.

In order to see this, let us begin by considering an interchange that takes place between Socrates and Meno. The *Meno* is a dialogue concerned with the issue of whether virtue can be taught. In the course of discussing this issue, Socrates pursues a number of other questions, including whether virtue is a form of knowledge and whether knowledge is teachable. As part of his in-quiry, Socrates demonstrates the plausibility of the idea that knowledge is a form of recollection by means of a prolonged session of questioning that he engages in with a slave boy. The result of Socrates' questioning of the slave boy is the boy's "remembering" of the Pythagorean theorem, an item of geo-metric knowledge that he did not possess at the outset of the dialogue.

In the broader context of the dialogue, however, Meno is not up to the verbal gymnastics whose course Socrates is expertly pursuing. Instead of giving up in frustration, as many of Socrates' discourse partners do, Meno turns to Socrates and charges him with using power to confuse his interlocutors:

> Socrates, even before I met you they told me that in plain truth you are a perplexed man yourself and reduce others to perplexity. At this moment I feel that you are exercising magic and witchcraft upon me and positively laying me under your spell until I am only just a mass of helplessness. If I may be flippant, I think that not only in outward appearance but in other respects as well you are exactly like the flat sting ray that one meets in the sea. Whenever anyone comes into contact with it, it numbs him, and that is the sort of thing that you seem to be doing to me now.[1]

In this passage, Meno accuses Socrates of exercising power over him. His in-vocation of magic and witchcraft signals his sense that he is no longer in full possession of his own faculties, that Socrates has him in his power. Although Meno is not sure what the point of this exercise of power is, other than simply befuddling him, he certainly views it as dangerous. The analogy he makes between Socrates and a sting ray points to his sense of a danger inherent in the interaction.

Meno's criticism of Socrates, then, is that he confuses people by talking with them. As one who is caught up in this process even as he protests against it, Meno is not able to fully understand it. Other interlocutors have a more definite view of Socrates' intentions. They feel that Socrates' attempts to befuddle them are intended to show them up as inferior to him in dialectical skills. One of the charges brought against Socrates at his trial is that he makes the weaker argument appear to be the stronger.[2] The interpretation of Socratic interrogation lying behind such a charge is that it is a pure power play whose goal is the establishment of Socrates as the knowledgeable superior.

Socrates does not think of himself as trying to show up the ignorance of his discourse partners, although he does intend to show them their ignorance. In defending himself against Meno's charges, Socrates presents an alternative interpretation of his practice: "It isn't that knowing the answers myself, I perplex other people. The truth is rather that I infect them also with the perplexity I feel myself."[3] With this statement, Socrates denies that he is trying to show up his interlocutors as lacking some knowledge that he has. He insists that he and his interlocutors are in the same boat in regard to knowledge; the sole difference is that Socrates is aware of this situation. It is this very awareness that Socrates claims he wants to bring to the other. Socrates accepts Meno's analogy with the sting ray in order to show that there is more truth in it than Meno realizes, asserting that he uses his ability to *help* rather than to harm the person whom he stings.

> So in perplexing him and numbing him like the sting ray, have we done him any harm? . . . In fact we have helped him to some extent toward finding out the right answer, for now not only is he ignorant of it [as he was before] but he will be quite glad to look for it . . . . Then the numbing process was good for him?[4]

Relying on his experience with the slave boy, Socrates gets Meno to admit that the numbing process to which he objects is part of a more comprehensive process whose goal is that of helping someone come to an awareness of his own ignorance and thus an awareness of the need to embark upon the search for truth.

Socrates' self-defense against Meno's charge of befuddling his interlocutors is based, then, on the claim that the befuddlement that they feel is a necessary stage in a larger process of personal growth. Socrates conceptualizes this process of growth in epistemic terms. His interlocutors begin not simply as ignorant people, but as ignorant people who are even ignorant of their own ignorance. The movement to a state of befuddlement is actually, *contra* Meno, an advance; for the individual in a state of befuddlement is, although still ignorant, at least *aware* of his own ignorance. As such, the creation of a state of befuddlement in a discourse partner marks a first step in the process of transformation that is the goal of Socrates' practice.

But if the creation of an awareness of ignorance is but the first step in a more comprehensive process, the nature of that larger process needs to be spelled out more clearly in order to show why such a problematic first step is necessary. Socrates justifies the creation of a sense of confusion in his interlocutors as a necessary step in getting them to reject their established way of life, one based upon a concern with "getting ahead", in order that they may come to embrace a new manner of living their lives in which their sense of themselves as human beings is the primary concern. As he puts it in his own defense at his trial: "I tried to persuade each of you not to think more of practical advantages than of his mental and moral well-being, or in general to think more of advantage than well-being in the case of the state or anything else." [5] Socrates claims here that the ultimate goal of his interactions with his fellow Athenians is to help them alter the basic end around which they orient their lives. Instead of seeing life as composed of a series of contests from which one emerges either advantaged or disadvantaged, Socrates tries to get his interlocutors to think about their lives in terms of the impact that their activities and choices will make upon their own sense of themselves.

Socrates' goal then, is to have his fellow citizens change the most basic assumption they make about their lives. Given this understanding of the point of Socrates' interrogations of his fellow citizens, it becomes clear that he is attempting to bring about a transformative power relationship with them. He wants his relationship with his interlocutors to result in a fundamental change in them, one that brings them to a more independent and autonomous stance. But this is precisely what a transformative power relationship aims at, namely the constitution of the other as a more independent being as a result of the relationship itself.

This is why Socrates needs to make his interlocutors discontented with their own manner of living. Again, using epistemic discourse, Socrates points out that it is only after a person has acknowledged his ignorance that he has any desire to search for the truth.[6] In less epistemic language, this means that one has no incentive to change the nature of his life so long as he thinks that he is pursuing it on a correct basis. Only when one has come to see that the assumed basis for his life will not bring about the results that are intended, when one realizes his "ignorance", will he have an incentive to bring about a restructuring of his life, to embark upon "the search for truth" that Socrates hopes to instigate. The process of befuddlement about which Meno complains is legitimated by seeing it as an element in a more general process of transformation.

On such an understanding of Plato's dialogues, Socrates emerges as someone who is attempting to exercise power in a transformative manner. He tries to exercise power over his fellow citizens by convincing them of something that they did not previously hold to be true, namely that their own welfare is more important than their position vis-à-vis others. If he is successful, he will have exerted a significant influence upon the course of their lives. As a result of a "successful" interaction with Socrates, his interlocutor will reorient his life.

A brief look at another Platonic dialogue, the *Phaedrus,* will substantiate this claim more fully. In the *Phaedrus,* Socrates discusses the nature of his relationship with his discourse partners by means of a discussion of the nature of love. Socrates conceives of the relationship between himself and his young interlocutors as a form of love.[7] Using the terminology of "lover" for the older partner and "beloved" for the younger one, Socrates gives the following characterization of the nature of the relationship between them: "Every lover is fain that his beloved should be of a nature like to his god, and when he has won him, he leads him on to walk in the ways of their god, and after his likeness, patterning himself thereupon and giving counsel and discipline to the boy."[8]

If Socrates' reference to "god" is taken to mean "ideal", then this passage can be seen to contain a clear description of how a transformative power relationship is able to transform someone. Because of the loving tutelage of the lover, the beloved is enabled to change himself into a different sort of being, one who now is shaped after a different pattern. Through his interaction with his lover, the beloved becomes empowered in so far as he is transformed into a more mature and self-determining person. This is the goal of the "patterning" that the lover undertakes in regard to the beloved, and that Plato praises as containing "blessings great and glorious".[9]

In the *Phaedrus,* Plato recognizes the transformative power that is implicit in Socrates' practice. Indeed, the relationship that Plato depicts between Socrates and Phaedrus mirrors the relationship that Socrates discusses in the dialogue itself.[10] Plato *shows* us the transformative power relationship between Socrates and his young, aristocratic, Greek, male disciple, Phaedrus, at the same time that Socrates describes the nature of such relationships to his audience. We see that Socrates' power over his "beloved" does not emanate from any good that he can promise or threaten him with. Rather, Socrates' power lies in his ability to get Phaedrus to acknowledge that Socrates can offer him the chance to come to a more adquate conception of how to live his life.

Plato clearly shows us that Socrates' power does not aim at domination, for Socrates uses his power with the welfare of the other as its object and in such a way as to develop the other into a more independent being. He is trying to get the members of his society—and here only ruling-class males are his targets—to opt for a different conception of how to live their lives.[11] The Socratic use of power is one in which the dominant agent uses his power over another to empower and transform the weaker agent, to enable him ultimately to see that he has the ability to determine the course of his own life.[12]

The Platonic dialogues also present evidence that Socrates himself saw his practice in the terms that I am using. That evidence comes from his use of a traditional female practice, midwifery, as a means of characterizing his own activity. In so doing, Socrates both associates himself with a traditional female role and gives a positive valuation to it. Such a move must have startled his fellow citizens, for Athenian society was still dominated by ideals of male virtue derived from warriors. For a male to associate himself with a traditionally female profession, one that was the profession of his mother to boot, was provocative.

By characterizing his own practice in this way, Socrates points to the distinctive nature of his relationships with his young followers. The midwife practices her own art or skill for the benefit of those whom she practices it, for by performing her skill she allows them to accomplish the act of giving birth to a child. Although the midwife has specialized knowledge and skill, she does not use it to place herself in a position superior to that of her patient, but rather as a means to guide her patient in the successful performance of the act of giving birth. Socrates uses this analogy to point out that he, too, uses his power over his followers for their benefit. Like a midwife, he can only help people deliver what is rightfully theirs, can only assist in a process that they must ultimately perform themselves.[13]

Socrates' own characterization of his practice thus points to a number of features that it shares with the transformative use of power as discussed by feminist theorists. The transformative use of power is a use of power in which the welfare of the other is the guiding motivation of the one who possesses power. But, even more than that, it is a use of power that aims at empowering others. Socrates' use of the metaphor of the intellectual midwife emphasizes the very same aspects of his own practice of elenchic interrogation. His attempt to create befuddlement in his discourse partners is part of a larger practice of transformative power that structures his manner of interacting with his fellow Athenians.

The Problematics of Transformative Power

My purpose in discussing the nature of Socrates' interaction with his fellow Athenians is to see more clearly certain central features of the transformative use of power that are not highlighted in the account of it presented by the feminist theorists of power. It is now time to explore how the picture of Socrates' practice that emerges from the Platonic dialogues can be used to enhance the understanding of the nature of transformative power relationships developed in the previous chapter.

The first thing to note about Socrates' practice is that his discourse partners are usually young men. Although the relationship between Socrates and these young men is not one of equality, it is a chosen relationship, one that can only exist as a result of the explicit decision of these young men to continue talking to Socrates. They always have the option of acting like Euthyphro and breaking off the conversation under the pretext of having pressing affairs that need tending.[14]

This is an important difference from the parenting[15] relationship, for a child cannot choose her parents and is not able to break off her relationship to them for a significant period of time during her development. By focusing upon the choice that Socrates' interlocutors make to allow themselves to enter into a transformative power relationship with him, I will display certain distinctive features of transformative power relationships that did not come to the fore in my discussion of the feminist theorists of power.

As I have said, Socrates' interlocutors have a real choice in their dealings with him. They can choose to see him as an intellectual bully, someone who is out to show that he is smarter than any of them. This charge has often been lodged against Socrates and is repeated by I. F. Stone in his controversial book on Socrates.[16] On such a view, Socrates is only interested in showing up his interlocutors, in getting them to acknowledge his superiority in arguing.

Nietzsche also shared this evaluation of Socrates. Indeed, he went so far as to claim that Socrates is a villain in Western culture, seeking to overpower the "strong" of Athenian culture by tricking them into playing his game of elenchic interrogation and thus disempowering themselves. On such an interpretation, two alternative modes of dominating power compete with one another for supremacy: the one involving competence at practical affairs; the other, the use of verbal and mental quickness.[17]

But Nietzsche is himself working with a notion of power-over as pure domination and is thus unable to see that the real objective of Socrates' power struggle is his interlocutor's self-evalution. Nietzsche simply sees Socrates as trying to get the "strong" of his culture to have second thoughts about the correctness of their actions. Such an interpretation of Socrates' practice fails to see the overall process in which he is engaged and of which the generation of confusion or ignorance is but a part. An interlocutor who has a sense of this overall practice is able to engage with Socrates in a different manner, one that accepts the engendering of confusion as a necessary step in a larger process.

But then the success of Socrates' interactions with his interlocutors depends upon their manner of interpreting his practice. Only if they allow Socrates to enter into a transformative power relationship with them, one based upon their acknowledgment of the nature of the process to which he is subjecting them, will that relationship actually be constituted as one involving transformative power in the first place.

In discussing various forms of power, I have laid a great deal of stress on the role that the subordinate agent plays in their constitution. My discussion of Socrates' practice demonstrates that, in the case of a transformative power relationship, the subordinate agent's role in the constitution of the relationship makes such relationships difficult to ground and tenuous to maintain. In discussing coercive power relationships, I showed how a dominant agent could resort to an instrumental use of force as a means for getting the subordinate agent to submit to her power. Such a resource is precisely what Socrates lacks. In order to constitute a transformative power relationship with an interlocutor, he must rely on the freely given acknowledgment of that interlocutor. If Socrates attempted to force such an acknowledgment, the very basis of the relationship would be eroded, for the interlocutor would perceive Socrates as attempting to dominate him. Although a government can force certain policies on an unwilling populace, Socratic power can only be successfully exercised through the willingness of the interlocutor to accede to it. The weaker person needs to open himself up to the stronger person in such a way that his power can be used in the relationship. Without such an acknowledgment, the power remains impotent.

This problem is heightened once we remember that the process of the transformative use of power may have some very uncomfortable aspects. In order for the process to be effective, the subordinate agent must continue to trust the dominant agent even in the midst of such discomfort. In the example of Socratic practice, we saw how the first stage of the process, the acknowledgment of one's ignorance, was a disconcerting experience for Meno.

The first feature of transformative power relationships that emerges from my consideration of Socrates' practice, then, is the importance of trust in their constitution and the difficulty of maintaining that trust in the course of their development. This feature of transformative power relationships allows us to understand more clearly how such relationships are constituted. The process that Socrates seeks to initiate, and that is definitive of any transformative power relationship, is one that is difficult for human beings to endure. It requires that a human being allow himself to be vulnerable to another human being and to allow that other to see him as he struggles to change himself. It also requires him to place himself in the control of someone else and to trust that other to use that control in a positive manner. Placing oneself in such a vulnerable position is difficult for human beings, but it is necessary if certain processes of growth are to take place.

Trust is central to the establishment of a truly empowering relation. So long as a discourse partner does not trust Socrates, he will be tied to a view of Socrates as trying to "numb" him. Once he opens himself to the possibility that there is something else motivating Socrates, he may be able to acknowledge a different possibility for interpreting Socrates' actions. Coming to such an awareness of what Socrates is doing is a permanent possibility for his interlocutors, although they rarely take it. Like God's love for St. Augustine, it is always there, simply waiting for one's acknowledgment. Nothing can force that acknowledgment, however. This sort of power depends on the recognition by the other that one is trying to help her, and such recognition cannot be gotten so long as one remains suspicious of the intentions of the powerful person. Openness cannot be forced; yet so much depends upon its achievement.

Because Socrates' power relies on the freely given acknowledgment of the other for its existence, if a particular individual refuses to accept the validity of Socrates' own interpretation of his actions, Socrates can do nothing to force him to accept it. It is for this reason that Socrates uses irony so frequently. By speaking ironically, Socrates leaves open the possibility that a discourse partner who does not accept Socrates' own understanding of his practice can change his mind upon seeing the point behind Socrates' ironic assertion.[18]

That is why it is so central to Socrates' character that he argue in the way that he does in the *Apology*. It is not that he is seeking to become a martyr or is bent on self-destruction; rather, Socrates' conception of his power (which he also presents as a gift of the gods) relies on others' accepting it. So his ironic comment at the trial about deserving a pension from the state needs to be seen as a straightforward continuation of his attempt to get his fellow citizen to see the point of his practice as he envisions it.

The role of trust in the development of a transformative power relationship emerges more clearly in Plato's dialogues than in the feminist discussion because the subordinate agents in Socrates' case are young adults. As such, the role of choice in determining their relationship to a dominant agent is more apparent. Even in the non-chosen relationship of child to parent, however, trust is important, for without that trust the relationship will not be transformative. For example, in Erikson's psychoanalytic accounts of child development, a parent's most basic task is the establishment of a sense of trust in a child.[19]

Plato's presentation of Socrates as someone who exercises transformative power over his young associates can also be used to supplement the account of the feminist theorists of power in another way. Plato explicitly presents certain aspects of this relationship as open to abuse. Since I have argued that the feminist theorists of power tend to idealize the mothering relationship and, with it, transformative power in general, Plato's realism in this regard will provide a useful corrective to this tendency.

In presenting Socrates as practicing the transformative use of power, Plato consistently shows us discourse partners who, like Meno, do not submit to Socrates' practice easily and without reservations. Often, these discourse partners do not fully trust Socrates, for they suspect that he is up to something whose nature they do not fully grasp.

So far, I have suggested that their skepticism about what he is doing results in their inability to see the actual nature of the process that he is attempting to generate. But their skepticism has another side to it, one that can provide new insights into the nature of transformative power. As we saw in the case of Meno, he realizes that his interaction with Socrates has left him vulnerable to Socrates in certain ways. While this vulnerability is an important feature of a transformative power relationship, a dominant agent can use it to her advantage, should she choose to. Indeed, this is why trust in the dominant agent is so crucial to the establishment of the power relationship in the first place. So although the vulnerability of the subordinate agent in a transformative power relationship is an important characteristic of such relationships, because of this vulnerability they present great dangers for the subordinate agent.

Plato explicitly acknowledges these dangers in the *Phaedrus*, the very dialogue in which he also presents such relationships as beneficial to the subordinate agents. In his first speech on love, Socrates paints a picture of a jealous lover who is only interested in himself and seeks to keep his beloved tied to him by any means possible. For example, Socrates states:

> he [the lover] is bound to be jealous, constantly debarring the boy not only, to his great injury, from the advantages of consorting with others,

which would make a real man of him, but, greatest injury of all, from consorting with that which would most increase his wisdom—by which I mean divine philosophy.[20]

This portrait of the jealous lover shows that a transformative power relationship with another human being can easily be turned into an attempt to dominate him or her, when the one who has the power loses sight of the appropriate grounding of that relationship. Socrates points out that a lover who is faced with the possibility of being deserted by his beloved may act in a dominating manner. The worried lover may no longer seek to empower his beloved, but rather to use any means available to him to keep the beloved within the scope of his power. When such a use of power becomes the predominant one in a relationship, it becomes a relationship of domination rather than one of transformation.

The presence of this alternative account of love in the *Phaedrus* shows us that Plato is aware of the dangerous nature of transformative power. Because one person is in the power of another, he lacks the normal means of control over his fate and thus can be made into a pawn of the more powerful person's desires.

By and large, this aspect of the transformative use of power has been ignored by the feminist theorists of power. Because of their idealization of the mothering role, feminist theorists of power have not attempted to conceptualize possible ways in which the transformative use of power could turn into a source of domination. When the maintenance of the relationship itself, rather than its eventual transcendence, becomes the goal of the dominant agent, the nature of the power relationship between the two agents can change from a transformative one to a dominating one.

The essential point that emerges from my discussion of Socrates' practice is that trust plays a crucial role in transformative power relationships. On the positive side, trust is a critical factor in the constitution of such relationships; without it, the agent offering a transformative power relationship will be misinterpreted by the agent to whom it is offered. On the negative side, the existence of trust makes it possible for the dominant agent to abuse the relationship by using the power to keep the subordinate agent subordinated. Whereas the point of a transformative power relationship is to empower the subordinate agent to such an extent that she can transcend her relationship to the dominant agent, the dominant agent's own desires can cause him to try to hold onto the subordinate agent instead of allowing her to achieve independence. Clearly, transformative power relationships, while an important use of power within society, are fraught with difficulties and problems that need to be acknowledged.

The Superposition of Power Relationships

I shall now explore another problem involved in the transformative use of power. I have singled out certain social practices as ones that involve the transformative use of power. In so doing, I have not meant to suggest that the transformative use of power is localized to these practices alone. Any social practice can be engaged in in a manner that opens up the possibility of engaging in transformative power relationships with others. In so far as one treats other human beings in a manner that encourages them to seek to develop their own potential, one can engage in transformative power relationships with them, regardless of the specific nature of the social relationship that one has to them.

Despite this, there are certain social practices whose characters are such that they have a more intimate tie to the transformative use of power than other social practices. While one could be a butcher without engaging in a transformative use of power, the social practices of mothering, teaching, and therapy are inherently tied to the transformative use of power. Each of these practices is hierarchical—that is, is constituted as involving a dominant and a subordinate agent. Moreover, these are relationships in which the subordinate agent is seen as being with a capacity for change, and the relationship is constituted in an attempt to foster such change in him or her. As a result, these practices are constituted so that the dominant agent be able to exercise power in a transformative manner—that is, bring about a process of growth in the subordinate agent.

The disturbing fact to which I would like now to call attention is that each of these practices has also been criticized as involving a form of domination. As I pointed out in the previous chapter, the idea of mothering as a locus of transformative power was actually developed in response to the claims of feminist theorists of domination that the family was a site of the reproduction of male domination and that women were complicit in their own domination by serving as mothers. The practice of mothering was indicted as an important means whereby the social domination of women was reproduced across generations.

In presenting my account of the situated conception of power, I also made it clear that teaching could be seen as playing an important role in social domination. Grading is used to give students selective access to jobs; moreover, it sets up a pattern of differential rewards based upon the extent to which they are able, in the opinion of their teachers, to master certain skills. By providing a dominant social alignment with social agents who are certified as capable of filling roles necessary for its maintenance, teaching too functions to maintain relationships of domination.

Although I have not explicitly discussed therapy up to this point, it is also an example of a transformative power relationship. In fact, many aspects of Socrates' practice make it closer to a therapeutic relationship than to a modern teaching one. A therapist is a person who seeks to bring another person to a more adequate manner of existing in the world, one in which the other is more independent and less ruled by fears and anxieties. As such, therapeutic practice fits the model of a transformative power relationship that I have developed in this chapter and the preceding one.

As with other forms of social practice that are tied to the idea of the transformative use of power, therapy has come in for a great deal of criticism from social theorists. In many ways this criticism is very similar to Ruddick's criticism of mothering practices: Just as Ruddick claims that many women's mothering of their children is constituted by an interest in acceptability, critics of therapy have argued that it is practiced with an interest in making individuals fit into society rather than with an interest in helping them.[21] That is, therapy is seen to be a means for handling those individuals who react negatively to an exploitative and unjust society. Instead of endorsing these negative reactions to an inadequate reality, therapy is criticized as a means of persuading these individuals to drop their resistance to that society and to accept life on the terms that society offers. The issue of whether the social practices of parenting, teaching, and therapy are the locus of a transformative or a dominating use of power is thus one over which social theorists disagree.

A fundamental source of this disagreement is the structure of the social practices of parenting, teaching, and therapy in contemporary society in which the transformative potential of these social practices is masked under a dominating aspect. This dominating aspect is constituted by the *superposition* of a situated power relationship upon the structure of a social relationship that could be, in the absence of such a superposition, a transformative power relationship.

My use of the term "superposition" can be illuminated by thinking about how one photographic image can be superimposed upon another. In this case, the resulting picture will contain two *superposed* images. Such a picture depicts physical reality as having a dual structure, one in which two objects occupy the same place at the same time. I want to suggest that, unlike physical reality, social reality needs to be thought about as actually constituted by superposed relationships. Two social practices, unlike two physical objects, can occupy the same space at the same time. I use the terminology of superposition to indicate this fact.

It is the presence of this core of a potentially transformative power relationship that the critics of the social practices of parenting, teaching, and therapy fail to notice. Concerned to show the harmful effects of the actual structure of these practices, they tend to ignore the presence of a potentially beneficial social practice that is overlaid with a different social structure.

I shall begin my argument for this view by returning to Ruddick's conception of the maternal mode of being. I want to suggest that the fissure that Ruddick points to in the practice of mothering can be explained by recourse to the idea of the superposition of a situated power relationship upon the practice of parenting. This means that the practice of parenting, which is one example of a transformative power relationship, takes place within a larger social context that is partially responsible for its nature. The larger social context alters the nature of the parenting relationship in a manner that fundamentally changes its orientation.

It is my contention that the idea of the superposition of a situated power relationship upon the practice of parenting provides a clear way of understanding how this works. To say that a situated power relationship is superposed upon the practice of parenting is to say that there is a social alignment that uses the outcome of that practice as a means for determining the child's access to certain social goods.

To see how this superposition affects the practice of parenting, think about an aspect of the parenting practice that seems relatively insignificant—teaching a child table manners. There is nothing about the practice of parenting itself that requires parents to be seriously concerned about their children's table manners. Nonetheless, this is often a serious issue between parents and their children. The reason for this, I want to suggest, is that table manners are an example of a practice used by a social alignment in subtle ways to judge the acceptability of individuals for certain social rewards. A person who exhibits bad table manners is often judged to be unacceptable for certain social tasks that have no relation to her manners. Manners are taken to be an indication of a person's suitability for, say, a job because they are taken to be indicative of her background and, hence, reliability.[22]

This seemingly trivial example shows that, in contemporary society, a parent who raises a child cannot simply be concerned to raise him in a manner that she believes is good for him; she must also be concerned with how that child will fare in society. While the former concerns constitute the parent as a wielder of transformative power in the parenting relationship, the latter concerns also have an effect on the manner in which she brings up her child. Since parents generally want their children to have access to various sorts of opportunities available within society, they bring their children up so as to be capable of getting these opportunities. In so far as a parent is trying to make her child into an acceptable member of society, one who has access to the benefits available within it, she will no longer be concerned only to develop that child into an adult who is self-determining; in so far as such a parent wants a child to "fit in" to the society in which the child is being reared, she will be concerned that the child adopt modes of action that will make him socially acceptable.

But this pattern of social relationship is precisely a situated power relationship. A situated power relationship is one in which a dominant agent's exercise of power over another agent is conditioned by the presence of a social alignment. In so far as a parent realizes that her child's chances for success are conditioned by such an alignment, she will exercise her power in a manner determined by its presence and not in a purely transformative manner.

By describing this situation as one in which the transformative power relationship between a parent and a child has a situated power relationship superposed upon it, I am suggesting that the interest in acceptability that Ruddick sees as an anomalous feature of actual parental practice is constituted by such a superposition. As a result of this superposition, parental practice comes to have a character that is non-unitary, for the situated power relationship comes to determine certain aspects of that practice.

Ruddick's discussion of the maternal mode of being can thus be seen to be a discussion of a social practice that is the result of the superposition of two distinct power relationships. On the one hand, the genuine practice of parenting, having as its goal the production of an independent, self-determining individual, is an example of a transformative power relationship; on the other hand, the concern for acceptability constitutes the parenting relationship as a situated power relationship. These two practices, though analytically distinguishable, are merged in the existing social practice of parenting. The very same actions that bring about one also bring about the other.

The idea that a specific social practice is really the result of the superposition of one power relationship upon another can also be seen by examining the nature of the teacher-student relationship. In order to see this, remember that my discussion of the teacher-student relationship in Chapter 7 explicitly left one aspect of that relationship out of consideration: the fact that teachers generally are teachers in virtue of some knowledge or skill that they possess and that students generally have an interest in coming to possess. In cases where a student actually has a desire to learn such a skill from a teacher, there are grounds for the existence of a power relationship between the two of them, one that is oriented around the goal of the teacher's transmitting that knowledge or skill to the student.

In Chapter 5 I described the type of relationship represented by this aspect of a teacher-student relationship as one of apprenticeship—that is, a power relationship between two agents based upon the expertise that an agent possesses and that she is able to transmit to another agent. At that point I argued that apprenticeship is a form of power grounded in the existing inequality between the master and the apprentice in regard to the knowledge or skill at issue as well as in the desire on the part of the apprentice to acquire it from the master. Because the apprentice lacks the skill or knowledge in question, the master is constituted as possessing power over her because she controls not only the knowledge or skill but also the pace and manner of conveying it.

Relationships of apprenticeship are a form of transformative power relationship. A teacher who is teaching a student who wishes to acquire a skill that the teacher has is seeking to develop that student into a more effective, more competent being. Thus, the teacher is engaged in a transformative use of power in her interactions with the student.

In contemporary society, however, teaching is not normally constituted purely as a form of apprenticeship. As in relationships of parenting, the social context has an important effect on the character of such relationships. Once again, the transformative character of such relationships is altered by the superposition of a situated power relationship upon them, so that the actions that a student and teacher engage in function in two distinct but related contexts. While, on the one hand, they are part of a potentially transformative power relationship, they are simultaneously part of a situated power relationship.

The precise nature of such a superposition emerges from a consideration of the role that the teacher's evaluation of the student plays in their relationship. In Chapter 7 I argued that, by virtue of the fact that a teacher was responsible for grading a student, a teacher existed in a situated power relationship with a student. However, a teacher's evaluation of a student has a different significance in the transformative power relationship between them. Within such relationships of apprenticeship, the teacher's evaluation of the student's performance also plays an important role. Since the student desires to achieve the sort of mastery that the teacher has, the teacher's evaluation—which signals her evaluation of the student's level of attainment of the skill or knowledge in question—will be very significant to the student. The student's sense of whether or not she is actually managing to attain the knowledge or skill that she wishes to will depend, at least in part, on the teacher's evaluation of her. In such relations, the evaluation functions as a form of communication, transmitting to the student the teacher's perception of her level of attainment.

Although the evaluation of one agent by another is an important component of both relationships of situated power and those of apprenticeship, it plays fundamentally different roles in these two types of relationship. In cases of apprenticeship, the evaluation of one agent by another is not the basis for that agent's power over the other. The power that the master possesses over the apprentice is based in the unequal possession of skill or knowledge; the evaluation functions within the context set by this more basic inequality and communicates to the apprentice the master's perception of the degree to which she is actually progressing in her desired acquisition. In teaching relationships that are constituted by situated power, on the other hand, the act of evaluation in the form of a grade plays a more central role, since the grading practice itself is constitutive of the empowered agent's power.

This discussion of the role of evaluation in both teaching relationships involving situated power and transformative power relationships of apprenticeship helps explain the possibility of the superposition of these two different relationships. The crucial factor in such a superposition is that the situated power relationship absorbs the structure of the transformative power relationship upon which it is superposed, but gives that structure a different meaning.[23] This is why each of these two distinct types of power relationship has, at its core, a relationship between two social agents that is homological to the other. Since the two types of power relationship have structural similarities, it is possible for a single social practice to instantiate aspects of both of them simultaneously.

In the case of teaching, both types of power relationship can be simultaneously present as features of the classroom. When a student faces a teacher, the teacher is able to represent the dominant agent in two very different types of power relationship. On the one hand, in so far as the student sees the teacher as someone who is able to transmit some desired knowledge or skill to her, the teacher will occupy the position of master in regard to the student. In this case, the student will see herself as standing in a relation of apprentice to the teacher-master. On the other hand, in so far as the student sees the teacher as someone whose evaluation of her plays an important role in her getting access to items that she desires, the teacher will occupy the position of the dominant agent in a situated power relationship. In this type of relationship, the teacher is seen as powerful because of her role in determining the student's access to social goods.

Although both a situated power relationship and a relationship of apprenticeship may be constituted by the same social practice, it makes sense to think of the situated power relationship as superposed upon the apprentice relationship because the latter relationship can be constituted simply through the presence of the two central agents. The situated power relationship, however, occurs through the overlaying of this original relationship with a social structure through which the master is given a new dimension of power, a specific form of social power.

Rather than entering into a full discussion of therapy as also fitting into this model, let me simply point out that one influential treatment of the therapeutic relationship ignores this possibility. In his discussion of psychoanalysis in Volume One of *The History of Sexuality,* Foucault treats it as a form of domination. Criticizing the image that psychoanalysis presents of itself as liberating individuals from the domination of their unconsciousnesses, Foucault argues that the practice of psychoanalysis is itself an "incitement of discourse" and part of a disciplinary practice that constitutes human beings as subject to the very desires from which it claims to liberate them.

Although it may be true that psychoanalysis first constitutes the human being as capable of apprehending itself as subject to certain desires, this does not mean that, in so doing, it is necessarily a form of social domination. The possibility that Foucault overlooks is that psychoanalysis, by means of this very constitution of the human being, could be providing a person with certain capabilities that enable her to live more fully and adequately. By conceiving of the therapeutic relationship as a form of transformative power, one asserts just this. The practice of reconstitution that is characteristic of psychoanalysis can be seen, *contra* Foucault, as part of a transformative power relationship in which the patient is given a greater degree of control over the vicissitudes of human existence.

This fact does not entail, however, that psychoanalysis is always practiced in such a manner. A great deal of psychoanalytic practice, as well as therapeutic practice more generally, can be seen as subject to precisely the same dilemma present in parenting and teaching, namely that the transformative practice is restructured as a result of its place within a social context. A therapist, just like a parent, may come to practice her art in a manner that aims at conformity with social roles rather than in a truly transformative manner. This possibility, however, needs to be kept distinct from the general analysis of the nature of therapeutic practice itself.

If my analysis of the superposition of situated power relationships upon relationships of transformative power is correct, it allows us to understand why the existence of transformative power has been so hard for social theorists to see. Once a transformative power relationship has had a situated power relationship superposed upon it, the basic character of the social practice is altered. As I have shown, the resulting practice is a divided practice, but one that normally performs a function in an overall pattern of domination.

In looking at Socrates' practice, I stressed how fragile transformative power relationships are, how difficult they are to constitute. Socrates' interlocutors had difficulty even seeing the possibility of their existence, for the possibility of domination tended to blind them to the existence of this alternative inherent in their relations with him.

The superposition of situated power relationships upon transformative power relationships makes the existence of the latter even more difficult to perceive. Because a subordinate agent sees her access to social goods as determined by the evaluation that she receives from the dominant agent, she will naturally interpret the relationship between the two of them as one involving situated power. As a result, she is significantly less likely to perceive the possibility of a transformative power relationship. The trust that is required for a transformative power relationship, already a fragile item, will not survive the recognition by the subordinate agent that the dominant agent is functioning as a means of access to certain social goods that she wants. The ontological structure of such practices is such that it is easy to ignore their transformative component and to see them simply as tools of social domination.

Power in Plurality

At this point, my exploration of the concept of power is complete. I have shown that power is a social phenomenon that exists in different forms and has different uses. In this chapter I have shown that the transformative use of power is both a crucial use of power in society and a difficult and problematic one. Although it may potentially benefit the agent over whom it is exercised, it also has the potential to dominate him. As a result, the transformative use of power can take its place alongside the dominating use of power as a fundamental phenomenon that social theory needs to acknowledge.

In casting a retrospective glance over the argument of this study, it becomes clear that the multiplicity of types and uses of power is one of the central ideas articulated by it. Indeed, this idea is one of the central features that differentiates my view of power from the views of many other social theorists. Unlike theorists who have been concerned to privilege one form of power as the only one to which social theory should pay attention, I have shown that it is important to see power as a general social phenomenon whose more specific instances embody a variety of forms. As a result, my theory of power is able to incorporate various views of power without claiming that one or the other of them is more basic.

If the task of a theory of power is to provide an account of power that is capable of being used by social theorists to criticize social practices and institutions, then the theory of power developed in this study accomplishes that task. By exploring the role of power in the constitution of individual social agents and society in general, it provides the social theorist with a tool for analyzing when power is present and what effects it has. Some analyses of power are structured more by the analyst's theoretical beliefs than by an actual investigation of the ways in which the concept of power functions in our own discursive practices and our social world. The theory of power developed here recognizes the ambiguous nature of power as a social presence and stresses the positive role that it plays in society. In so doing, it supplies social theorists with a more adequate understanding of this significant social phenomenon.

Notes

Chapter 1

1. Hannah Arendt, *On Violence* (New York: Harcourt Brace Jovanovich, 1969, 1970), p. 41.

2. David West, "Power and Formation: New Foundations for a Radical Concept of Power", *Inquiry* 30 (1987): 137.

3. Niklas Luhmann, *Macht* (Stuttgart: Enke, 1975), p. 1; my translation.

4. See, for example, Michel Foucault, *Power/Knowledge: Selected Interviews and Other Writings, 1972–1977,* ed. Colin Gordon (New York: Pantheon, 1980).

5. Steven Lukes, *Power: A Radical View* (London and Basingstoke, Eng.: Macmillan, 1974), p. 9.

6. William E. Connolly, *The Terms of Political Discourse* (1974; 2nd ed., Princeton, N.J.: Princeton University Press, 1983), p. 126.

7. W. B. Gallie, "Essentially Contested Concepts", *Proceedings of the Aristotelian Society* 56 (1955–56), p. 167.

8. *Ibid.*, pp. 172–73. It should be clear that Gallie's own definition of such concepts is needlessly restrictive. For example, there is no reason to limit the concept to "achievements"; concepts for negative accomplishments can also be thought of this way, as the theorists of power attempt to do.

9. *Ibid.*, pp. 184–85.

10. This view of concepts goes back at least as far as Aristotle's theory of definition and can be seen to dominate philosophical theories of concepts and language through modern times.

11. This is a central claim of Ludwig Wittgenstein, *Philosophical Investigations*, trans. G. E. M. Anscombe (New York: Macmillan, 1968).

12. Anthony Giddens, *Central Problems in Social Theory: Action, Structure, and Contradiction in Social Analysis* (Berkeley and Los Angeles: University of California Press, 1979), pp. 89–90.

13. Connolly points out the relation between the thesis of essentially contested con-

cepts and deconstruction. See his *Terms of Political Discourse,* ch. 6. This seems to me an important point, for it shows the linguistic basis of the thesis.

14. I have not specifically addressed Connolly's restriction of the thesis of essential contestability to power-over. Suffice it to say that I see my general argument against that thesis as also applicable to his view.

15. *The Oxford English Dictionary* (Oxford, Eng.: Oxford University Press, 1971), p. 1213.

16. Nancy Hartsock, to cite but one example, articulates her views concerning power in terms of such a distinction. See her *Money, Sex, and Power: Towards a Feminist Historical Materialism* (New York and London: Longman, 1983).

17. *The Oxford English Dictionary,* p. 1213. The *O.E.D.* distinguishes six different meanings of the term "power".

18. The source of this quote is given as John Stuart Mill, *Human Mind* (n.p., 1869), bk. 2, ch. 21, p. 208.

19. Hannah Pitkin, *Wittgenstein and Justice* (Berkeley, Los Angeles, and London: University of California Press, 1972), pp. 276–77; emphasis added.

20. Talcott Parsons, "On the Concept of Political Power", in Roderick Bell, David V. Edwards, and R. Harrison Wagner, eds., *Political Power: A Reader in Theory and Research* (New York: Free Press, 1969), p. 251.

21. Plato, *Sophist* 247e, trans. F. M. Comford, in Edith Hamilton and Huntington Cairns, eds., *The Collected Dialogues of Plato* (Princeton, N.J.: Princeton University Press, 1961), p. 992.

22. John Locke, *An Essay Concerning Human Understanding* (New York: Dover, 1959), bk. 2, ch. 7, ¶ 8.

23. *Ibid.,* bk. 2, ch. 21, ¶ 2.

24. For one example of such a theorist, see Jean Baker Miller, "Colloquium: Women and Power", Stone Center for Developmental Services and Studies, *Work in Progress,* no. 882-01, 1982, p. 2.

25. Thomas Hobbes, *Leviathan,* ed. Michael Oakshott (Oxford, Eng.: Blackwell, 1946), p. 56.

26. Recent attempts by feminist theorists to reintroduce a conception of power that stresses its nature as an ability are based upon this sense of the concept. I shall discuss these attempts in Chapter 9.

27. Bertrand Russell, *Power* (New York: Norton, 1938), p. 35. Both Hannah Arendt and Talcott Parsons give accounts of power that follow Russell's active usage, although for them power is properly predicated only of groups. See Arendt, *On Violence,* and Parsons, "On the Concept of Political Power".

28. A further problematic feature of Russell's definition is his use of the term "intended" to qualify the effects brought about by the use of power. This results in his claiming that power is exercised only when an individual intends the results that he brings about.

29. I mention this fact in order to reiterate the inability of the thesis of essential contestability to illuminate the dispute about power within social theory.

30. Nicos Poulantzas, *Political Power and Social Classes* (London: New Left, 1973), p. 104.

31. Baruch Spinoza, *Tractatus Politicus,* ch. 2, ¶ 2, in A. G. Wernham, ed. and trans., *The Political Works* (Oxford, Eng.: Clarendon, 1958).

32. *Ibid.*, ch. 2, ¶ 9.

33. James Mill, *An Essay on Government,* ed. E. Barker (Cambridge, Eng.: Cambridge University Press, 1937), p. 37; quoted in C. B. Macpherson, *Democratic Theory: Essays in Retrieval* (Oxford, Eng.: Oxford University Press, 1973), pp. 42–43; emphasis added.

34. Harold Laswell and Abraham Kaplan, *Power and Society* (New Haven, Conn.: Yale University Press, 1950), p. 75. But note their assimilation of power-over to political power.

35. I discuss these theorists in Chapter 3.

36. Max Weber, *Wirtschaft und Gesellschaft: Grundriss der Verstehenden Soziologie* (5th ed.; Tübingen: Mohr, 1985), p. 28; my translation. There has been some controversy, centered on the meaning of the term *"Chance"* in this definition.

37. The notion of coactive power, or power-with, is one that Dorothy Emmet takes from Mary Parker Follett. See Emmet, "The Concept of Power", *Proceedings of the Aristotelian Society* 54 (1953-4), p. 9.

38. I discuss the idea of empowerment in my "Beyond Babies and Banners: Towards an Understanding of the Dynamics of Social Movements", *New Political Science* 14 (Winter 1985–86): 157–171.

39. I shall examine a more specific example of this tendency in discussing Hannah Arendt's view of power in the following chapter.

40. Macpherson, *Democratic Theory,* p. 42.

41. *Ibid.*, p. 47.

42. *Ibid.*, p. 49.

43. C. B. Macpherson, *The Political Theory of Possessive Individualism: Hobbes to Locke* (Oxford, Eng.: Oxford University Press, 1962).

44. Hartsock, *Money, Sex, and Power,* p. 12.

45. *Ibid.*, p. 210.

46. As my discussion of the history of the concept of power shows, not all male theorists have neglected the concept of power-to, power as ability, as Hartsock asserts. This casts some doubt on her view that the failure of contemporary theorists to address this side of power is simply a result of male bias.

47. I shall discuss this issue more extensively in Chapter 9.

Chapter 2

1. Hannah Arendt, *On Violence* (New York: Harcourt Brace Jovanovich, 1969, 1970), p. 35.

2. *Ibid.*

3. *Ibid.*, p. 37.

4. Cf. Plato, *Republic* 343b–344c. Arendt discusses Plato's view of political power in the essay "What Is Authority?" in *Between Past and Future: Eight Exercises in Political Thought* (Harmondsworth, Eng.: Penguin, 1954), pp. 91–142. Arendt's criticism of Plato's own view of political power is that he lacks the consensual model of power and is thus forced to use inadequate models for thinking of political power or, as she puts it in this essay, authority.

5. *Ibid.*, p. 41.

6. *Ibid.*, pp. 48–49.

7. *Ibid.*, p. 50.

8. Steven Lukes, *Power: A Radical View* (London and Basingstoke, Eng.: Macmillan, 1974), p. 30.

9. *Ibid.*, p. 31.

10. Although many social theorists treat Arendt's view of power as identical with that of Talcott Parsons, this is not true in all respects. For example, as Jürgen Habermas has pointed out, Parsons' theory does not address the character of the consensus that legitimates power, while Arendt consistently stresses its uncoerced nature. See his "Hannah Arendts Begriff der Macht", in *Philosophisch-politische Profile* (Frankfurt: Suhrkamp, 1981), pp. 244–45.

11. Talcott Parsons, "On the Concept of Political Power", in Roderick Bell, David V. Edwards, and R. Harrison Wagner, eds., *Political Power: A Reader in Theory and Research* (New York: Free Press, 1969), p. 257.

12. Parsons does give an argument of sorts to justify his conclusion, namely that traditional views of power have serious defects that his view does not. Nonetheless, his failure to see the difference between theories of political and social power vitiates the force of this argument.

13. Jürgen Habermas, *The Theory of Communicative Action*, vol. 1: *Lifeworld and System: A Critique of Functionalist Reason*, trans. Thomas McCarthy (Boston: Beacon, 1987), p. 268.

14. Although many critics of Arendt simply dismiss her view, Nancy Hartsock is one critic who does not. Despite her agreement with Arendt's critics, she finds much that is useful in Arendt's work. See *Money, Sex, and Power: Towards a Feminist Historical Materialism* (New York and London: Longman, 1983), pp. 211–222.

15. Dennis Wrong points out that there is another aspect to such a situation: "There is also the need for *discretionary judgment* in deciding which tasks should be carried out, which immediate goals pursued, in concrete situations. Discretion differs from coordination in that it involves what is done rather than how it is done, the choice of goals rather than their implementation, strategical rather than tactical decision-making" (*Power: Its Forms, Bases, and Uses* [Oxford, Eng.: Blackwell, 1979], pp. 248–49). The purely "technical" need for a decision-maker in a group is therefore overlaid with a need to decide which of a given set of alternative courses of action is the best one for the group as a whole to pursue. To give a single agent decision-making power is to allow her to make such a substantive choice as well.

16. *Ibid.*, p. 39.

17. Arendt, *On Violence*, p. 50.

18. This question of the dynamics of power is one that I discuss at length in Chapter 8.

19. A literary example of such a situation is that of the "good servants" in *King Lear*, who both follow Cornwall's orders in helping to blind Gloucester and yet later admit their wish that the blinding had not come to pass.

20. Anthony Giddens makes a similar criticism of Parsons for adopting too simplistic an understanding of power relations: "But it is surely beyond dispute that positions of power offer to their incumbents definite material and psychological rewards, and thereby stimulate conflicts between those who want power and those who have it" (*Central Problems in Social Theory: Action, Structure, and Contradictions in Social Analysis* [Berkeley and Los Angeles: University of California Press, 1979], p. 264). By failing to conceptualize the relations between the formal structure of power and the concomitant rewards open to those in power, Parsons' conceptualization bypasses central issues concerning the nature of power.

21. Throughout this discussion, I pass over the important question of whether a universal consensus would itself entail legitimacy for a particular political regime. To pursue this would raise the question of the production of consent, a topic whose discussion requires some of the distinctions I make in Chapter 5.

22. It is worth remembering that Arendt is worried about the student movement of the sixties, with its tendency to see violence as a necessary part of the strategy of attaining power.

Chapter 3

1. See, for example, Heidegger's critique of Descartes' understanding of the nature of corporeal substance in ¶¶ 20–21 of Martin Heidegger, *Being and Time*, trans. John Macquarrie and E. S. Robinson (New York: Harper and Row, 1962).

2. C. Wright Mills, *The Power Elite* (Oxford, Eng.: Oxford University Press, 1956).

3. *Ibid.*, p. 4.

4. *Ibid.*, p. 20.

5. See, for example, Nelson W. Polsby, "How to Study Community Power: The Pluralist Alternative", in *Community Power and Political Theory* (New Haven, Conn.: Yale University Press, 1980), pp. 112–21; and Robert A. Dahl, "A Critique of the Ruling Elite Model", in Roderick Bell, David V. Edwards, and R. Harrison Wagner, eds., *Political Power: A Reader in Theory and Research* (New York: Free Press, 1969), pp. 36–41.

6. Dahl, "Critique of the Ruling Elite Model", p. 38.

7. Robert Dahl, "The Behavioral Approach in Political Science: Epitaph for a Monument to a Successful Protest", *American Political Science Review* 55 (1961): 767. Let me note that the terms "social science" and "political science" are themselves somewhat controversial in that they presuppose the scientific character of the disciplines at issue.

8. For a good, general presentation of this view of scientific theories, see, for example, Ernest Nagel, *The Structure of Science* (New York: Harcourt Brace Jovanovich, 1974).

9. David Truman, "The Implications of Political Behavior Research", Social Science Research Council *Items,* 1951, p. 38, quoted by Dahl in "Behavioral Approach", p. 767; italics are Dahl's.

10. David Easton, "The Current Meaning of Behavioralism," in James C. Charlesworth, ed., *Contemporary Political Analysis* (New York: Free Press, 1967), pp. 11–31. I would like to thank Terence Ball for pointing this fact out to me.

11. Gilbert Ryle, *The Concept of Mind* (New York: Harper and Row, 1949).

12. Robert Dahl, "The Concept of Power", in Bell et al., eds., *Political Power,* p. 80.

13. William Domhoff subjects Dahl's study to an extensive critique in *Who Really Rules: New Haven and Community Power Re-examined* (Santa Monica, Calif.: Goodyear, 1978).

14. Peter Bachrach and Morton S. Baratz, "Decisions and Non-decisions: An Analytical Framework", in Bell et al., eds., *Political Power,* pp. 100–109.

15. Bertrand de Jouvenal, *On Power: Its Nature and the History of Its Growth* (Boston: Beacon, 1945). C. B. Macpherson also notes this use in *Democratic Theory: Essays in Retrieval* (Oxford, Eng.: Oxford University Press, 1973).

16. Steven Lukes, *Power: A Radical View* (London and Basingstoke, Eng.: Macmillan, 1974), pp. 24–25; italics in original.

17. *Ibid.*

18. *Ibid.,* p. 23.

19. In "Power, Repression, Progress: Foucault, Lukes, and the Frankfurt School", in *Foucault: A Critical Reader* (Oxford, Eng.: Blackwell, 1986), pp. 123–47, David Hoy points out that Lukes's extension of the concept of power is an attempt to legitimate the idea of ideology as a domain in which power is exercised.

20. Lukes, *Power,* pp. 26–27.

21. *Ibid.,* p. 34. Lukes's claim here suggests that the core difference between the three views of power is their understanding of what the interests of a human being amount to. In this sense, Lukes is unwittingly supporting my contention that there is a fundamental ontological understanding of human agency common to all these views.

22. Anthony Giddens, *Central Problems in Social Theory: Action, Structure, and Contradiction in Social Analysis* (Berkeley and Los Angeles: University of California Press, 1979), p. 90.

23. David West criticizes Lukes for much the same reason as this. See his "Power and Formation: New Foundations for a Radical Concept of Power", *Inquiry* 30 (1987): 137–54.

24. My understanding of the issues involved here has benefited from the work of Terence Ball and Jeffrey C. Isaac. Both of them assess the debate in terms of broad philosophical issues of the sort that I discuss here. For their views, see Ball, "Power, Causation, and Explanation", *Polity* 8 (1975): 189–214, and Isaac, *Power and Marxist Theory: A Realist View* (Ithaca, N.Y., and London: Cornell University Press, 1987).

25. The thesis that the views of these philosophers have resulted in a new perspective for social theory has been argued by, among others, Richard J. Bernstein in *Beyond Objectivism and Relativism: Science, Hermeneutics, and Praxis* (Philadelphia: University of Pennsylvania Press, 1983).

26. See, in particular, Jürgen Habermas' *Knowledge and Human Interests* (Boston: Beacon, 1971) and Charles Taylor's "Interpretation and the Sciences of Man", *Review of Metaphysics* 25 (Fall 1971): 4–51.

27. The lack of clarity on the distinction between possessing and exercising power, another feature of the power debate, is aided by this model.

28. Lukes certainly intends his view to do more than this. However, his failure to see the issues involved at a sufficient level of generality causes his definition to betray his own intentions.

29. I will return to the lordship-bondage relationship in my subsequent discussion of power.

30. "Consciousness" is the hero of Hegel's philosophic novel.

31. The contrast that I draw between an interventional and a structural model of power has parallels in Terence Ball's distinction between an agency and a structural model of coercion. See his "Two Concepts of Coercion", *Theory and Society* 15 (Jan. 1978): 97–112.

32. Ball, "Power, Causation, and Explanation", pp. 189–214.

Chapter 4

1. The fact that the husband has economic power over his wife in a traditional marriage does not mean that she does not have a different type of power over him. In fact, such stereotypical female behavior as "shrewishness" can be analyzed as an attempt by wives to achieve a countervailing form of power over their husbands. Both of these types of power need to be acknowledged if one is interested in analyzing the total array of power in such a relationship.

2. In my earlier work on the concept of power, I accepted such a dispositional analysis of the possession of power. See, for example, my "The Forms of Power", *Analyse und Kritik* 10 (1988): 3–31.

3. Within the history of metaphysics, Locke's *Essay Concerning Human Understanding* (New York: Dover, 1959) marks the *locus classicus* for a discussion of the dispositional properties of objects. See his discussion of the distinction between primary and secondary qualities of objects in book 2. Although Locke does not make this distinction in its full generality, he clearly distinguishes occurrent properties from dispositional ones, thus making an ontological advance in the understanding of objectivity. In so doing, he develops Aristotle's distinction between actuality and potentiality, albeit in a specifically modern context.

4. James Agee begins *Let Us Now Praise Famous Men* (Boston: Houghton Mifflin, 1941) with three vignettes in which this aspect of the existence of power is given a forceful portrayal in the context of race and economic relations.

5. For an interesting discussion of this assumption and its conflict with structural

views of power, see Steven Lukes, "Power and Structure", in *Essays in Social Theory* (New York: Macmillan, 1977), ch. 1.

6. This characterization can be found in Aristotle's *De Anima* as well as Marx's *Economic Philosophical Manuscripts*. The characterization of the human being as rational has generally been the dominant strand within traditional thought.

7. For the purposes of this chapter, I will use the imprecise term "group" as a shorthand for various forms of social collectivities.

8. Dahl, "The Concept of Power", in Roderick Bell, David V. Edwards, and R. Harrison Wagner, eds., *Political Power: A Reader in Theory and Research* (New York: Free Press, 1969), p. 80.

9. Steven Lukes, *Power: A Radical View* (London and Basingstoke, Eng.: Macmillan, 1974), p. 39. Lukes's usage follows Dahl's in "The Concept of Power".

10. There are important questions about how to understand a group as a social agent. My discussion in the previous chapter of men's having power over women reflects these problems. The terminological choice only highlights these issues as ones that need to be discussed.

11. The reader may have already noticed this practice in the previous chapters.

12. Aristotle, *Nichomachean Ethics* 1109b34–1110a4, in J. L. Ackrill, ed., *The New Aristotle Reader* (Princeton, N.J.: Princeton University Press, 1987), pp. 386–87.

13. One theorist who makes a similar point in his discussion of power is William Connolly. In the third chapter of *The Terms of Political Discourse* (1974; 2nd ed, Princeton, N.J.: Princeton University Press, 1983), Connolly argues that there is a conceptual tie between the concept of power and that of responsibility. My reservation about Connolly's claim is that he does not distinguish clearly between the metaphysical and ethical levels of analysis.

14. The one exception is what I call "force". I will discuss this, as well as other types of power, in the following chapter.

15. Since I develop the idea of two courses of actions being alternatives, I need to define the entire set of action-alternatives as composed of pairs of actions, any of which are alternative to one another.

16. In this definition, an agent may have a reason to pursue an action that she is not aware of as possible for her to pursue. This means that the specification of an agent's action-alternatives cannot be made solely from the point of view of the agent, but must include a more idealized perspective.

17. This problem is even more marked in social contexts where the coordination of other agents is required for an action to be taken, as the "paradoxes" of social agency point out.

18. See, for example, my discussion of influence in the following chapter.

19. Heidegger's discussion of the fundamental ontology of *Dasein* in *Being and Time,* trans. John Macquarrie and E. S. Robinson (New York: Harper and Row, 1962), is an attempt to present the human being as having a fundamentally different relation to its possibilities than the intellectualist tradition assumes. Within the pragmatist tradition, the role of doubt in the generation of belief marks a similar attempt to deny the

intellectualist model of action. Aristotle's distinction between voluntary action and choice is another marking of this distinction.

20. In the following chapter, I will distinguish force from such other types of power as coercion and influence. This social theortic use of the term "force" is, of course, different from the use I have made of it in this chapter as an ontological category.

21. Sartre's story "The Wall", in Lloyd Alexander, trans., *Intimacy* (New York: Berkeley, 1948), pp. 59–80, depicts just such a case with ironic implication.

22. For Aristotle's view, see his discussion of the difference between voluntary action and choice in book 3 of the *Nichomachean Ethics*.

23. Locke discusses these two aspects of human freedom in his discussion of "free will" in the *Essay*, bk. 2, ch. 21.

Chapter 5

1. The awkward nature of this last phrase is an attempt to conceptualize the sort of example that follows, in which force is used to get an agent's body to behave in a way that he would not actively choose.

2. This fact about force does not mean that there are no intentional concepts that are necessary for a justified application of that term. Consider the example of the farmer whose fields are burned down by the local villain in order to keep him from paying the mortgage. If that farmer is actually looking for a way to justify leaving town and moving to New York to pursue a career as a writer, the villain's burning his fields would not amount to an exercise of force in my sense since it provides the farmer with a way of realizing the action-alternative that he most wishes to realize. Even a force relationship requires an understanding of the intentional states of the two agents who take part in it.

3. The notion of an "economy" of power is one that Foucault uses to talk about power. See his *Discipline and Punish* (New York: Vintage, 1975). The present analysis is meant to capture some of the essentials of his analysis without having to treat power as a substance that has autonomous existence and interests, as Foucault sometimes does. The use of the term "economy" is also similar to Freud's use of that term in regard to the drives. See, for example, *A General Introduction to Psychoanalysis* (New York: Washington Square, 1920), ch. 18.

4. This point is noted by Jack Lively in his "The Limits of Exchange Theory" in Brian Barry, ed., *Power and Political Theory: Some European Perspectives* (London: Wiley, 1976), p. 8.

5. I want to call attention to a type of power that is analogous to force but that operates "negatively"—that is, through the failure of the dominant agent to perform an action. For example, a doctor who is the only one who can administer a life-saving drug to me can exercise this type of power over me by choosing not to give me the drug. Such a use of power is similar to force in that it changes my action-environment

directly. This type of power has no English term to designate it and has not been widely studied by theorists of power.

6. I shall ignore the idea of coercive offers. For an interesting discussion of this concept, see Robert Nozick, "Coercion", in Peter Laslett, W. G. Runciman, Quentin Skinner, eds., *Philosophy, Politics, and Society* (4th ser.; Oxford, Eng.: Oxford University Press, 1972), pp. 101–35.

7. This particular example was suggested to me by Ruth Anna Putnam.

8. A full account of the effect of the threat would have to consider the likelihood of an agent's being harmed by the maker of the threat. At this point, I shall simply treat the threat as having a categorical effect, weakening this assumption in my further discussion.

9. Again, I shall treat the situation at this point as less complex than it really is. Although the fact that the police may react to a demonstration by arresting the demonstrators is itself a possible ground for demonstrating, I shall ignore such aspects of the situation for now.

10. It is perhaps unrealisic to consider threat situations in which there is a real trade-off for the victim. Often, the threatener will be in a position to make the negative effect accrue to the victim regardless of the action-alternative he chooses. In such cases, the threat amounts to saying either you do this or I will make it happen to you.

11. Let me just note that the attempt to coerce an agent can be as morally problematic as successfully doing so. My analysis does not claim that only successful acts of coercion are morally blameworthy.

12. Dennis Wrong, for example, in *Power: Its Forms, Bases, and Uses* (Oxford, Eng.: Blackwell, 1979), obscures the element of mutual understanding by seeing the presence of a gun as sufficient by itself to constitute a coercive relation.

13. These four conditions have certain similarities to Peter Blau's conditions necessary for an exchange that results in the creation of power. In this sense, I agree with his idea that power is created by the "rational" response of the victim. Rationality does not, however, as Blau seems to believe, imply legitimacy. See his *Exchange and Power in Social Life* (2nd ed.; New Brunswick, N.J.: Transaction, 1986).

14. The account I have just presented could be amplified by developing various features of coercive power—for example, the scope of the actions controlled by an agent or the cost of controlling such actions. For my purposes, however, there is no need to do so.

15. Robert Nozick, in his study of coercion, fails to see the productive nature of coercion because of his tendency to conceptualize coercion in negative terms—that is, coercing *B* not to do something. See his "Coercion".

16. Ongoing relations of coercion differ from single events of coercion in the amount of resistance they are likely to engender.

17. Marxist theories of ideology, for example, seek to expose such miscognition and show how coercion is concealed by them. I will explore this theme in greater depth in Chapter 8.

18. These distinctions will also be useful in Chapter 10, where I discuss the superposition of power relationships.

19. Note that at least some cases of distributive expertise are not instances of power since the doctor simply has knowledge that he can make available to a patient, allowing the patient to act as she sees fit.

20. Baruch Spinoza, *Tractatus Politicus,* in A. G. Wernham, ed. and trans., *The Political Works* (Oxford, Eng.: Clarendon, 1958), ch. 2, ¶ 10, pp. 273–74. I would like to thank Paul Ricoeur for calling this work to my attention.

21. See Wrong, *Power.*

22. Carl J. Friedrich, *Man and His Government: An Empirical Theory of Politics* (New York: McGraw-Hill, 1963), p. 163.

Chapter 6

1. In this chapter, I shall use the concept of domination to characterize a use of power in which the dominant agent harms the subordinate agent. Thus, although my concern will be to define "domination", I do so in a way that will recognize oppression as a specific form of domination.

2. Max Weber, *Wirtschaft und Gesellschaft: Grundriss der Verstehenden Soziologie* (5th ed.; Tübingen: Mohr, 1985), pp. 28–29; my translation.

3. Cf. Arendt's worry about the command-obedience model discussed in Chapter 2.

4. My discussion of transformative power in Chapter 9 will discuss related issues.

5. See my "Marx and the Social Constitution of Value", *Philosophical Forum* 16, no. 4 (1985): 249–73.

6. The present discussion supplements that in Chapter 3, by showing how this section presents Hegel's view of domination. I once again am using A. V. Miller's translation of Hegel's term "Herrschaft und Knechtschaft." As I have mentioned, the term "Herrschaft" has more general connotations than does "lordship" and is often translated as "domination". Hegel's term could therefore with some justification be translated as "dominance and subordination".

7. G. W. F. Hegel, *Phenomenology of Spirit,* trans. A. V. Miller (Oxford, Eng.: Oxford University Press, 1977), pp. 113–14.

8. Let me explicitly note that Hegel's model of the life-and-death struggle actually has a degree of "innerness" that I am ignoring here, namely that the two consciousnesses do attain a form of mutual recognition in their very struggle to the death. This aspect of their consciousness, according to Hegel, exists only *in-itself* and not *for* these consciousnesses themselves. I also want to acknowledge the possibility of seeing this analysis on a more symbolic level than I am currently expounding.

9. Hegel, *Phenomenology,* p. 115. Hegel uses the concept of the "thing" to refer to this complex set of circumstances that determine the bondsman's relation to the lord. Let me also note that a full discussion of the lordship-bondage relationship would entail a look at, among other things, Hegel's notion of *desire held in check.*

10. It is in this context that the moment of recognition within the struggle itself is

important. This aspect of Hegel's analysis has interesting implications for thinking about so-called competitive sports.

11. See Carl J. Friedrich, *Man and His Government: An Empirical Theory of Politics* (New York: McGraw-Hill, 1963), ch. 11, for an elaboration of this concept. However, Friedrich treats anticipatory reaction as a form of influence rather than as a form of coercion. William E. Connolly, *The Terms of Political Discourse* (1974; 2nd ed., Princeton, N.J.: Princeton University Press, 1983), p. 131, n. 6, mistakenly attributes to Bachrach and Baratz the recognition of this form of power in modern social theory.

12. The dominant agent will, of course, have to do whatever is necessary to reproduce the ability that creates the possibility of his actually threatening the subordinate agent.

13. Although Hegel's discussion of such benefits in terms of the labor of the bondsman might give the impression that such benefits are material in nature, there is no reason to restrict our understanding of the productivity of domination to material benefits. A relationship of domination can also give the dominant agent such psychological benefits as are available in unequal relationships of recognition. It is important to keep in mind the psychological origin that Hegel gives to relationships of domination.

14. Once again, for my purposes in this chapter, I do not distinguish exploitation from domination.

15. For a more detailed exploration of Marx's views, see my article "Marx and the Social Constitution of Value", *Philosophical Forum* 16, no. 4 (1985): 249–73.

16. I discuss Foucault's claims more fully in the appendix to this chapter.

17. See Antonio Gramsci, *The Prison Notebooks*, trans. Quintin Hoare and Geoffrey Nowell Smith (New York: International Publishers, 1971).

18. For the purposes of this study, I will focus only on Nietzsche's account of domination as a means of social ascendancy.

19. Although not all characteristics of a good student are necessarily justifiable from this perspective, I wish to present them as such in order to explain Nietzsche's view. Such actions as "doing one's homework" can also be seen as useful to the student herself. I will take up such ideas when I discuss the concept of a transformative use of power.

20. Friedrich Nietzsche, *The Birth of Tragedy and the Genealogy of Morals*, trans. Francis Golffing (New York: Doubleday, 1956). In future references, I will give the book and section number, followed by the page number of the translation.

21. *Ibid.*, 1, x, p. 170.

22. *Ibid.*, 1, vii, p. 167.

23. *Ibid.*, 1, xi, p. 174.

24. *Ibid.*, 1, x, pp. 170–71.

25. The idea of a perspectiveless view of reality is one that characterizes the entire rationalist tradition in philosophy and distinguishes it from the empiricist view, a fact that many Continental philosophers fail to acknowledge.

26. Habermas seems to miss this aspect of Nietzsche's claim when he assimilates Nietzsche's treatment of evaluations to aesthetic judgments conceived as expressions

of taste or preferences. See Jürgen Habermas, *The Philosophical Discourse of Modernity,* trans. Frederick Lawrence (Cambridge, Mass.: MIT Press, 1987), ch. 4.

27. Marx's analysis of capitalism is also an attempt to show that force does not play an important role in that system of domination. Nonetheless, in such an analysis coercive relations are still present.

28. Foucault has shown us a means of translating these terms of Nietzsche's into more concrete histories of social institutions and practices. But the conception of power at work in Foucault's writings is self-acknowledgedly Nietzschean. It is a form of power whereby social agents are constituted by means of a conceptual valuation that presents certain values to them in a concealed manner. Unlike Nietzsche, however, Foucault does not see such domination as occurring by means of the action of a dominant group.

29. To be fair, Nietzsche is less guilty of this than Hegel in that he does distinguish the priestly valuation from the aristocratic one, thus admitting the possibility of alternative modes of domination.

30. Michel Foucault, *Power/Knowledge: Selected Interviews and Other Writings, 1972–1977,* ed. Colin Gordon (New York: Pantheon, 1980), p. 93.

31. Michel Foucault, *The History of Sexuality,* vol. 1: *An Introduction,* trans. Robert Hurley (New York: Pantheon, 1978), pp. 142–43; emphasis in original.

Chapter 7

1. Brian Fay, *Critical Social Science* (Ithaca, N.Y.: Cornell University Press, 1987), p. 120; my emphasis.

2. Both the example that I am using and the model that I am developing are necessarily abstract. In order to see how situated power works, both at the theoretical level and in terms of the example of grading, I shall abstract from various other features of the concrete situation in which teachers and students find themselves in order to focus my attention upon the manner in which a set of social relationships external to the student-teacher relationship constitutes that relationship as a power relationship. I will examine these assumptions in the following chapter.

3. There are institutions of higher education like Hampshire College that evaluate rather than grade their students. I leave out of consideration how such a divergence affects the power relationship between students and teachers. The teacher-student relationship that I am discussing here is intended to be the standard one in American higher education.

4. Fay, *Critical Social Science,* p. 120.

5. Fay's use of "causal outcome" in his definition of power is also problematic. My telling you that today is a holiday may have as a causal outcome a change in your actions, but this does not mean that I exercised power over you.

6. Previous social theorists have talked about "anticipatory reaction" in this context. Cf. note 11, Chapter 6. The problem with this concept is that it makes the existence of such power depend solely upon the subordinate agent.

7. What counts as a low grade will depend both on the student's perceptions and on her desires. A student who believes that a "B-" is a sign of intellectual failure will react differently to that grade than one who sees it as a sign of success. Although the meaning of grades is not subjective, there is a subjective factor in the assessment of them.

8. Let me stress once again that I have abstracted from the purely evaluative aspect of the grade and am considering it solely as a social measure of a student's success. Cf. my earlier separation of evaluation as a universal feature of teaching relationships from grading as a particular means of evaluation.

9. I use quotation marks to indicate that, although I have used language that implies that the peripheral agents intentionally cooperate with the empowered agent, power can be constituted without such intentions' playing a part in them. Agents who use the grades received by a student as a reason for giving or denying her access to items that they control are not thereby intending to give the teacher power over the student. Rather, their use of the grade has this effect without their explicitly intending that it have it. In this sense, my account of power conceptualizes it as non-intentional: An agent can have power over another agent without the intentional assistance of other agents; only a structure of differential response is necessary as a ground for the existence of a situated power relationship.

10. It is worth mentioning that the act of evaluation can ground the teacher's power in ways other than that upon which I am focusing here. A student who desires to learn a skill from a teacher will experience the teacher as powerful because the teacher is able to measure how well the student has learned the skill. My point is that this type of power can be analytically distinguished from the power that the teacher has as a result of the social role that a grade plays.

11. It is in this context that I would place Freud's notion of introjection. Freud's use of this concept is geared to the idea that the structure of the individual's consciousness is a reflection of certain relationships of power in the external world.

12. My description should make it clear that I have in mind the situation of certain minority groups in this country and that the source of this problem is not the educational system.

13. See my discussion of this notion in Chapter 2.

14. David Hume, *A Treatise of Human Nature,* ed. L. A. Selby-Bigge (Oxford, Eng.: Clarendon, 1888), p. 312. Hume's use of "authority" as the basis of the ascription of power, though the term is not used in a contemporary sense, raises certain problems that I shall simply pass over. William McBride called my attention to this feature of Hume's claim.

15. David Hume, *Enquiries Concerning the Human Understanding and Concerning the Principles of Morals,* L. A. Selby-Bigge (2nd ed.; Oxford, Eng.: Clarendon, 1902), sec. 7, pt. 1, p. 69.

16. *Webster's Seventh New Collegiate Dictionary,* (Springfield, Mass.: Merriam, 1963), p. 22.

17. All the claims made in this discussion should be read as including a *ceteris paribus* clause.

18. I discuss this issue in my "Marx, Class Consciousness, and Social Transformation", *Praxis International* 2 (1982): 52–69.

19. Marx, of course, sees starvation as the only alternative that laborers have. In contemporary capitalist society, this claim must be amended to something like what I have proposed.

20. For a more thorough development of the role of relations of power in the employment relation see Samuel Bowles and Herb Gintis, "Structure and Practice in the Labor Theory of Value," *Review of Radical Political Economics* 12, no. 4 (Winter 1981): 1–26. In my discussion, I omit their insightful consideration of the problems of actually extracting labor from the laborer.

21. See, for example, Michel Foucault, *The History of Sexuality,* vol. 1: *An Introduction,* trans. Robert Hurley (New York: Pantheon, 1978).

Chapter 8

1. Of course, possession is itself not as simple a relation as my use of it in this disanalogy assumes.

2. I use the term "(re)production" in order to indicate that the very act that is evidence for the existence of power (i.e., produces it) is also an act that reproduces it (i.e., makes it a social reality for future actors). I explain the point of this locution in the following discussion.

3. See, for example, Anthony Giddens, *The Constitution of Society* (Cambridge, Eng.: Polity, 1984).

4. I discuss this view in my "Marx and the Social Constitution of Value", *Philosophical Forum* 16, no. 4 (1985): 249–73, where I characterize Marx's view as "social idealism". I now find the term "interactive nominalism" less misleading.

5. The latest version of Habermas' criticism of Marx is in *The Philosophical Discourse of Modernity;* trans. Thomas McCarthy (Boston: Beacon, 1987), ch. 3.

6. The fact that Marx distinguishes between simple and expanded *reproduction* shows that he does not think of reproduction as inherently stable.

7. Michel Foucault, *The History of Sexuality,* vol. 1: *An Introduction,* trans. Robert Hurley (New York: Pantheon, 1978), p. 95. I use the concept of resistance as simply an example of Foucault's focus on power as a dynamic social reality. His whole view of power as essentially relational seeks to give priority to a dynamic view of it.

8. I use the concept of horizon here in order to indicate that it does not function as an objective limit on the power of the dominant agent, but rather as a factor that he needs to take account of in his actions.

9. I called this the "contextual view" of power in the previous chapter. For an example of this specific claim, see Robert A. Dahl, "The Concept of Power", in Roderick Bell, David V. Edwards, and R. Harrison Wagner, eds., *Political Power: A Reader in Theory and Research* (New York: Free Press, 1969), pp. 79–93.

10. Of course, not all athletes will finally wind up in such a situation. Discussion of that problem is beyond the scope of this study.

11. For an interesting collection of essays that highlight the importance of these movements, see *Social Research* 52, no. 4 (Winter 1985).

12. It is worth noting that the presence of an alternative alignment can actually change the nature of the dominant practice by successfully challenging the dominance of that practice. Such is the case in certain aspects of medical practice.

13. Of course, the specific expectations that the (parents of) clients of an educational institution will have depend on the class, race, and gender of the client (and/or parent). I am also dealing with expectations that parents have only if their children have successfully met the demands of the institution. Further, this social view of the service is not fully determinative of the nature of the practice. Many parents and students expect other things from an educational institution as well—for example, that some knowledge will be disseminated by it.

14. The importance of competing institutions is that they function to keep a particular institution from making its decisions independently of the market conditions.

15. Agents in the aligned institutions are themselves in a similar situation with respect to the agent within the central institution. The point is not to displace the position from which power is exercised but to see that the site where it is exercised is dispersed over a whole set of social practices and institutions.

16. There are aspects of the teacher-student relationship that I have not considered, such as the student's desire to learn from the teacher and the teacher's desire to have a genuine student. Chapter 10 will touch upon these.

Chapter 9

1. This particular locution shows the dangers of using the dominant/subordinate dichotomy to conceptualize the positions in a relationship of power-over. Recall that I do not treat the dominance of the dominant agent as identical with domination.

2. Cf. my discussion of this idea in Chapter 5.

3. Alison M. Jaggar, *Feminist Politics and Human Nature* (Totowa, N.J.: Rowman and Allanheld, 1983).

4. See, for example, Angela Y. Davis, *Women, Race, and Class* (New York: Vintage, 1981).

5. These are collected in Marilyn Frye, *The Politics of Reality* (Trumansburg, N.Y.: Crossing Press, 1983).

6. See, for example, Ann Ferguson, "On Conceiving Motherhood and Sexuality", in Joyce Trebilcot, ed., *Mothering: Essays in Feminist Theory* (Totowa, N.J.: Rowman and Allanheld, 1983), pp. 153–82.

7. Mary G. Dietz, "Citizenship with a Feminist Face: The Problem with Maternal Thinking", *Political Theory* 13, no. 1 (Feb. 1985): 19. I will take issue with Dietz's identification of the site of the family with mothering practices later in this study.

8. The distinction between theorists of domination and theorists of power is, like any dichotomy, too coarse to capture the subtlety of the analyses of writers whom I put in either category. In reality, there are two different tendencies among feminist theorists and not the two absolute positions that my categories suggest. Also, certain earlier

women theorists did talk about positive uses of power in a different context. See, for example, Dorothy Emmet, "The Concept of Power", *Proceedings of the Aristotelian Society,* 1953, pp. 1–25.

9. I have already discussed this use in Chapter 2.

10. Jean Baker Miller, "Colloquium: Women and Power", Stone Center for Developmental Services and Studies *Work in Progress,* no. 882-01, 1982, p. 2.

11. The question of whether power is "zero-sum" is one that has been a focus of controversy since Parsons' critique of Mills.

12. This is the idea that motivates Hegel's discussion of the life-and-death struggle. Cf. my discussions in Chapters 3 and 6.

13. Nancy Hartsock, *Money, Sex, and Power: Towards a Feminist Historical Materialism* (New York and London: Longman, 1983), p. 257.

14. Chodorow's views are expounded in Nancy Chodorow, *The Reproduction of Mothering: Psychoanalysis and the Sociology of Gender* (Berkeley: University of California Press, 1978).

15. Eléanor H. Kuykendall, "Toward an Ethic of Nurturance: Luce Irigaray on Mothering and Power", in Trebilcot, ed., *Mothering,* p. 264; emphasis added.

16. There is some question about whether Irigaray allows for transformative power relations to exist between mothers and sons or only between mothers and daughters.

17. Such a conception of power is widespread. See Bertrand de Jouvenal, *On Power: Its Nature and the History of Its Growth* (Boston: Beacon, 1945), and Dennis Wrong, *Power: Its Forms, Bases, and Uses* (Oxford, Eng.: Blackwell, 1979), for two examples of it.

18. A more precise discussion of this valuation would have to take account of the fact that the social valuation of such practices has been contradictory, seeing that work as important but not requiring special skill for its realization and, in any case, as fit only for women.

19. Foucault's two key works in this regard are *Discipline and Punish* (New York: Vintage, 1975) and *The History of Sexuality,* vol. 1: *An Introduction,* trans. Robert Hurley (New York: Pantheon, 1978). Although he sees power as constituting, Foucault does not see it as positive in the sense that I am using that term to characterize the views of the feminist theorists of power.

20. In *The Philosophical Discourse of Modernity,* trans. Frederick Lawrence (Cambridge, Mass.: MIT Press, 1987), chs. 9 and 10, Habermas makes a similar point against Foucault, arguing that Foucault's work shows only one side to the developments of modernity.

21. Sara Ruddick, "Maternal Thinking", in Trebilcot, ed., *Mothering,* p. 224.

22. *Ibid.*, p. 215.

23. Habermas expounded this view in *Knowledge and Human Interests* (Boston: Beacon, 1971). In her account of maternal thinking, Ruddick seems to vacillate between two different ways of making her point. In one, she describes a set of "social practices" that women have developed in order to fulfill their role as the primary caretakers of children; in the other, she uses the more idealistic discourse of a mode of

"thinking". I will simply assume that she means to see the practices as constitutive of this model of "thought".

24. Cf. Martin Heidegger, *Being and Time,* trans. John Macquarrie and E. S. Robinson (New York: Harper and Row, 1962), pt. 1, div. 1, ch. 6.

25. Ruddick, "Maternal Thinking", pp. 220–21.

26. *Ibid.,* p. 226.

27. A good general account of these developments is contained in Jay R. Greenberg and Stephen A. Mitchell, *Object Relations in Psychoanalytic Theory* (Cambridge, Mass.: Harvard University Press, 1983). See also Alice Miller, *Thou Shalt Not Be Aware: Society's Betrayal of the Child* (New York: New American Library, 1984), for a more popular discussion of the importance of narcissism for social theory.

28. An additional problem is that the position of the child is often conceived of as powerless. Although this may be true at birth, the child is always developing more and more ability to cope with her environment. The relationship has a dynamic quality that needs to be fully incorporated into the discussion. For some startling evidence about the child's ability to affect the mother's behavior at ages of less than one year, see Joanne L. Gusella, Darwin Muir, and Edward Z. Tronick, "The Effect of Manipulating Maternal Behavior During an Interaction on Three- and Six-Month Olds' Affect and Attention", *Child Development* 59 (1988): 1111–24.

29. Dietz, "Citizenship with a Feminist Face", p. 19. Although she takes the term "maternal thinking" in her title from Ruddick, Dietz focuses her criticism upon Jean Elshtain.

Chapter 10

1. Plato, *Meno* 80a. All translations of Plato's works in this chapter are taken from F. M. Cornford, trans., and Edith Hamilton and Huntington Cavins, eds., *The Collected Dialogues of Plato* (Princeton, N.J.: Princeton University Press, 1961).

2. Plato, *Apology* 19b.

3. Plato, *Meno* 80a.

4. *Ibid.,* 84b–84c.

5. Plato, *Apology* 36c.

6. Plato, *Meno* 84c.

7. This is also confirmed by Socrates' discussion of love in the *Symposium.*

8. Plato, *Phaedrus* 253b.

9. *Ibid.* 256e.

10. The central difference between my account and Plato's is that he seeks to provide a metaphysical interpretation of this phenomenon that places the central responsibility for this power in a supra-human world. I intentionally ignore this feature of his account.

11. In describing Socrates' practices, I ignore their racist, classist, and sexist base. In not questioning these aspects of his culture, Socrates has certainly not fully transcended its historical limitations.

12. A model of power that comes close to this transformative use of power is the Christian idea of the power of love. In Augustine's *Confessions,* God's love is portrayed as having a transformative effect on Augustine. Once he is able to accept God's love, Augustine becomes a different person, one not troubled in the way he was before. See *Confessions,* trans. R. S. Pine-Coffin (Baltimore: Penguin, 1961).

This type of love is often described as unconditional love because, as Augustine says, there is nothing that he can do that will cause God not to love him. But it is not a blind, uncritical love because it is based on a recognition of possibilities in Augustine that God knows since he created him. In a non-religious language, we can talk about such love as recognizing a potential within a person and as asking him to live up to that potential. It is the ability to remain in love with someone while also asking of him that he justify that love. So the love is unconditional in the sense of not being able to be lost, but conditonal in that it makes demands.

13. This aspect of a transformative power relationship distinguishes it from the attempt simply to influence someone else for one's own benefit. While the sophists certainly were interested in influencing others, and in the teaching of this skill, they saw such influence as benefiting not the others, but rather those who did the influencing.

14. Plato, *Euthyphro* 15e.

15. At this point, I will use the term "parenting" to refer to the caretaking role that a parent assumes in regard to a child. I do this to avoid the sexist implications of the term "mothering", which suggests that the caretaking role is suitable exclusively for women.

16. I. F. Stone, *The Trial of Socrates* (Boston and Toronto: Little, Brown, 1988), *passim,* but especially ch. 6.

17. This is the picture of Socrates that emerges in *The Birth of Tragedy,* for example. For an interesting discussion of the grounds for Nietzsche's ambiguous assessment of Socratic practice, see Alexander Nehamas, *Nietzsche: Life as Literature* (Cambridge, Mass.: Harvard University Press, 1985), ch. 1.

18. A full discussion of Socratic irony would take us beyond the issues I am concerned with here. I shall address it in a later paper.

19. See, for example, Erik H. Erikson, *Childhood and Society* (2nd ed; New York: Norton, 1963), p. 247–51.

20. Plato, *Phaedrus* 239b.

21. R. D. Laing's *The Divided Self* (Harmondsworth, Eng.: Pelican, 1965) is a classical example of such a criticism.

22. They also show a person's class, an issue that I will sidestep at this point.

23. Readers familiar with Hegel's use of the concept *Aufheben* ("supersession") will understand my discussion to be an explanation of the claim that the superposition of a situated power relationship upon a transformative power relationship results in the latter's being superseded. Unlike Hegel, however, I claim that the original relationship is not fully canceled by its supersession. It remains a problematic social presence in the same social practice.

Bibliography of Works Cited

Agee, James. *Let Us Now Praise Famous Men*. Boston: Houghton Mifflin, 1941.

Arendt, Hannah. *On Violence*. New York: Harcourt Brace Jovanovich, 1969, 1970.

————. "What Is Authority?" Pages 91–141 in *Between Past and Future: Eight Exercises in Political Thought* (Harmondsworth, Eng.: Penguin, 1954).

Aristotle. *Nichomachean Ethics*. In J. L. Ackrill, ed., *The New Aristotle Reader*. Princeton, N.J.: Princeton University Press, 1987.

Augustine, Saint. *Confessions,* trans. R. S. Pine-Coffin. Baltimore: Penguin, 1961.

Bachrach, Peter and Morton S. Baratz. "Decisions and Non-decisions: An Analytical Framework". Pages 100–109 in Roderick Bell, David V. Edwards, and R. Harrison Wagner, eds., *Political Power: A Reader in Theory and Research* (New York: Free Press, 1969).

Ball, Terence. "Power, Causation, and Explanation". *Polity* 8 (1975): 189–214.

————. "Two Concepts of Coercion", *Theory and Society* 15 (Jan. 1978): 97–112.

Barry, Brian. *Power and Political Theory: Some European Perspectives*. London: Wiley, 1976.

Bell, Roderick, David V. Edwards, and R. Harrison Wagner, eds. *Political Power: A Reader in Theory and Research*. New York: Free Press, 1969.

Bernstein, Richard J. *Beyond Objectivism and Relativism: Science, Hermeneutics, and Praxis*. Philadelphia: University of Pennsylvania Press, 1983.

Blau, Peter. *Exchange and Power in Social Life*. 2nd ed. New Brunswick, N.J.: Transaction Books, 1986.

Bowles, Samuel, and Herb Gintis, "Structure and Practice in the Labor Theory of Value", *Review of Radical Political Economics* 12, no. 4 (Winter 1981): 1–26.

Charlesworth, James C., ed. *Contemporary Political Analysis*. New York: Free Press, 1967.

Chodorow, Nancy. *The Reproduction of Mothering: Psychoanalysis and the Sociology of Gender*. Berkeley: University of California Press, 1978.

Connolly, William E. *The Terms of Political Discourse*. Princeton, N.J.: Princeton University Press, 1974 and 1983.

Dahl, Robert A. "The Behavioral Approach in Political Science: Epitaph for a Monu-
    ment to a Successful Protest". *American Political Science Review* 55 (1961):
    763–72.
———. "The Concept of Power". Pages 79–93 in Roderick Bell, David V. Edwards,
    and R. Harrison Wagner, eds., *Political Power: A Reader in Theory and Research*
    (New York: Free Press, 1969).
———. "A Critique of the Ruling Elite Model". Pages 36–41 in Roderick Bell,
    David V. Edwards, and R. Harrison Wagner, eds., *Political Power: A Reader in
    Theory and Research* (New York: Free Press, 1969).
Davis, Angela Y. *Women, Class and Race.* New York: Vintage, 1981.
de Jouvenal, Bertrand. *On Power: Its Nature and the History of Its Growth.* Boston:
    Beacon, 1945,
Dietz, Mary G. "Citizenship with a Feminist Face: The Problem with Maternal Think-
    ing". *Political Theory* 13, no. 1 (Feb. 1985): 19–38.
Domhoff, William. *Who Really Rules: New Haven and Community Power Re-
    examined.* Santa Monica, Calif.: Goodyear, 1978.
Easton, David. "The Current Meaning of Behavioralism". Pages 11–31 in James C.
    Charlesworth, ed. *Contemporary Political Analysis* (New York: Free Press, 1967).
Emmet, Dorothy. "The Concept of Power". *Proceedings of the Aristotelian Society*
    54 (1953–54): 1–25.
Erikson, Erik H. *Childhood and Society.* New York: Norton, 1963.
Fay, Brian. *Critical Social Science.* Ithaca, N.Y.: Cornell University Press, 1987.
Ferguson, Ann. "On Conceiving Motherhood and Sexuality". Pages 153–82 in Joyce
    Trebilcot, ed., *Mothering: Essays in Feminist Theory* (Totowa, N.J.: Rowman and
    Allenheld, 1983).
Foucault, Michel. *Discipline and Punish.* New York: Vintage, 1975.
———. *The History of Sexuality,* vol. 1: *An Introduction,* trans. Robert Hurley. New
    York: Pantheon, 1978.
———. *Power/Knowledge: Selected Interviews and Other Writings, 1972–1977,* ed.
    Colin Gordon. New York: Pantheon, 1980.
Freud, Sigmund. *A General Introduction to Psychoanalysis.* New York: Washington
    Square, 1920.
Friedrich, Carl J. *Man and His Government: An Empirical Theory of Politics.* New
    York: McGraw-Hill, 1963.
Frye, Marilyn. *The Politics of Reality: Essays in Feminist Theory.* Trumansburg,
    N.Y.: Crossing Press, 1983.
Gallie, W. B. "Essentially Contested Concepts". *Proceedings of the Aristotelian So-
    ciety* 56 (1955–56): 167–98.
Giddens, Anthony. *Central Problems in Social Theory: Action, Structure, and Con-
    tradiction in Social Analysis.* Berkeley and Los Angeles: University of California
    Press, 1979.
———. *The Constitution of Society.* Cambridge, Eng.: Polity, 1984.
Gramsci, Antonio. *The Prison Notebooks,* trans. Quintin Hoare and Geoffrey Nowell
    Smith. New York: International Publishers, 1971.

Greenberg, Jay R., and Stephen A. Mitchell. *Object Relations in Psychoanalytic Theory*. Cambridge, Mass: Harvard University Press, 1983.

Gusella, Joanne L., Darwin Muir, and Edward Z. Tronick. "The Effect of Manipulating Maternal Behavior During an Interaction on Three- and Six-Month-Olds' Affect and Attention". *Child Development* 59 (1988): 1111–24.

Habermas, Jürgen. "Hannah Arendts Begriff der Macht". Pages 228–48 in *Philosophisch-politische Profile* (Frankfurt: Suhrkamp, 1981).

———. *Knowledge and Human Interests*. Boston: Beacon, 1971.

———. *The Philosophical Discourse of Modernity*, trans. Frederick Lawrence. Cambridge, Mass.: MIT Press, 1987.

———. *The Theory of Communicative Action*, vol. 1: *Lifeworld and System: A Critique of Functionalist Reason*, trans. Thomas McCarthy. Boston: Beacon, 1987.

Hartsock, Nancy. *Money, Sex, and Power: Towards a Feminist Historical Materialism*. New York and London: Longman, 1983.

Hegel, G. W. F. *Phenomenology of Spirit*, trans. A. V. Miller. Oxford, Eng.: Oxford University Press, 1977.

Heidegger, Martin. *Being and Time*, trans. John Macquarrie and E. S. Robinson. New York: Harper and Row, 1962.

Hobbes, Thomas. *Leviathan*, ed. Michael Oakshott. Oxford, Eng.: Blackwell, 1946.

Hoy, David. "Power, Repression, Progress: Foucault, Lukes, and the Frankfurt School". Pages 123–47 in *Foucault: A Critical Reader*, ed. Hoy (Oxford, Eng.: Blackwell, 1986).

Hume, David. *Enquiries Concerning the Human Understanding and Concerning the Principles of Morals*, ed. L. A. Selby-Bigge. 2nd ed. Oxford. Eng.: Clarendon, 1902.

———. *A Treatise of Human Nature*, ed. L. A. Selby-Bigge. Oxford, Eng.: Clarendon, 1888.

Isaac, Jeffrey C. *Power and Marxist Theory: A Realist View*. Ithaca, N.Y., and London: Cornell University Press, 1987.

Jaggar, Alison M. *Feminist Politics and Human Nature*. Totowa, N.J.: Rowman and Allanheld, 1983.

Köhler, Wolfgang. *Gestalt Psychology*. New York: Liveright, 1947.

Kuydendall, Eleanor H. "Toward an Ethic of Nurturance: Lucy Irigaray on Mothering and Power". Pages 263–74 in Joyce Trebilcot, ed., *Mothering: Essays in Feminist Theory*. Totowa, N.J.: Rowman and Allanheld, 1983.

Laing, R. D. *The Divided Self*. Harmondsworth, Eng.: Pelican, 1965.

Laswell, Harold, and Abraham Kaplan. *Power and Society*. New Haven, Conn.: Yale University Press, 1950.

Lively, Jack. "The Limits of Exchange Theory". Pages 1–13 in Brian Barry, ed., *Power and Political Theory: Some European Perspectives* (London: Wiley, 1976).

Locke, John. *An Essay Concerning Human Understanding*. New York: Dover, 1959.

Luhmann, Niklas. *Macht*. Stuttgart: Enke, 1975.

Lukes, Steven. *Power: A Radical View*. London and Basingstoke, Eng.: Macmillan, 1974.

————. "Power and Structure". Pages 3–23 in *Essays in Social Theory* (New York: Macmillan, 1977).

Macpherson, C. B. *Democratic Theory: Essays in Retrieval*. Oxford. Eng.: Oxford University Press, 1973.

————. *The Political Theory of Possessive Individualism: Hobbes to Locke*. Oxford, Eng.: Oxford University Press, 1962.

Marx, Karl. *The Economic and Philosophic Manuscripts of 1844*, ed. Dirk J. Struik. New York: International Publishers, 1964.

Miller, Alice. *Thou Shalt Not Be Aware: Society's Betrayal of the Child*. New York: New American Library, 1984.

Miller, Jean Baker. "Colloquium: Women and Power". Stone Center for Developmental Services and Studies, *Work in Progress*, no. 882–01, 1982.

Mills, C. Wright. *The Power Elite*. Oxford, Eng.: Oxford University Press, 1956.

Nagel, Ernest. *The Structure of Science*. New York: Harcourt Brace Jovanovich, 1974.

Nehamas, Alexander. *Nietzsche: Life as Literature*. Cambridge, Mass.: Harvard University Press, 1985.

Nietzsche, Friedrich. *The Birth of Tragedy and the Genealogy of Morals*, trans. Francis Goffing. New York: Doubleday, 1956.

Nozick, Robert. "Coercion". Pages 101–35 in Peter Laslett, W. G. Runciman, and Quentin Skinner, eds. *Philosophy, Politics, and Society* (4th ser.; Oxford, Eng.: Oxford University Press, 1972).

The Oxford English Dictionary. Oxford, Eng.: Oxford University Press, 1971.

Parsons, Talcott. "On the Concept of Political Power". Pages 251–84 in Roderick Bell, David V. Edwards, and R. Harrison Wagner, eds., *Political Power: A Reader in Theory and Research* (New York: Free Press, 1969).

Pitkin, Hannah. *Wittgenstein and Justice*. Berkeley, Los Angeles, and London: University of California Press, 1972.

Plato. *The Collected Dialogues of Plato*, trans. F. M. Cornford and ed. Edith Hamilton and Huntington Cairns. Princeton, N.J.: Princeton University Press, 1961.

Polsby, Nelson W. "How to Study Community Power: The Pluralist Alternative". Pages 112–21 in *Community Power and Political Theory* (New Haven, Conn.: Yale University Press, 1980).

Poulantzas, Nicos. *Political Power and Social Classes*. London: New Left, 1973.

Ruddick, Sara. "Maternal Thinking". Pages 213–30 in Joyce Trebilcot, ed., *Mothering: Essays in Feminist Theory* (Totowa, N.J.: Rowman and Allanheld, 1983).

Russell, Bertrand. *Power*. New York: Norton, 1938.

Ryle, Gilbert. *The Concept of Mind*. New York: Harper and Row, 1949.

Sartre, Jean Paul. "The Wall". Pages 59–80 in *Intimacy*, trans. Lloyd Alexander (New York: Berkley, 1948).

Shakespeare, William. *King Lear*, ed. Kenneth Muir. London and New York: Methuen, 1985.

Social Research 52, no. 4 (Winter 1985).

Spinoza, Baruch. *Tractatus Politicus*. Pages 256–445 in A. G. Wernham, ed. and trans., *The Political Works* (Oxford, Eng.: Clarendon, 1958).

Stone, I. F. *The Trial of Socrates*. Boston and Toronto: Little, Brown, 1988.

Taylor, Charles. "Interpretation and the Sciences of Man". *Review of Metaphysics* 25 (Fall 1971): 4–51.

Trebilcot, Joyce, ed. *Mothering: Essays in Feminist Theory*. Totowa, N.J.: Rowman and Allanheld, 1983.

Truman, David. "The Implications of Political Behavior Research". Social Science Research Council *Items* 5 (1951): 37–39.

Wartenberg, Thomas. "Beyond Babies and Banners: Towards an Understanding of the Dynamics of Social Movements". *New Political Science* 14 (Winter 1985–86): 157–171.

———. "The Forms of Power". *Analyse und Kritik* 10 (1988): 3–31.

———. "Marx and the Social Constitution of Value". *Philosophical Forum* 16, no. 4 (1985): 249–73.

———. "Marx, Class Consciousness, and Social Transformation". *Praxis International* 2 (1982): 52–69.

Weber, Max. *Wirtschaft und Gesellschaft: Grundriss der Verstehenden Soziologie*. 5th ed. Tübingen: Mohr, 1985.

West, David. "Power and Formation: New Foundations for a Radical Concept of Power". *Inquiry* 30 (1987): 137–54.

Wittgenstein, Ludwig. *Philosophical Investigations*, trans. G. E. M. Anscombe. New York: Macmillan, 1968.

Wrong, Dennis. *Power: Its Forms, Bases, and Uses*. Oxford, Eng.: Blackwell, 1979.

Index

For Better, For Worse

To One Spouse
and Many Friends